SUSTAINABILITY
A WAY FORWARD

SUSTAINABILITY
A WAY FORWARD

Editor
SURENDER MOR

Bhagat Phool Singh Mahila Vishwavidyalaya

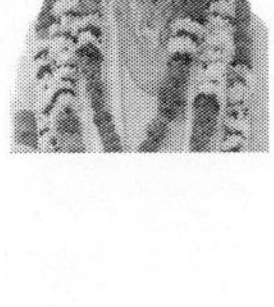

B L O O M S B U R Y
NEW DELHI • LONDON • OXFORD • NEW YORK • SYDNEY

BLOOMSBURY INDIA
Bloomsbury Publishing India Pvt. Ltd
Second Floor, LSC Building No. 4, DDA Complex,
Pocket C – 6 & 7, Vasant Kunj,
New Delhi 110070

BLOOMSBURY, BLOOMSBURY INDIA and the Diana logo are trademarks of Bloomsbury Publishing Plc

First published in India 2022
This edition published 2022

ISBN: 978-93-54359-07-1
2 4 6 8 10 9 7 5 3 1

Printed and bound in India by Replika Press Pvt. Ltd

To find out more about our authors and books, visit www.bloomsbury.com and sign up for our newsletters

CONTENTS

FOREWORD

The issue of sustainability, rightly and undoubtedly, has, by now, emerged as the buzzword in the discourse on socio-economic transformation in the 21st Century, regardless of the stage of development of the country concerned. In this process the role of United Nations, *inter alia* by its Agenda 2030 as manifested in the declaration on Sustainable Development Goals, cannot be overemphasised. It is also notable that that the term sustainable development overtime has also undergone substantial transformation. While the earlier focus was on narrow ecological sustainability, dealing mainly with the limits to development set by the limited natural resources, today we find a much broader perspective that goes beyond ecological sustainability to encompass economic and social suitability. To the extent that the countries and societies do vary with respect to their level of development and social transformation, the problematic of sustainability, naturally, is contingent on the socio-economic and the institutional specificities of the context concerned.

In a large developing country like India, where nearly 50 percent of the population is dependent of rainfed agriculture or depends on Himalayan rivers for irrigation and having one of the longest coastline, the impact of changes in the rainfall pattern, flood on account of the melting of glaziers or rise in the sea level on account of global warming need no elaboration. Hence, despite being a poor country that has not been a significant contributor to carbon emission, there is no room for compromising on the issue of ecological sustainability. At the same time, when we consider sustainability by taking into account the issue of feeding the largest number of poor, we are taken to the door steps of various socio economic institutions that generate and sustain multiple spaces of exclusion that perpetuates poverty and deprivation. Hence one also wonders whether a blind adoption of sustainability as articulated in the first world, wherein equal emphasis given to the needs of the yet to be born generation and present generation that enjoys all the luxuries of the world, is of any consequence for the developing country context.

There is reason to believe that at the root of the sustainability discourse is the nexus between ecology, economy, technology and society. While the advances in the science, technology and innovation could be seen as the single most important factor that facilitated the unscrupulous exploitation of exhaustible resources, the final solution for the problem at hand could also be found in science, technology and innovation, seen in a broader perspective to encompass organisational, institutional and other relevant innovations.

It is in this context that I value the contribution of the present volume, edited by Professor Surender More, which is collection of 16 well-articulated articles at instance of scholars from within and outside India. The most important common theme that attracted me in a number of chapters is their focus on innovation. It is all the important to note that the studies in this volume, while dealing with the bearing of technologies that comes under rubric of Industry 4.0, also focus innovation, that too in a broader perspective by taking the agenda beyond the narrow confines of technological innovation. Especially notable is the special focus on issues relating to sustainable agriculture, indicative of the concern of the authors with the rural, agrarian ad the less privileged in our country.

I congratulate the Editor and the contributors for coming up with this timely book which I consider a must read for the scholars, policy makers and the students at large.

Prof. K.J. Joseph
Director, Gulati Institute of Finance and Taxation (GIFT)
Thiruvananthapuram, Kerala, India

FROM THE EDITOR'S DESK

This book titled 'Sustainability: A Way Forward' is based on the papers received for the International Conference on the theme '*Economics to Earthonomics: Shifting Paradigms, Policy Paralysis, and Worsening Sustainability*' held on 9–11 March 2022. The book examines the process of transition from economic development to sustainable development. It revolves around the issue of sustainability across the globe in the wake of climate change. Environment and development are indispensable when one talks about sustainability based on three economic, social, and ecological sustainability pillars. Classical economists to modern economists believe that economic activities are constrained by nature. Hence, the debate between economic growth and the environment led to the evolution of sustainable development. The notion of weak and strong sustainability has fetched attention because sustainable development must meet the needs of the present generations without compromising the future generations. Hence, sustainability represents a trade-off between the aspirations of humanity towards a better life and the limitations imposed by natural resources. The book comprises three sections, highlighting a particular aspect related to sustainability.

Section-I deals with articles exploring the role of technology in affecting the environment and humanity. The world looks to technology like Artificial Intelligence, 5G, machine learning, Internet of Things (IoT), and industry 4.0 to save the planet and a fossil-fuel-free world. Information and communications technology affect environmental sustainability, blockchain technology-enhanced supply chain sustainability and mobile technology influence sustainability in industries. The technology has many pros and cons, and the cons are its carbon footprints or unsustainability. *Sunita Devi* highlights the spirit of environmental protection and practises sustainable development, mentioned in Kautilya's *Arthashastra. At the same time, Ruth Taplin* focused on the beneficial effects of Artificial Intelligence (AI) in mitigation with climate change. The paper by *Mario B. Curatolo* talks about resilience as a sustainability strategy for businesses in the post-covid era. At the same time, *Cornelia Caseau* examines the environmental challenges of France's blackcurrant sector to build territorial resilience. *Swati Mehta's* chapter deals with the role of Innovation, Industry and Infrastructure in emerging Asian economies in compliance with the sustainable development goals, whereas *Rengarajan* calls for rethinking and revitalising our pathways to sustainable human welfare and a safe planet.

Section II incorporates articles focussing on the role-played organisation to promote sustainability. Various corporate practices contribute a lot to climate management, like ISO 14001 & 14002, green marketing, eco-labelling, and digitalisation. Sustainable practices have been found to play a role in environmental and non-environmental sustainability. Countries ranked higher in economic, financial and social indicators stand worst on sustainability. *Sanjay Bhayana and Sapna Arora* discuss corporate governance rating as a tool for the global strategy for good corporate governance. The paper by *Rashmi Tyagi and Jatesh Kathpalia* explore the antecedents of self-help groups in the rural area of Haryana state of India, whereas *Sarita Adhikari and Radhe Shyam Pradhan* examine the effect of innovation and technology on productivity and profitability on commercial banks of Nepal. *Parmod Malik* discusses the case of Solid Waste of Rohtak Municipal Corporation in the Haryana State of India. *Anita Sapkota and Nar Bahadur Bista* examine the significance of microfinance in promoting women's empowerment in the Kathmandu Valley of Nepal.

Section III consists of articles related to various agricultural practices contributing to climate management, especially crop residue burning in rice cultivation in India, laser levelling techniques & drip irrigation technology for water-saving, and 'Happy Seeder' farm technology for sustainable agriculture. The agriculture sector is one of the forerunners to deploy AI, enhancing efficiency in agricultural production and minimising the adverse impacts on the environment. The deployment of AI leads to improved crop monitoring, better soil health, weeds, pests & insect control, higher crop yields, reduction of the manual labour force, and improvement in the food supply chain. *Preeti Sihan, Ashok Kumar, Neelam Kumari, and Shivam* discussed the paddy straw management techniques given widescale burning of crop residue, especially in rice cultivation in Haryana. *Priya and Jaswinder Singh Brar* analyse the Laser Levelling Technology for Sustainable Irrigation leading to improved water productivity, reduced cost of irrigation, and higher crop yield in wheat crops. The paper by *Vinod Kumari and Subhash Chander* elaborates on the impacts of drip Irrigation Technology for efficient water use and Sustainable Crop Production in the Haryana State of India. At the same time, *Jatesh Kathpalia, Rashmi Tyagi, Vinod Kumari and Anil Kumar Saroha* discusses the economic benefits of the adoption of 'Happy Seeder' farm technology for sustainable agriculture in Haryana, India.

Surender Mor

ACKNOWLEDGEMENTS

I wish to express my deepest gratitude to my revered teacher, Prof. T. R. Kundu, for guiding me at each life and academic career stage. Further, I owe gratitude to Prof. Arvind Ashta (Burgundy School of Business, France) and Prof. Shyam S. Lodha (Professor Emeritus, Southern Connecticut State University, USA) for initiating the idea of organizing the International Conference at Bhagat Phool Singh Mahila Vishwavidyalaya (BPSMV), Khanpur Kalan, Sonepat.

I wish to place on record a special vote of thanks for the continuous support and blessings received from Prof. Rajenderkumar Anayath, Former Vice-Chancellor, Bhagat Phool Singh Mahila Vishwavidyalaya for his keen interest, encouragement at various stages of publication of book and organization of the International Conference at Bhagat Phool Singh Women University, Khanpur Kalan, Sonipat.

I am sincerely grateful to Prof. Lakhwinder S. Gill (Former Professor, Punjabi University, Patiala), Prof. Ranjan Aneja (Central University of Haryana), Prof. Manas Choubey (Central University of Sikkim), Prof. P.K. Mishra (Central University of Punjab), Prof. Supran Kumar Sharma (Sri Mata Vaishno Devi Univesity, Katra, J&K), Prof. Jaswinder Singh Brar (Professor, Punjabi University, Patiala), Prof. Sonu Madan (Indira Gandhi University, Rewari, Haryana), Prof. Radhey Shyam Pradhan (Tribhuvan University, Kathmandu Nepal) and Prof. N.K. Bishnoi (Guru Jambeshwer University of Science and Technology, Hisar, Haryana) for their excellent assistance and cooperation in reviewing the papers for the present academic endeavour. Without their continuous support, it would not have been possible to maintain the academic quality and credibility of the book.

My special thanks go to the Faculty and Staff of the Department of Economics, Bhagat Phool Singh Mahila Vishwavidyalaya, for their hard work and contribution to the publication of this book. I am also thankful to the contributors for adding rich manuscripts and elevating the standard of the book with their academic work. I am also grateful to Bloomsbury India for their behind-the-scenes help, and marvellous job editing and getting the book printed excellently.

Surender Mor

CONTRIBUTORS

Anil Kumar Saroha, Assistant Professor, Department of Farm Machinery & Power Engineering, Chaudhary Charan Singh Haryana Agricultural University, Hisar, Haryana

Anita Sapkota, Student, Uniglobe College, Pokhara University, Kathmandu, Nepal

Ashok Kumar, Associate Director, Department of Extension Education, Chaudhary Charan Singh Haryana Agricultural University, Hisar, Haryana

Cornelia Caseau, Professor, Burgundy School of Business, Université Bourgogne Franche-Comté, Dijon, France

Jaswinder Singh Brar, Professor, Centre for Research in Economic Change, Punjabi University Patiala

Jatesh Kathpalia, Assistant Scientist, Department of Sociology Chaudhary Charan Singh Haryana Agricultural University, Hisar

Mario Curatolo-CEO, Management Business Consultants, Dino, Switzerland

Nar Bahadur Bista, Director, Uniglobe College, Pokhara University, Kathmandu, Nepal

Neelam Kumari, Ex-Student, Department of Extension Education, Chaudhary Charan Singh Agricultural University, Hisar, Haryana

Parmod Malik, Assistant Professor, Department of Law, BPS Women University, Khanpur Kalan, Sonepat, Haryana

Preeti Sihan, Department of Extension Education, Chaudhary Charan Singh Haryana Agricultural University, Hisar, Haryana

Priya, Research Fellow, Department of Economics, Punjabi University Patiala

Radhe Shyam Pradhan, Professor of Management, Tribhuvan University, Kathmandu, Nepal

Rashmi Tyagi, Assistant Professor, Department of Sociology, Chaudhary Charan Singh Haryana Agricultural University, Hisar

Ruth Taplin, Chief Editor, Interdisciplinary Journal of Economics and Business Law (IEBL), United Kingdom

Sanjay Bhayana, Professor, Department of Food Business Management and Entrepreneurship, Development (FBMED), NIFTEM, Kundli, Haryana

Sapna Arora, Assistant Professor, Department of Food Business Management and Entrepreneurship, Development (FBMED), NIFTEM, Kundli, Haryana

Sarita Adhikari, Student, Uniglobe College, Pokhara University, Kathmandu, Nepal

Shivam, Ex-Student, Kedarnath Aggarwal Institute of Management, Charkhi Dadri, Haryana

Subhash Chander, Assistant Professor, Department of Sociology, Chaudhary Charan Singh Haryana Agricultural University, Hisar, Haryana

Sunita Devi, Assistant Professor in Economics, Government College, Mohna, Faridabad, Haryana

Surender Mor, Professor, Department of Economics, BPS Women University, Khanpur Kalan, Sonepat, Haryana

Swati Mehta, Assistant Professor, Punjab School of Economics, Guru Nanak Dev University, Amritsar, Punjab, India

V. Rengarajan, Former Consultant, Madras Institute of development Studies, Chennai

Vinod Kumari, Professor, Department of Sociology, Chaudhary Charan Singh Haryana Agricultural University, Hisar, Haryana

'SUSTAINABILITY' – A WAY FORWARD: AN INTRODUCTION

Environment and development are indispensable when one talks about sustainability. The concept of sustainability is used for natural resources, both stock and flow, that people can continue to count on their yield for a long period. Sustainability denotes the ability of something to sustain or maintain itself over time and represents both climate and sustainable development. In a broader sense, sustainability encompasses building a more sustainable world in the long run, while sustainable development involves only specific processes and methods to achieve these goals. Sustainable development connects environmental and social issues for the North and the South. The Brundtland Commission Report "Our Common Future" defines sustainable development to ensure that it meets the needs of the present without compromising the ability of future generations to meet their own needs (Brundtland, 1987).

The early literature on sustainability discussed its social and ecological perspective with the economic status quo and later attempted to reconcile it with economic growth to devise solutions to social and economic problems (Purvis et al., 2019). Sala et al. (2015) addressed the broad environmental, economic and social context of sustainability on scientific sustainability evaluation, whereas Mor et al. (2017) systematically developed a comprehensive definition of sustainability based on definitions already used in the literature. Nagatsu et al. (2020) connected sustainability scientists and philosophers of science and raised concerning issues of science sustainability, which leads to its advancement. Sustainability science can effectively bridge the gap between natural and social sciences in addressing sustainability challenges (Jerneck et al., 2011). Abson et al. (2017) related sciences, politics and humanity, which largely remained on an unsustainable development path owing to tangible but weak sustainability interventions. The study calls for linking people to nature, reorganising institutions, and reconsidering how knowledge is created and used in pursuit of sustainability.

Research indicates that sustainability embodies a trade-off between the aspirations of humanity towards a better life and the limitations imposed by nature (Kuhlman & Farrington, 2010). The central theme of sustainability has been found in the United Nations Conference on Environment and Development policy forums and the United Nations Conference on Sustainable Development (Fuchs, 2017). Eizenberg and Jabareen (2017) opined that sustainability relates to risk resulting primarily from climate change and its succeeding uncertainties pose serious social, spatial, structural, and physical threats to contemporary human societies and their living spaces. If humans want to last long on this planet, the quantum of pollution must be reduced. Bennich et al. (2021) assessed and implemented sustainability measures using interlinkage between agenda 2030, bio-based economy and robust sustainability approach and found them mutually interacting. Ives et al. (2020) related sustainability with the inner world of the people and identifies a powerful transformative capacity for system change.

Sustainability permeates the idea that humans should not degrade global commons for realising the short-term benefits as these are essential for life on the planet. The ongoing process of climate change, ozone depletion, melting glaciers, rising sea levels, acid rain and loss of biodiversity fetched a significant momentum of the world policymakers since last 1970s. The concept also signifies that we need to be fair to our gifts of nature in pursuing our economic activities. Sustainability encompasses three dimensions, namely, economic, social and environmental and is concerned with the well-being of future generations.

Economic sustainability is closely related to natural resources, both renewable and exhaustible, which provide physical inputs for economic activities. It requires societies to pursue a growth path that generates an optimal flow of income while maintaining their basic stock of manmade capital, natural capital and human capital. There is a debate on the economic dimension of sustainability as economic growth/economic development implies the use of natural resources in the development/growth path. Suppose economic growth is sustained, then how to ensure welfare for all especially developing countries, as they try to develop fast. Even SDG 8 envisages that economic growth often brings societal progress as well as wellbeing. Economic sustainability requires internalising all costs associated with production and consumption.

Social sustainability often gets less attention than environmental sustainability. But it's just as important as the later. Social sustainability is defined as a measure of human welfare. It is based on the twin principles of justice and equality, i.e., for a development path to be sustainable in the long run period, wealth, resources, and opportunities should be equitably shared. Social sustainability focuses on the human effects of economic systems, and the category includes attempts to eradicate poverty and hunger, as well as to combat inequality. In this pillar, poverty has been assumed a major cause of the environmental degradation in a broader sense—social sustainability matters for individuals as well as for society.

Environmental sustainability, the third pillar in sustainability, focus more on environmental sustainability with more emphasis on the life support system like soil and atmosphere that need to be preserved with economic growth/development vis-a vis quality of human life. It requires sustainable resource use, efficient sink function and maintenance of a stock of natural capital. It also implies that the environment should perform these functions efficiently and uninterruptedly in such a way the ecological stability is maintained and resilience remains unaffected. Increasing pollution in the last century forced world nations to talk about and resolve the issue of GHGs, ozone depletion, loss of biodiversity and climate change posing dangerous anthropogenic effects on humanity.

The three dimensions of sustainability are interdependent and follow the rules of sustainable development, which explains the substitutability of various factors between them, namely weak and strong sustainability. The essential condition for sustainability is that the stock of capital (manmade, human and natural) should not decline over time. The intergenerational equity as envisaged in the Stockholm Declaration can be maintained in three ways. The first aspect requires that the next generation should inherit the same level of manmade and natural capital, the second aspect expects only natural capital, and the third includes all three types of capital, human, manmade and natural capital. There are two variants of this rule, weak sustainability and strong sustainability.

Weak Sustainability rule implies that total stocks of manmade, human and natural capital are non-declining through time. Further, it assumes that the natural capital can be substituted by way of manmade capital, i.e., we can inherit less natural capital, and more manmade capital to the next generation. Hence, the weak sustainability rule assumes perfect substitutability between natural and human capital, which is actually not there.

Strong sustainability rules imply that the stock of natural capital should be non-declining over time. In other words, the strong sustainability criterion requires constancy of natural capital stock of natural capital (environmental resources) and environmental quality, which implies that the environment should not be degraded over the years; rather, improvement is expected. The concept of strong sustainability, on the other hand, states that natural capital provides some functions that are not replaceable by manmade capital. It envisages resources once lost, cannot be recovered or repaired within a reasonable time scale, such as biodiversity or loss of certain species, pollination, fertile soils, assimilation capacity, clean air, clean water, climate regulation.

Organizational Sustainability: The concept of sustainability is equally applied to businesses where two types of sustainable business practices are being followed in businesses or organizations. One considers the effect a business has on the environment, while the other considers the effect a business has on society, with the motto of casting a positive impact on at least one of those areas through adopting sustainable business practices. In this era of cutthroat competition, the concept is one of the critical drivers of change in the organizational, marketplace and business strategy. It applies to organizational activities and classified known as business for sustainability, sustainable organization and sustainable business as (Wikström (2010), socially sustainable practices affect economic sustainability performance in supply chains (Sudusinghe & Seuring, 2020) and quality improvement into a systematic approach to an organization's sustainability (Schalock et al., 2016). Further, it impacts various knowledge risks related to business sustainability (Durst & Zieba, 2020), develop pathways to organize elements of sustainability transition (Williams & Robinson, 2020) and the value creation process of firms excelling in sustainability (Brozovi et al., 2020).

Studies call for redesigning the financial risk management process in fiscal governance. (Tofan et al., 2020) and ensuring community-based programs for the targeted communities, where the impacts of this programme will be reduced when the sustainability of such programme declines (Ceptureanu et al., 2018) and sustainability and social justice remain elusive even though each is unattainable without the other (Haedicke, 2019). Jadoon et al. (2021) disclosed that investors value corporate sustainability performance gained through social, economic, and corporate governance dimensions only and the quality of sustainability reporting. Fry and Egel (2021) confirmed that global leaders for sustainability become more committed to moving beyond satisfying stakeholders' demands for economic returns toward a more sustainable, triple bottom line, balanced approach; Nezami and Yildirim (2013) found that a sustainability-based approach significantly affects a company's personnel, energy, material, and overall costs.

Technology and sustainability are the emerging areas where the world is looking to counter the ill effects of global warming. Gouvea et al. (2018) showed that information and communications technology (ICT) and human development have significant effects on environmental sustainability. Technological innovations help businesses minimize their adverse environmental impacts besides inducing sustainable behaviours (Vacchi et al., 2021). The role of digital Industry 4.0 technologies in sustainability accounting revealed that accounting for economic values is well-considered; however, it does not perform comprehensive environmental and social accounting (Klymenko et al., 2021). Saunila et al. (2019) found corporate sustainability strategy and smart technologies linked to each other and smart technologies do not have a direct influence on environmental or social sustainability. Zhang et al. (2021) reported that policy interventions in taxes and subsidies are still required to foster sustainability in the industry.

Economics and Sustainability

History of Economics can be traced the times of Kautilya's Arthashastra which is now evolved to modern economic science. Arthashastra was written by Kautilya focusing on broad discussion about ancient statecraft, economic policy and military strategy. Ancient economic thought also comprised of physiocrats and mercantilists, that latterly became the force behind imperialism by the western world shaping the larger part of world history.

Modern economic science deals with the efficient use of limited resources and trade-offs. Economic science is dominated by the neoclassical school of thought which is the basis of all microeconomic analysis. Neoclassical economics analyse the process of price determination by assuming the economy as a closed system that finds no limits.

However, some classical economists like Malthus (1798), Ricardo (1817), and Mill (1857) Marx (1867) believed that economic activities are constrained by nature. In the 1970s a debate was started on social and environmental limits to economic growth with the advent of limit to growth theory (Club of Rome 1972). This awareness of the actual conflict between economic growth and the environment led to the birth of the concept of sustainable development.

In Economics we have branches like Resource Economics, Environmental Economics and Ecological Economics which emphasize upon environmental sustainability, green accounting, natural resources and environmental ethics. However, policymaking and real-life economic decisions are still based on the traditional concept of growth which is the consistent rise of per capita income without environmental considerations. In view of this, there is a need to contemplate the inclusion of environmental and sustainability considerations into real-world policy implementation. The environment should be the foremost concern of economic planners; so, focus must shift from Economics to Earthonomics which is the need of the hour. Nowadays, everyone is experiencing the effect of climate change which is mainly due to anthropogenic reasons. It is the result of unplanned economic thoughts dominated by the Western Economic thoughts, since the advent of the Industrial Revolution. The world cannot afford to follow the same path if, we want to save human existence on earth. There is a need to rethink and revisit our way of modelling by making sustainability a major component.

Sustainable development was a key theme of the United Nations Conference on Human Environment in Stockholm in 1972. Sustainable development is a process of improving economic well-being and quality of life while enabling the next generations. Sustainable development aims to lessen the likelihood of dynamic natural and/or manmade systems exceeding tipping points when exposed to disturbances (Bloesch et al., 2015). Sustainable development is taken to mean improving the quality of life. If development were to mean growth, then it could not be sustained over the long term (Munn, 1992). Katunian (2019) discussed sustainable development at societal, organizational, and individual levels, where sustainable human development can bring broader development in organizations and society. The United Nation's sustainable goals (SDGs) have been considered a benchmark for sustainable development, where these goals seek to eradicate poverty, malnutrition, hunger and vulnerability, equitable educational opportunities, and access green energy. Barbier and Burgess (2017) revealed that the 17 SDGs are primarily attributed to the environmental, economic or social system.

Transition to Earthonomics

The concept of sustainable development suggests that it is possible to achieve economic growth without environmental damage. Over the decades sustainable development thinking is evolved through World Conservation Strategy (1980), The Brundtland Report (1987) United Nations Conference on Environment and Development in Rio (1992), Kyoto protocol and Agenda-21 and the most recent Paris Agreement. The unsustainable development process creates a delusion in the history of development. Studies of development must, of course, consider economic factors, particularly in the case of societies who suffer from the pollution of poverty; However, cultural and environmental factors are equally important. In fact, development is not sustainable over the long term if it is not ecologically sustainable (Munn, 1992).

Climate Change and Sustainability: The ongoing process of global warming increased the Earth's global average surface temperature by about 1 degree Celsius (°C), which could increase the global mean temperature up to 2°C-4°C by the year 2100, compared to pre-industrial levels (National Oceanic and Atmospheric Administration (2021). Research confirmed an inverted 'U' shaped relationship between environment and economic growth, thereby suggesting that the growth of per capita tends to improve the environmental quality (Mor & Jindal, 2012; Mor, 2014). Therefore, the nations can opt for the present value of higher future growth and a better-quality environment in future at the cost of the current rate of degradation of environmental resources (Mor & Singh, 2019). Climate change trigger a potential hidden disaster for the agriculture sector (Panghal & Mor, 2020), leading to more vagaries for small size farm (Mor, 2017a) and reduced crop revenue (Mor, 2017b).

The mitigation of GHGs concentration has become a first-order issue for decision making in environmental sustainability resembles the policy documents of the IPCC and UNFCCC. The rigour of global mitigation efforts is seen from the series of Conferences of the Parties (COP) and resulting agreements like Kyoto Protocol and Paris Agreement

(Seo, 2017), where countries can meet their mitigation commitments and environmental objectives through multiple instruments (Mele et al., 2021).

Kyoto Protocol became a legally binding treaty on 16th February 2005 and implemented the first international top-down mechanisms and provided mitigation incentives for both Annex I and non-Annex I parties (Kuriyama & Abe, 2018). It established a flexible, broad-based, international mechanism (Böhringer, 2003), and parties ratifying it should be environmentally efficient compared to those who do not ratify it (Feroz et al., 2009). Research showed the Kyoto Protocol have a measurable reducing effect on CO_2-e emissions Grunewald and Martinez-Zarzoso, 2016), while Rosen (2015) regarded it as a fundamentally flawed agreement that set back solutions on climate change by two decades. The protocol termed as obsolete as it was not ratified by the largest emitter of the world (Singh, 2006).

Paris Agreement was adopted at the annual gathering of parties to the UNFCCC in December 2015, and its goal is to limit global warming to well below 2°C, preferably to 1.5°C, compared to pre-industrial levels. The agreement is described as a breakthrough in international climate policy by accepting the predominance of domestic climate change (Falkner, 2016), representing a marked shift in emission reduction spheres (Janetschek et al., 2020) and sets forth a new international legal regime to strengthen the global response to climate change (Horowitz, 2016). However, the Earth's temperature is still set to increase by 3-4°C, almost double the agreement limiting it to 1.5-2.0°C even if all national pledges are fully realized (Young, 2016).

Introduction of Chapters in the Book

Part-I: Technology and Sustainability

The first part of the book begins with the role of technology in affecting the environment and humanity. The world looks forward to technology to mitigate the emissions of GHGs and stabilise climate changes without compromising on the economic growth of nations (Nguyen et al., 2017). The technology, Artificial Intelligence (AI), 5G, machine learning, Internet of Things (IoT), and industry 4.0 can contribute to this endeavour to save the planet Earth and prepare the world for a fossil-fuel-free society (Ekholm, 2019). Information and communications technology and human development have significant effects on environmental sustainabilit(Gouvea et al., 2018). Blockchain technology improved supply chain sustainability performance (Park & Li, 2021) and mobile technology impacted sustainability in many other industries (Bai et al., 2020). Luccioni et al. (2020) revealed that advancements in AI make lives simpler, faster, and less complicated, whereas Iafrate (2018) pointed out that AI minimises human work errors, mistakes and intentional misconduct by automating various tasks and activities at the same time, instead of reducing human jobs. Research indicates that it is time to move beyond that and to address the sustainability of developing and using AI systems, a growing effort towards achieving sustainable development goals (van Wynsberghe, 2021).

Research talks about the pros and cons of technology deployment due to their carbon footprints or unsustainability. Tussyadiah and Miller (2020) narrated the future states of technology, reflecting the expectation of technical feasibility of artificial intelligence (AI), and found a critical link between advancements in technology and sustainability, while Fuchs (2017) cortices the use of information technology sustainability as it should transform, the sustainability concept into a critical notion of un/sustainable information technology sustainability in the context of the information society. The development of a framework for technology assessment was exploded by integrating the three key elements: technology development, sustainable development, and dynamic systems approach and demonstrated that incorporating the system dynamics methodology in energy technology assessment theory and practice exists within the context of sustainable development (Musango & Brent, 2011). (Ranjbari et al., 2021) examined the impact of COVID-19 on the three pillars (economic, social, and environmental) of sustainability and found a negative impact on sustainable development. The increasing mean annual global temperature requires long term strategies to cope with. The resilience strategies may differ in case of local environmental problems like residue burning or river pollution; however, it may be global in case of GHGs emission, depletion of Ozon layers loss of biodiversity.

The first chapter, authored by **Sunita Devi**, revisits Kautilya's Philosophy on Sustainable Development. She talks about Kautilya-a teacher, philosopher, economist and administrator, who wrote the book *Arthashastra* around 300 BC, which contains many references on environmental protection, ecological balance, rainfall phenomena, weather cycles, and related concepts. The paper highlights the spirit of environmental protection and practise sustainable development, mentioned in Arthashastra by recognising the need for current and future times. Without productive economic activity, current prosperity and future growth will be destroyed. The author citing 'Arthashastra' state, pinpointed eight great calamities like fire, floods, disease, famine, rats, wild animals, serpents and evil spirits. The paper talks about the state's role in protecting produce-forests, elephant-forests, irrigation works and mines and demanded punishments and penalties specified for injuring and killing the living creatures. The paper reveals that many Environmental protection and pollution control legislations are based on Kautilya's philosophy like Article 51-A and 48-A of the Constitution of India, which prescribes environmental protection as a fundamental duty of every citizen and protection of the environment and to safeguard the forests and wildlife of the country.

In the second chapter of this section, **Ruth Taplin** discusses some sustainability lessons based on Innovations in Artificial Intelligence AI to Mitigate Climate Change. The paper focused on the beneficial effects of Artificial Intelligence (AI) in mitigation with climate change and promotes sustainability efforts globally. She revealed that climate change negatively affects the economies and societies in many developing countries like India. Her study further pinpoints that the AI solutions like Machine learning (ML), Global Positing Systems (GPS) and Mobile Apps can effectively be deployed to generate data on pollution, flooding and land degradation, locust and swarm warning, which thereby by cumulatively reduce the emission.

The third chapter authored by **Mario B. Curatolo** talks about resilience as a sustainability strategy for businesses in the post-covid era. Resilience is defined as the ability of individuals, groups, communicates, firms and organisations to adapt and adjust to unpredicted changes. It implies the ability to predict unexpected future scenarios, which may be short terms like the Covid outbreak and long terms like recession and climate change. He terms the Covid outbreak as a "wake-up call" for businesses to think out of the box and take consciousness about the impossibility to postpone any longer the way they allocated human and physical resources. The paper suggests that resilience is to be promoted as a sustainability strategy for the transformation of businesses, and at the same time, resilience by design will need to be embedded too as part of the board social business culture of the modern firm.

The fourth chapter by **Cornelia Caseau** examines the twin question- the territorial and environmental challenges of the blackcurrant sector in Burgundy-Franche-Comté (France) and the assets of the Blackcurrant Actors to build territorial resilience. Her study dialogues the Territorial resilience of the Blackcurrant Actors in Burgundy/France in the face of the impacts of climate change. She elaborates on the role of the Burgundy-Franche-Comté region, which is the third-largest producer of blackcurrants in 2021 and an important segment in the supply of fruits to the Dijon and Burgundy liqueur makers, including blackcurrant cream annually. The paper reveals that the Blackcurrant Actors do not have sufficient financial support hampering their potential owing to climate change.

Swati Mehta's chapter deals with the role of Innovation, Industry and Infrastructure in emerging Asian economies in compliance with the sustainable development goals, especially on SDG 9, which focuses on 3Is, Infrastructure, Industries and Innovation. She attributes SDGs as a promising roadmap for inclusive and sustainable growth, where firms, industries, sectors and economies all are striving for long-run growth. The paper reveals that industrialisation backed with innovation and robust infrastructure is the key to development, where Asia is growing fast amid a changing landscape.

V. Rengarajan, author of the sixth paper of this section, calls for rethinking and revitalising our pathways to sustainable human welfare and a safe planet. The paper focused on the social achievement of the economic model's ultimate goal. The engineering approach is primarily concerned with logistics issues based on Amartya Sens's definition of economics as the study of ethics and politics. He suggests that the promotion of ancient indigenous knowledge on sustainability on the one hand and an alternate pathway for integrated socially inclusive green finance development, one the other. The alternate pathway to sustainability should base on environment social governance like no poverty, zero hunger, reduction in inequality, affordable clean energy and gender equality—the former posse mor humanitarian perspective during the later governance one.

Part-II: Organization and Sustainability

The part II of the book deals with the crucial role of organization in good governance and promoting sustainability. Research by Fouché and Brent (2020) focused on the participatory planning approach for local energy sustainability of South Africa and revealed that both the local governments as well as institutions were aspiring for sustainability. Barometer of Sustainability, a tool for monitoring the sustainability process, has been examined by Batalhão et al. (2018) who found that the municipality is more concerned with socioeconomic issues than environmental issues in Brazil. Hallin et al. (2021) assessed the sustainability concept based on ten years-long digital footprints of Stockholm Royal Seaport and revealed that sustainability is local, temporal and political in the case of Stockholm Royal Seaport.

Sustainable practices have been found to play a vital role among newly enrolled engineering students in Denmark to environmental and non-environmental sustainability issues and regarded sustainability equally important in engineering (Haase, 2014); Chakraborty et al. (2021) discussed the strategy for adoption of sustainable strategies in Ashoka University in India and found its commitment towards sustainability in courses, research and operations.

Finance is essential to keep businesses and economies moving and make them sustainable and viable. Lagoarde-Segot and Paranque (2018) regarded finance as a shared resource, and the present financial structure and system indices inequalities lead to ecological crises (Jager and Schmidt, 2020). Ziolo et al. (2019) found that traditional finance does not care for society and the environment; however, sustainable development reduces negative externalities. Many financial indicators are associated with economic, social and environmental sustainability, especially externalities. Countries ranked higher in terms of economic, financial and social indicators (Belgium, Germany, Luxembourg, the Netherlands and the United Kingdom) stand worst on sustainability. Research showed that finance helps small South African enterprises manage risks and promote sustainable practices (Kimanzi & Gamede, 2020). Therefore, green finance can be an effective panacea for climate management.

The first paper by **Sanjay Bhayana** and **Sapna Arora** discusses corporate governance rating as a tool for the global strategy for good corporate governance. They talked about media interest in corporate governance, where reports of corporate governance failures are integral to the news. The authors evidence that the rating services are critical in disseminating motivation among the stakeholders & investors and companies. The paper further reiterated that multiple benefits accrue to investors from advising on transparency and disclosure practices for investors, whereas GCR help companies in terms of improving image and valuation, stock exchange listing, transactions with creditors and so on. Resultantly, the Companies can use/set as a standard for further improvement, and the outcome of the rating can be used to enhance the long-term shareholder value.

Partha Naskar, in the second chapter of this section, talks about the notion of thinking-planning-execution as the crux of organizational excellence for sustainable development. The paper investigates four categories of employees A, B, C & D based on a research scale in the name of "Potential Assessment of Organizational Planning-Public Department" and act as a benchmark tool of assessment of organizations. The author reveals the role of organizational planning for economic progression in sustainable global business practices, especially in the current COVID period of turmoil. Further, the study reveals robust implications in understanding the extent of real-life application of planning in the government departments in the West Bengal state of India. The paper recommends that the authorities and senior managerial officials in the Government of West Bengal can understand the core areas where improvement is necessary for planning considering the four categories of employees in the public departments in the West Bengal Government.

The second paper by **Rashmi Tyagi** and **Jatesh Kathpalia** explore the antecedents of self-help groups and their activities in rural area of Fatehabad and Kurukshetra Districts of

Haryana state of India. The study reveals that the majority of the farmers possess a low level of socio-economic status leading to a low level of socio-economic empowerment and vice-versa. Further, social participation was found to be significantly associated with the Level of socio-economic empowerment, and farmers with low mass media exposure experience a medium level of socio-economic empowerment. The study findings reveal that respondents' monthly income, monthly expenditure, and savings have increased after joining SHGs, which enhance their decision-making power, i.e., empowerment. Moreover, most sample respondents opined that their power has increased in taking decisions after joining SHGs either inside or outside their family.

Sarita Adhikari and *Radhe Shyam* Pradhan examines the effect of innovation and technology on productivity and profitability using data from 160 respondents from 25 commercial banks of Nepal. The study depicts that internet banking positively impacts the bank productivity and profitability of Nepalese commercial banks. Furthermore, ATMs have been found to have a positive impact on bank productivity and profitability, indicating higher efficiency of banks having a more significant number of ATMs. The finding confirms that mobile banking, point of sale services, and e-payment technology positively impact bank productivity and profitability in commercial banks of Nepal.

The fourth paper by **Parmod Malik** discusses the case of Solid Waste of Rohtak Municipal Corporation in Haryana State of India using secondary data on municipal waste and its disposal. He regards Swatch Bharat Abhiyan as a paradigm shift towards India's environmental policy and municipal waste disposal. The paper further talks about the potential benefits of municipal waste disposal legislation for sustainable development in developing countries, especially India. The Government has enforced the Solid Waste Management Rules, 2016, to monitor the proper and adequate disposal of the solid wastes generated. Local bodies such as Municipal Corporations are held responsible for collection, transportation and composting, treatment, segregation and disposal of solid waste. Landfilling is only allowed for non-biodegradable wastes.

Anita Sapkota and *Nar Bahadur* Bista examines the significance of microfinance in promoting women's empowerment in the Kathmandu Valley of Nepal. Based on primary data from 154 respondents, the study employs regression models on various dependent variables like financial independence, decision making and self-confidence and entrepreneurial skills, access to resources, leadership skills, and self-efficacy. The findings report a positive impact that entrepreneurial skills have on financial independence, decision-making, and self-confidence. Further, access to resources positively affects financial independence, decision-making, and self-confidence. The conclusion further reveals that leadership skills positively impact financial independence, decision making, and self-confidence. Similarly, self-efficacy positively affects financial independence, decision-making, and self-confidence.

Part-III: Agriculture and Sustainability

The third part is devoted to the significance of agricultural activities in climate management. AI-enabled solutions are becoming popular nowadays in agriculture besides finance, transport, energy and healthcare (Tolamise, 2020), which caters for more reliable and improved harvesting (Bisen, 2019). The agriculture sector is one of the forerunners to deploy AI as stems for the numerous startups in the agrarian sector, which is enhancing efficiency in agricultural production and at the same time minimizes the adverse impacts on the environment (Mathew, 2019). Faggella (2020) opined that AI deployment leads to improved crop monitoring, better soil health, weeds, pests & insect control, higher crop yields, reduction of the manual labour force, and improvement in the food supply chain. It helps farmers detect plant diseases, forecast climate changes, respond smartly and apart from processing the agricultural data and reduce carbon footprints by 20 per cent (Gupta, Vemireddy, & Pingali, 2019). With the deployment of AI-enabled digital solutions, the distresses and vulnerabilities caused by climate change can be effectively minimized (Mor et al., 2020).

Neelam Luhach, Preeti Sihan, Ashok Kumar, Neelam Kumari, and **Shivam** discussed Haryana's paddy straw management techniques. The burning of crop residue, especially in rice cultivation, has created havoc, causing air pollution in Northern Haryana in the paddy harvesting season (October-November). The authors report that farmers find the most effective way of disposing of the residue by burning biomass in the paddy field. The paper is based on the sampled 120 farmers from four villages in Sonipat and Karnal districts of Haryana state by employing a random sampling technique. The authors collected information through a well-structured interview schedule of 11 variables, namely, age, education, socio-economic status, landholding, farm Implements, mass media exposure, extension contact, irrigation facilities, risk orientation, cropping system, soil health card knowledge, adoption and constraints perceived by the farmers in adoption of paddy straw management techniques. The conclusions reveal that most farmers possess high to medium knowledge in paddy straw management Techniques in Haryana.

Priya and Jaswinder Singh Brar analyse the Laser Levelling Technology for Sustainable Irrigation which impacted water productivity, cost of irrigation, and crop yield in wheat crops. They selected primary data for 56 farms, out of which 36 adopted this technology and 20 non-adopters from the Jalandhar district in Punjab state of India. The authors establish that the farmers who had adopted this technique realized better water productivity, saved on the front of cost and realized better returns. Furthermore, highly educated and large farm households have adopted the latest irrigation technique. The study argues that for the adoption of this technology with apparent benefits. Therefore, the government needs to adopt policies and incentives aimed at water use to ensure sustainable development of the agricultural sector.

The third chapter of the section by **Vinod Kumari and Subhash Chander** elaborates the impacts of drip Irrigation Technology in Citrus Cultivation for efficient water use and Sustainable Crop Production in the Haryana State of India. The authors opines that Drip irrigation effectively delivers water directly to the root zone, reduces water wastage, and is considered a feasible alternative for crops requiring much water. The study calls for improving adoption of drip irrigation besides mass-media exposure, extension contacts and training and education among farmers as most farmers possess a low level of education. Further, the authors suggest that enhancing the regular electricity supply, more subsidy and provisioning training to farmers regarding operations, maintenance, repair, and water-soluble fertilizers are necessary may promote the use of adoption of the Drip Irrigation System. They conclude that this water-saving technology must be expanded to all regions to elucidate the benefit of drip irrigation through proper extension services so that farmers can get higher crop productivity using limited water resources and benefit economically.

The fourth chapter discusses the economic benefits of the adoption of 'Happy Seeder' farm technology for sustainable agriculture by **Jatesh Kathpalia, Rashmi Tyagi, Vinod Kumari and Anil Kumar Saroha.** The study pertains to 160 farms, including 80 'Happy Seeder' adopters and 80 non-adopters farmers, from the Fatehabad district of Haryana. The study concludes that 48.75 per cent of the respondents had a high level of adoption rest (18.75 per cent of the respondents had a low level of the adoption of Happy seeder farm technology. The authors report that age, education, annual family income, landholding and mass media exposure were found significantly associated with adoption level.

In a nutshell, the world is required to devise long term strategies for the global commons, and the use of the word Sustainability in international politics resumes it (World Commission on Environment and Development, 2017). The concept of sustainable development pertains to the ability of the biosphere to absorb the ills effects of human activities where technology and societal organizations can play an essential role in managing the global emissions and enhancing the economic growth of nations (Brundtland, 1987). Indeed, the essence of sustainable development envisages that the dividends of economic growth need to be distrusted equitably among the poor and vulnerable in a sustainable manner. Further, it requires that the affluent society manage their lifestyle within limits set by the earth's natural reoccurs, and the goal of sustainable development can be achieved when the economic growth and population growth are in harmony without disturbing the ecosystem.

References

1. Abson, D. J., Fischer, J., Leventon, J., Newig, J., Schomerus, T., Vilsmaier, U., von Wehrden, H., Abernethy, P., Ives, C. D., Jager, N. W., & Lang, D. J. (2017). Leverage points for sustainability transformation. *Ambio*, 46(1). https://doi.org/10.1007/s13280-016-0800-y
2. Barbier, E. B., & Burgess, J. C. (2017). The sustainable development goals and the systems approach to sustainability. *Economics*, 11. https://doi.org/10.5018/economics-ejournal.ja.2017-28
3. Batalhão, A. C. da S., Teixeira, D., de Godoi, E. L., & Prates, G. Ap. (2018). Exploring the Local Sustainability Approach Using Indicators. *Journal of Management and Sustainability*, 8(4). https://doi.org/10.5539/jms.v8n4p39
4. Bennich, T., Belyazid, S., Stjernquist, I., Diemer, A., Seifollahi-Aghmiuni, S., & Kalantari, Z. (2021). The bio-based economy, 2030 Agenda, and strong sustainability – A regional-scale assessment of sustainability goal interactions. *Journal of Cleaner Production, 283*. https://doi.org/10.1016/j.jclepro.2020.125174
5. Bisen, V. S. (2019). How AI Can Help in Agriculture- Five Applications and Use Cases. Retrieved December 10, 2020, from https://medium.com/vsinghbisen/how-ai-can-help-in-agriculture-five-applications-and-use-cases-f09c3dc326c9

6. Bloesch, J., von Hauff, M., Mainzer, K., Mohan, S. V., Renn, O., Risse, V., Song, Y., Takeuchi, K., & Wilderer, P. A. (2015). Sustainable development integrated in the concept of resilience. *Problemy Ekorozwoju, 10*(1).
7. Böhringer, C. (2003). The Kyoto Protocol: A review and perspectives. *Oxford Review of Economic Policy*, 19(3). https://doi.org/10.1093/oxrep/19.3.451
8. Böhringer, C. (2003). The Kyoto Protocol: A review and perspectives. Oxford Review of Economic Policy, 19(3). Retrieved from https://doi.org/10.1093/oxrep/19.3.451
9. Brozovi, D., D'Auria, A., & Tregua, M. (2020). Value creation and sustainability: Lessons from leading sustainability firms. *Sustainability (Switzerland)*, 12(11). https://doi.org/10.3390/su12114450
10. Brundtland, G. (1987). UN Brundtland Commission Report. *Our Common Future*.
11. Ceptureanu, S. I., Ceptureanu, E. G., Luchian, C. E., & Luchian, I. (2018). Community based programs sustainability. a multidimensional analysis of sustainability factors. *Sustainability (Switzerland), 10*(3). https://doi.org/10.3390/su10030870
12. Chakraborty, A., Kumar, S., Shashidhara, L. S., & Taneja, A. (2021). Building sustainable societies through purpose driven universities: A case study from ashoka university (India). *Sustainability (Switzerland), 13*(13). https://doi.org/10.3390/su13137423
13. *Daniel Faggella (2020). Author Page | Emerj*. (2020). Retrieved April 21, 2021, from https://emerj.com/author/dan/
14. Durst, S., & Zieba, M. (2020). Knowledge risks inherent in business sustainability. Journal of Cleaner Production, 251. https://doi.org/10.1016/j.jclepro.2019.119670
15. Eizenberg, E., & Jabareen, Y. (2017). Social sustainability: A new conceptual framework. *Sustainability (Switzerland)*, 9(1). https://doi.org/10.3390/su9010068
16. Ekholm, B (2019). Want to cut greenhouse gas emissions? Look to digital technologies | World Economic Forum. Retrieved December 8, 2020, from https://www.weforum.org/agenda/2019/09/want-to-exponentially-reduce-ghg-emissions-look-to-digital-tech-solutions/
17. Falkner, R. (2016). The Paris agreement and the new logic of international climate politics. *International Affairs*, 92(5). https://doi.org/10.1111/1468-2346.12708
18. Feroz, E. H., Raab, R. L., Ulleberg, G. T., & Alsharif, K. (2009). Global warming and environmental production efficiency ranking of the Kyoto Protocol nations. *Journal of Environmental Management, 90*(2). https://doi.org/10.1016/j.jenvman.2008.05.006
19. Feroz, E. H., Raab, R. L., Ulleberg, G. T., & Alsharif, K. (2009). Global warming and environmental production efficiency ranking of the Kyoto Protocol nations. Journal of Environmental Management, 90(2). Retrieved from https://doi.org/10.1016/j.jenvman.2008.05.006
20. Fouché, E., & Brent, A. (2020). Explore, design and act for sustainability: A participatory planning approach for local energy sustainability. *Sustainability (Switzerland)*, 12(3). https://doi.org/10.3390/su12030862
21. Fry, L. W., & Egel, E. (2021). Global leadership for sustainability. Sustainability *(Switzerland), 13*(11). https://doi.org/10.3390/su13116360
22. Fuchs, C. (2017). Information technology and sustainability in the information society. *International Journal of Communication, 11*.
23. *Global Climate report. (2021) report Global Temperature | Vital Signs – Climate Change: Vital Signs of the Planet*. (2021). https://climate.nasa.gov/vital-signs/global-temperature/
24. Gouvea, R., Kapelianis, D., & Kassicieh, S. (2018). Assessing the nexus of sustainability and information & communications technology. *Technological Forecasting and Social Change, 130*. https://doi.org/10.1016/j.techfore.2017.07.023

25. Grunewald, N., & Martinez-Zarzoso, I. (2016). Did the Kyoto Protocol fail? An evaluation of the effect of the Kyoto Protocol on CO2 emissions. *Environment and Development Economics*, 21(1). https://doi.org/10.1017/S1355770X15000091
26. Gupta, S., Vemireddy, V., & Pingali, P. L. (2019). Nutritional outcomes of empowerment and market integration for women in rural India. Food Security, 11(6), 1243–1256. https://doi.org/10.1007/s12571-019-00978-z
27. Haase, S. (2014). Engineering students' sustainability approaches. *European Journal of Engineering Education, 39*(3). https://doi.org/10.1080/03043797.2013.858103
28. Haedicke, M.A. (2019). Sustainability: Approaches to Environmental Justice and Social Power. *Contemporary Sociology: A Journal of Reviews, 48*(5). https://doi.org/10. 1177/00943 06119867060nn
29. Hallin, A., Karrbom-Gustavsson, T., & Dobers, P. (2021). Transition towards and of sustainability—Understanding sustainability as performative. Business *Strategy and the Environment, 30*(4). https://doi.org/10.1002/bse.2726
30. Höhne, N., Kuramochi, T., Warnecke, C., Röser, F., Fekete, H., Hagemann, M., Day, T., Tewari, R., Kurdziel, M., Sterl, S., & Gonzales, S. (2017). The Paris Agreement: resolving the inconsistency between global goals and national contributions. *Climate Policy,* 17(1). https://doi.org/10.1080/14693062.2016.1218320
31. Horowitz, C. A. (2016). Paris Agreement. *International Legal Materials*, 55(4). https://doi.org/10.1017/s0020782900004253
32. Iafrate, F. (2018). Artificial Intelligence and Big Data: The Birth of a New Intelligence. In *Artificial Intelligence and Big Data:* The Birth of a New Intelligence (Vol. 8). wiley. https://doi.org/10.1002/9781119426653
33. Ives, C. D., Freeth, R., & Fischer, J. (2020). Inside-out sustainability: The neglect of inner worlds. *Ambio*, 49(1). https://doi.org/10.1007/s13280-019-01187-w
34. Jadoon, I. A., Ali, A., Ayub, U., Tahir, M., & Mumtaz, R. (2021). The impact of sustainability reporting quality on the value relevance of corporate sustainability performance. *Sustainable Development*, *29*(1). https://doi.org/10.1002/sd.2138
35. Jager, J., & Schmidt, L. (2020). Global green finance and sustainability: Insights for progressive strategies. *Journal Fur Entwicklungspolitik*, *36*(4). https://doi.org/10.20446/JEP-2414-3197-36-4-4
36. Janetschek, H., Brandi, C., Dzebo, A., & Hackmann, B. (2020). The 2030 Agenda and the Paris Agreement: voluntary contributions towards thematic policy coherence. *Climate Policy*, *20*(4). https://doi.org/10.1080/14693062.2019.1677549
37. Jerneck, A., Olsson, L., Ness, B., Anderberg, S., Baier, M., Clark, E., Hickler, T., Hornborg, A., Kronsell, A., Lövbrand, E., & Persson, J. (2011). Structuring sustainability science. *Sustainability Science*, *6*(1). https://doi.org/10.1007/s11625-010-0117-x
38. Katunian, A. (2019). Sustainability as a new approach for the human resource development in tourism sector. *Public Policy and Administration*, *18*(4). https://doi.org/10.13165/VPA-19-18-4-03
39. Kimanzi, M. K., & Gamede, V. W. (2020). Embracing the role of finance in sustainability for SMEs. *International Journal of Economics and Finance Studies*, *12*(2). https://doi.org/10.34109/ijefs.202012213
40. Klymenko, O., Halse, L. L., & Jæger, B. (2021). The enabling role of digital technologies in sustainability accounting: Findings from norwegian manufacturing companies. *Systems*, *9*(2). https://doi.org/10.3390/systems9020033

41. Kuhlman, T., & Farrington, J. (2010). What is sustainability? In *Sustainability* (Vol. 2, Issue 11). https://doi.org/10.3390/su2113436
42. Kuriyama, A., & Abe, N. (2018). Ex-post assessment of the Kyoto Protocol – quantification of CO2 mitigation impact in both Annex B and non-Annex B countries. *Applied Energy, 220*. https://doi.org/10.1016/j.apenergy.2018.03.025
43. Lagoarde-Segot, T., & Paranque, B. (2018). Finance and sustainability: From ideology to utopia. *International Review of Financial Analysis, 55*. https://doi.org/10.1016/j.irfa.2017.10.006
44. Luccioni, A., Lacoste, A. & Schmidt, V. (2020). Estimating Carbon Emissions of Artificial Intelligence. Retrieved December 2, 2020. Available at: https://technologyandsociety.org/estimating-carbon-emissions-of-artificial-intelligence/
45. Mathew, K. (2019). Precision Farming: AI and Automation Are Transforming Agriculture. Retrieved December 14, 2020, from https://datacenterfrontier.com/precision-farming-ai-and-automation-are-transforming-agriculture/
46. Mele, A., Paglialunga, E., & Sforna, G. (2021). Climate cooperation from Kyoto to Paris: What can be learnt from the CDM experience? *Socio-Economic Planning Sciences, 75*. https://doi.org/10.1016/j.seps.2020.100942
47. Mor, S. (2014). Estimation of Environmental Kuznets Curve for India. *EPRA International Journal of Environmental Economics, Commerce and Educational Management*, 1(1), 10–16.
48. Mor, S. (2014). Estimation of Environmental Kuznets Curve for India. *EPRA International Journal of Environmental Economics, Commerce and Educational Management, 1*(1), 10–16.
49. Mor, S. (2017a). Climate Change and Land Revenue: Evidences from Indian Agriculture. *Disaster Advances, 10*(12), 21–27.
50. Mor, S. (2017b). Climate Change and Land Revenue: Evidences from Indian Agriculture. *Disaster Advances*, 10(12), 21–27.
51. Mor, S., & Jindal, S. (2012). *Estimation of Environmental Kuznets Curve and Kyoto Parties: A Panel Data Analysis. IJCEM International Journal of Computational Engineering & Management* (Vol. 15).
52. Mor, S., & Jindal, S. (2012). Estimation of Environmental Kuznets Curve and Kyoto Parties: A Panel Data Analysis. In *IJCEM International Journal of Computational Engineering & Management* (Vol. 15).
53. Mor, S., & Singh, G. (2019). Does Growth affect environment? Evidence from the World. *Journal of International Economics*, 10(1), 42–49.
54. Mor, S., Madan, S., & Prasad, K. D. (2021). Artificial intelligence and carbon footprints: Roadmap for Indian agriculture. *Strategic Change*, 30(3), 269–280. Retrieved August 8, 2021 from https://doi.org/10.1002/JSC.2409
55. Munn, R. E. (1992). Towards sustainable development. *Atmospheric Environment Part A, General Topics, 26*(15). https://doi.org/10.1016/0960-1686(92)90007-8
56. Musango, J. K., & Brent, A. C. (2011). A conceptual framework for energy technology sustainability assessment. *Energy for Sustainable Development, 15*(1). https://doi.org/10.1016/j.esd.2010.10.005
57. Nagatsu, M., Davis, T., DesRoches, C. T., Koskinen, I., MacLeod, M., Stojanovic, M., & Thorén, H. (2020). Philosophy of science for sustainability science. *Sustainability Science, 15*(6). https://doi.org/10.1007/s11625-020-00832-8
58. Nezami, F. G., & Yildirim, M. B. (2013). A sustainability approach for selecting maintenance strategy. *International Journal of Sustainable Engineering*, 6(4). https://doi.org/10.1080/19397038.2013.765928

59. Nguyen, K., Sahin, O., Stewart, R. and Zhang, H. (2017). Smart Technologies in Reducing Carbon Emission: Artificial Intelligence and Smart Water Meter. https://doi.10.1145/3055635.3056566
60. Panghal, A., & Mor, S. (2020). Climate Variability and Wheat Crop Yield: Forecasting Indian Scenario till 2100 AD. *Disaster Advances*, *13*(11), 31–41.
61. Park, A., & Li, H. (2021). The effect of blockchain technology on supply chain sustainability performances. *Sustainability (Switzerland)*, *13*(4). https://doi.org/10.3390/su13041726
62. Purvis, B., Mao, Y., & Robinson, D. (2019). Three pillars of sustainability: in search of conceptual origins. *Sustainability Science*, *14*(3). https://doi.org/10.1007/s11625-018-0627-5
63. Ranjbari, M., Shams Esfandabadi, Z., Zanetti, M.C., Scagnelli, S.D., Siebers, P.O., Aghbashlo, M., Peng, W., Quatraro, F., & Tabatabaei, M. (2021). Three pillars of sustainability in the wake of COVID-19: A systematic review and future research agenda for sustainable development. *Journal of Cleaner Production*, *297*. https://doi.org/10.1016/j.jclepro.2021.126660
64. Rosen, A. M. (2015). The wrong solution at the right time: The failure of the kyoto protocol on climate change. *Politics and Policy*, *43*(1). https://doi.org/10.1111/polp.12105
65. Sala, S., Ciuffo, B., & Nijkamp, P. (2015). A systemic framework for sustainability assessment. *Ecological Economics*, *119*. https://doi.org/10.1016/j.ecolecon.2015.09.015
66. Saunila, M., Nasiri, M., Ukko, J., & Rantala, T. (2019). Smart technologies and corporate sustainability: The mediation effect of corporate sustainability strategy. *Computers in Industry*, *108*. https://doi.org/10.1016/j.compind.2019.03.003
67. Schalock, R. L., Verdugo, M., & Lee, T. (2016). A systematic approach to an organization's sustainability. *Evaluation and Program Planning*, *56*. https://doi.org/10.1016/j.evalprogplan.2016.03.005
68. Seo, S. N. (2017). Beyond the Paris Agreement: Climate change policy negotiations and future directions. Regional Science Policy and Practice, 9(2). Retrieved from https://doi.org/10.1111/rsp3.12090
69. Singh, S. (2006). The Kyoto Protocol: Toothless and Obsolete. *Panjab University Research Journal (Arts)*, October, 33–42.
70. Sudusinghe, J.I., & Seuring, S. (2020). Social sustainability empowering the economic sustainability in the global apparel supply chain. *Sustainability (Switzerland)*, *12*(7). https://doi.org/10.3390/su12072595
71. Tofan, M., Onofrei, M., & Vatamanu, A.F. (2020). Fiscal responsibility legal framework—new paradigm for fiscal discipline in the EU. *Risks*, *8*(3). https://doi.org/10.3390/risks8030079
72. Tolamise, J.K. (2020). The Role of Artificial Intelligence in Agricultural Sectors. https://datafloq.com/read/the-role-of-artificial-intelligence-in-agricultural-sectors/8700
73. Tussyadiah, I., & Miller, G. (2020). Imagining the future of travel: Technology and sustainability transitions. *E-Review of Tourism Research*, *17*(5).
74. UNFCCC (2015). *The Paris Agreement | UNFCCC*. https://unfccc.int/process-and-meetings/the-paris-agreement/the-paris-agreement
75. Vacchi, M., Siligardi, C., Demaria, F., Cedillo-González, E. I., González-Sánchez, R., & Settembre-Blundo, D. (2021). Technological sustainability or sustainable technology? A multidimensional vision of sustainability in manufacturing. *Sustainability (Switzerland)*, *13*(17). https://doi.org/10.3390/su13179942
76. van Wynsberghe, A. (2021). Sustainable AI: AI for sustainability and the sustainability of AI. *AI and Ethics*, *1*(3). https://doi.org/10.1007/s43681-021-00043-6
77. Wikström, P.A. (2010). Sustainability and organizational activities – Three approaches. *Sustainable Development*, *18*(2). https://doi.org/10.1002/sd.449

78. Williams, S., & Robinson, J. (2020). Measuring sustainability: An evaluation framework for sustainability transition experiments. *Environmental Science and Policy, 103*. https://doi.org/10.1016/j.envsci.2019.10.012
79. Wirth, D. A. (2017). The Paris agreement as a new component of the UN climate Regime48. *International Organisations Research Journal*, *12*(4). https://doi.org/10.17323/1996-7845-2017-04-185
80. World Commission on Environment and Development. (2017). Brundtland Report - Our common future. *Our Common Future*.
81. Young, O. R. (2016). The Paris agreement: Destined to succeed or doomed to fail? Politics and Governance, 4(3). Retrieved from https://doi.org/10.17645/pag.v4i3.635
82. Zhang, B., Zhang, Y., & Zhou, P. (2021). Consumer attitude towards sustainability of fast fashion products in the uk. *Sustainability (Switzerland)*, *13*(4). https://doi.org/10.3390/su13041646
83. Ziolo, M., Filipiak, B. Z., Bak, I., Cheba, K., Tîrca, D. M., & Novo-Corti, I. (2019). Finance, sustainability and negative externalities. An overview of the european context. *Sustainability (Switzerland)*, *11*(15). https://doi.org/10.3390/su11154249

PART I: TECHNOLOGY AND SUSTAINABILITY

KAUTILYA'S PHILOSOPHY ON SUSTAINABLE DEVELOPMENT

Sunita Devi

Abstract

Sustainable development was a key theme of the United Nations Conference on Human Environment in Stockholm in 1972. The concept suggests that it was possible to achieve economic growth without environmental damage. In India, sustainable development has been emphasized since ancient times. It has a long tradition. It is interesting to note that Arthashastra has several references on environmental protection, ecological balance, rainfall phenomena, weather cycles, and related concepts that directly indicate the high level of awareness of Kautilya and people of that time. Kautilya protected and respected the environment and practiced sustainable development. He recognized the needs of both current and future times. In his Arthashastra, Kautilya emphasized the protection of environment while achieving economic development. Based on the famous Indian treatise on political economy, Kautilya's Arthashastra, the present paper attempts to describe and explain the different aspects of sustainable development in ancient India. In this paper, the policies of environmental protection, ecological balance, rainfall phenomena, weather cycles, and related concepts, as accomplished by Kautilya, will be examined. This paper demonstrates the relevance of these policies during modern era.

Keywords: *Sustainable Development, Kautilya, Arthashastra*

Introduction

Kautilya was an Indian teacher, noble advisor, philosopher, economist and practical administrator. He was the teacher and guardian of Chandragupta Maurya (322 B.C.-298 B.C.), the greatest ruler in Indian history. In fact he was the founder of the Maurya Empire. Kautilya was the first and great Indian economist. Kautilya's *Arthashastra* has a memorabilia place in the melting pot. It is a famous treatise of ancient India which was composed around 300 B.C. in *Arthashastra* there are several references on environmental protection, ecological balance, rainfall phenomena, weather cycles, and related concepts. It indicates the high level of awareness of Kautilya and people of that time. Kautilya protected and respected the environment and practiced sustainable development. He recognized the needs of both current and future times. In *Arthashastra* it is advised that the state should be ever active in the management of the economy, because in the absence of fruitful economic activity, both current prosperity and future growth will be destroyed. To quote:

तस्मान्नित्यो उत्थितो राजा कुर्याद् अर्थानुशासनम् ।
अर्थस्य मूलम् उत्थानम् अनर्थस्य विपर्ययः॥
अनुत्थाने ध्रुवो नाशःप्राप्तस्यानागतस्य च ।
प्राप्यते फलम् उत्थानाल्लभते चार्थसम्पदम् ॥

(Tasmaatnityo utthito raja kuryad arthanushasnam.
Arthasya moolam utthaanm anarthasya viparyayah.
Anutthane dhruvo naashah praptsyanagtasya cha.
Prapyate falam utthanlabhte chaarthsampdam.)

{1.19.35, 36}

The *slokas* state that-

"Therefore, being ever active, the king should carry out the management of material wellbeing. The root of material well-being is activity; of material disaster its reverse. In the absence of activity, there is certain destruction of what is obtained and of what is not yet received. By activity reward is obtained, and one also secures abundance of riches."

Arthashastra reveals a full awareness of the undesirable effects of environmental degradation, whether caused by human activities or natural factors. It was the responsibility of the State to protect its citizens from these calamities.

दैवान्यष्टौमहाभयानि-अग्निरुदकम्व्याधिर्दुर्भिक्षम् मूषिका व्याला: सर्पारक्षाम्सीति ।
तेभ्यो जनपदम् रक्षेत्।

(Daivanyastau mahabhayani-agnirudakam vyadhirdurbhikshm moosika vyalah sarparakshamseeti.
Tebhyo janpadam rakshet.)

{4.3.1, 2}

The *slokas* state that-

"There are eight great calamities of a divine origin: fire, floods, disease, famine, rats, wild animals, serpents and evil spirits. From them the state should protect the country."

दैवपीडनम्-अग्निरुदकम् व्याधिर्दुर्भिक्षम् मरक इति ।

(Daivpeednam-agnirudakam vyadhirdurbhikshm marak iti.)

{8.4.1}

The *sloka* states that-

"Visitations from the god are: fire, floods, disease, famine and epidemic."

The environmental protection and ecological balance was understood to be one of the main functions of the state. Injuring or killing the birds and animals were strictly prohibited. There were also punishments for causing pollution and unfriendly sanitation. In *Arthashastra* there are various *slokas* advising protection of animals, trees and forests:

एवम् द्रव्यद्विपवनम् सेतुबन्धमथाकरान् ।
रक्षेत्पूर्वकृतान् राजा नवांश्चाभिप्रवर्तयेत् ॥

(Evam dravyadvipawanam setubandhmathakran.
Rakshetpoorvkritan raja navanshrchabhipravartyet.)

{2.1.39}

The *sloka* states that-

"Thus the state should protect produce-forests, elephant-forests, irrigation works and mines that were made in ancient times and should start new ones."

Punishments and penalties were specified for injuring and killing the living creatures:

क्षुद्रपशूनाम् काष्ठादिभिर्दु:खोत्पादने पणो द्विपणो वा दण्ड:,शोणितोत्पादने
महापशूनामेतेष्वेव स्थानेषु द्विगुणो दण्ड: समुत्थानव्ययश्च ।

(*Kshudrapashoonam kasthaadibhirduhkhotpadne pano dwipano va dandah, shonitotpadne dwigunah.*
Mahapashoonametesvev sthanesu dviguno dandah samutthanvyayashrch.)

{3.19.26, 27}

The *slokas* state that-

"For causing hurt to small animals with wood and other things, the fine shall be one *pana* or two *panas*, double that for causing bleeding. For these same offences concerning big animals, the fine shall be double and payment of expenses for treatment and cure."

मृगद्रव्यवनान्मृगद्रव्यापहारे शत्यो दण्ड:।
बिम्बविहारमृगपक्षिस्तेये हिंसायाम् वा द्विगुणो दण्ड: ।
(*Mrigdravyavanammrigdravyaphare shatyo dandah.*
Bimbviharmrigpakshisteye hinsayam va dwiguno dandah.)

{4.10.4, 5}

The *slokas* state that-

"In case of theft of deer or objects from deer-parks or produce-forests, there shall be a fine of one hundred. In case of theft of deer or birds (intended) for show or pleasure or in case of killing these, the fine shall be double."

सर्वातिथिमृगम् प्रत्यन्ते चान्यन्मृगवनम् भूमिवशेन वा निवेशयेत्।

(*Sarvatithimrigam pratyante chanyanmrigvanam bhoomivashen va niveshyet.*)

{2.2.4}

The *sloka* states that-

"And he should establish on its border or in conformity with the (suitability of the) land, another animal park where all animals are (welcomed) as guests (and given full protection)."

All of the tree parts were considered significant and punishments were fixed according to the damage of the specific part of the tree. To quote:

पुरोपवनवनस्पतीनाम् पुष्पफलच्छायावताम् प्ररोहच्छेदने षट्पण:,क्षुद्रशाखाच्छेदने
द्वादशपण:,पीनशाखाच्छेदने चतुर्विंशतिपण:,स्कन्धवधे पूर्व:साहसदण्ड:,
समुच्छित्तौ मध्यम: ।
पुष्पफलच्छायावद्गुल्मलतास्वर्धदण्ड:,पुण्यस्थानतपोवनशमशानद्रुमेषु च ।

(*Puropvanvanspateenam puspflachchhayavtam prarohchchhedne stpanah, kshudrashakhachchhedne dwadaspanah, peenshakhachchhedne chaturvinshtipanah, skandhvadhe poorvah sahasdandah, samuchchhittau madhyamah. Puspfalachchhayavadgulmlatasvardhdandah, punyasthantapovanshmashaandrumesu cha.*)

{3.19. 28, 29}

The *slokas* state that-

"For cutting the shoots of trees in city parks that bear flowers or fruit or yield shade (the fine shall be) six *panas*, for cutting small branches twelve *panas*, for cutting stout branches twenty four *panas*, for destroying trunks the lowest fine for violence, for uprooting (the tree) the middle (fine). In case of bushes and creepers bearing flowers or fruit or yielding shade the fine shall be half, also in the case of trees in holy places, penance-groves and cremation grounds."

सीमवृक्षेषुचैत्येषुद्रुमेष्वालक्षितेषुच।
तएवद्विगुणादण्डा: कार्याराजवनेषुच॥

(*Seemavrikshesu chaityesu drumeswalakshitesu cha.
Ta eva dwiguna dandah karya rajvanesu cha.*)

{3.19. 30}

The *sloka* states that-

"In the case of trees at the boundaries, in sanctuaries, and of trees that are prominent, these same fines doubled shall be imposed, also (in the case of trees) in royal parks."

Kautilya realized the importance of forests and appointed a high officer (the Director of Forests) to look after the forests. He advised that forests should be established, preserved and protected.

कुप्यप्रदिष्टनाम् च द्रव्याणामेकैकशो वनानि निवेशयेत्,
द्रव्यवनकर्मान्तानटवीश्च द्रव्यवनापाश्रया: ।

(*Kupyapradistanam cha dravyanammekaikasho vanani niveshayet,
dravyavankarmantantaveeshrch dravyavanapashrayah.*)

{2.2.5}

The *sloka* states that-

"The state should establish forests, one each for the products indicated as forest produce, as well as factories for goods made from forest produce, and (settle) foresters, attached to the produce forests."

Kautilya devoted a full chapter (Remedial Measures during Calamities) in *Arthashastra* to suggest measures for preventing the natural hazards, e.g. Fire hazards, Flood hazards, Famines and Draughts hazards

Relevance of Kautilya's Ideas in Modern ERA

In essence, Kautilya's *Arthashastra* is the most glorious chapter in the Indian history for environmental and ecological protection. Environmental protection and pollution control were made duties for the whole society instead of the responsibility of an individual or the king alone. Article 51-A of the Constitution of India also prescribes environmental protection as a fundamental duty of every citizen:

"It shall be the duty of every citizen of India to protect and improve the natural environment including forests, lakes, rivers and wildlife and to have compassion for living creatures." (Article 51-A, Constitution of India)

Maintenance of cleanliness, sanitation and hygiene was a part of house building regulations. For sustainable development, Kautilya recommended the active participation of State. Kautilya put great importance on environment sustainability since he realized that for a balanced growth of humanity, protection of environment was important. He had advised to co-exist with the environment and had an ecological balance. The environmental issues described by Kautilya are highly relevant in modern era. During modern era most discussions on environmental protection in our country begin with the Stockholm Conference held in 1972. But, Kautilya's *Arthashastra* shows that our ancient society paid much more attention to protecting the environment than we can imagine. During modern era also, the need is felt for conservation of environment and ecology in order to promote the level of social and economic welfare as mentioned in the Directive Principles of State Policy of the Constitution of India:

"The State shall endeavour to protect and improve the environment and to safeguard the forests and wildlife of the country". (Article 48-A, Constitution of India)

References

1. Ali, S.S. (2006). Kautilya and the Concept of Good Governance. *The Indian Journal of Political Science*, 67(2), 375-380. Retrieved from https://www.jstor.org
2. Basu R.L. & Sen, R. K. (2008). *Ancient Indian Economic Thought Relevance for Today*. New Delhi: Rawat Publications.
3. Basu, R. L. (2011). *Kautilya's Arthashastra (300 B.C.): Economic Ideas*. Retrieved from https://www.smashwords.com
4. Bhalachandran, G. (2011). Kautilya's Model of Sustainable Development. *Humanomics*, 27(1), 41-52.
5. Chamola, S. D. (2006). *Arthashastra* and its Relevance. In R. K. Sen & R. L. Basu, *Economics in Arthashastra* (pp. 21-35). New Delhi: Deep & Deep Publications.
6. Chamola, S. D. (2011). *Economic Development and Ethics- Indian Experience since Independence*. New Delhi: Global Vision Publishing House.
7. Kangle, R. P. (1965). *The Kautilya Arthashastra, Part I, II and III*. Delhi: Motilal Bnarsidas.
8. Ramamurthy. (2004). Ancient Indian Economic Thought in Kautilya. *87th conference volume of IEA*.
9. Rangarajan, L.N. (1992). *Kautilya -The Arthshastra*. New Delhi: Penguin Books India Pvt. Ltd.
10. Sharma, S. K. (2005). Indian Idea of Good Governance: Revisiting Kautilya's *Arthashastra*. *Dynamics in Administration, 17*(1), 8- 9. Retrieved from https://www.academia.edu

11. Sharma, sunil sen. (2000). *Kautilya's Arthashastra- in the light of Modern Science and Technology*. New Delhi: DK Printwood.
12. Shastri, U. (1970). *Kautaleeya Arthashastra*. New Delhi: Meharchandra Lachamandas Publications, शास्त्री, उ. (1970). *कौटलीय अर्थशास्त्र.* नईदिल्ली: मेहरचन्द्र लछमन दास पब्लिकेशन्स्।
13. The Constitution of India, Part IV. Ministry of Law & Justice. Retrieved from http://lawmin.nic.in
14. The Constitution of India. Retrieved from, http://lawmin.nic.in
15. Veerabhadraswami, M. R. (2006). Relevance of *Arthashastra* in Modern Times. In R. K. Sen & R. L. Basu, *Economics in Arthashastra* (pp. 58-63). New Delhi: Deep & Deep Publications.

Websites Visited

http://agriculture.gov.in
http://agriharyana.gov.in
http://envfor.nic.in/
http://www.nsdcindia.org
https://www.india.gov.in/topics/agriculture

SUSTAINABILITY LESSONS: AI INNOVATIONS TO MITIGATE CLIMATE CHANGE

Ruth Taplin

Artificial Intelligence (AI) can be used to good effect to assist in climate change mitigation and sustainability efforts globally. As climate change is negatively affecting countries' economies and societies such as India, AI can be used to lower carbon emissions and provide data to assist in ending severe air pollution, flooding and land degradation and assist with the needs of rural communities to warn of plagues of plant destroying pests or when lightning strikes will occur which kill many in India annually.

Mitigating air Pollution

AI in a recent example of climate mitigation technology is using satellite tracking to understand where severe air pollution is emanating from through monitoring carbon emissions. This is particularly important for countries such as India which are trying to move away from highly polluting coal fired power plants. Such monitoring can be used to understand other sources of air pollution in industrial and electricity plants, the data of which can be used to levy taxes on the heaviest polluters or convince financial backers and the government to finance lesser polluting companies and plants.

Human activity, mainly through intensive use of fossil fuels to run industries, the use of petroleum derived products such as plastics coupled with reliance of gas and oil for energy requirements have led to unprecedented carbon emissions. These heat-trapping gases termed greenhouse gases are at a higher level than in the last 800,000 years of planet earth's existence.

Carbon dioxide emissions have increased by a third since the Industrial Revolution, warming the planet so rapidly that nature cannot change in parallel time. Previously, the environment had thousands of years to evolve to deal with volcanic eruptions for example which affected the climate.[1] Therefore, solutions to these climate problems must be accomplished quickly and that is why AI can offer the most effective and efficient solutions rapidly at pace.

Electricity Systems

AI because it is data driven is and will play a key role in climate change mitigation through a number of key energy systems. As the chapter in my last book dealing with cyber risk and smart grids[2] AI has been radically changing energy systems to create electricity based smart grids that enable low carbon electricity. There are two types of electricity systems that can produce low carbon emissions with the help of Machine Learning (ML). (It is probably more accurate to use ML because among many experts on AI it is ML which can be used more readily to change systems such as smart grids through reinforced learning AI methods). One is variable such as energy derived from the sun or wind and the other is controllable such as nuclear or geothermal which can be turned on or off.

The bulk of electricity is delivered to consumers through an electric grid where every second of energy consumed is met by power generated. The problem with this system is that power generation is assured largely through carbon emitting buffer systems known as spinning reserves provided by coal and natural gas plants. To reduce the carbon emissions to a level that will mitigate climate change, there is a movement to new energy storage technologies including batteries, and pumped hydro water systems. AI based technologies will be used to lower carbon emissions through shaping forecasting, scheduling and control to create variable electric systems that are flexible in relation to demand.

To assist with fluctuations in electricity generation and demand scheduling must be made in real time to reduce reliance on polluting standby plants. The basic forecasting techniques which most electric grids rely on at present are not accurate enough and do not operate in real time which AI techniques use to allow efficient forecasting with certainty. AI techniques with their advanced algorithms will be able to improve the accuracy of climate modelling and weather forecasting for solar, wind and water from rivers, driven sources of energy to power electric grids.

At present electric grid system operators use slow and complex scheduling systems called scheduling and dispatch. As scheduling moves to even more complex systems based on increased storage, variable generators and flexible demand, AI can progress a more rapid use of power optimisation systems improving both the quality and speed of optimisation systems.

For example, dynamic scheduling and safe reinforcement systems can be utlised to balance the electric grid in real time. Another way in which AI can be used is to decentralise scheduling and dispatch by creating local algorithms for storage and price. For example, AI can be used to determine real time prices that optimise for lower carbon emissions.

Using AI to create storage facilities using new materials for solar energy storage and improvements in lithium battery storage can be improved through AI methods using AI based modelling.[3]

Industrial Organisation

The global industrial sector including manufacturing, building materials and logistics contributes heavily to the production of greenhouse gases. However, for ML to deal with climate mitigation in this sector, it is made easier because it is data driven. ML has the potential to reduce carbon emissions by improving the quality of production, streamlining supply chains, optimising heating and cooling systems, and predicting machine breakdowns. Yet, the use of ML will not have the desired effect unless industry has the incentives for example, to choose clean electricity over fossil fuels.

Other choices that can accelerate the use of ML is predicting with accuracy supply and demand for goods. Many industries inaccurately overproduce goods which are then wasted.

This includes the fashion industry that manufactures high amounts of waste that produce greenhouse gases through the disposal of unwanted garments because fashions are not predicted correctly. India still has a very large textile sector that produces such waste.

Food waste is also astronomical with 1.3 billion metric tons of food wasted globally through inadequate storage, estimating supply and demand for certain food products incorrectly, not taking into account time spans to prevent spoiling of certain foods and inadequate refrigeration. ML can be used through sensors to detect when food is about to spoil or a part of food stored with fresher produce will ruin the entire shipment so it can be quickly removed. This is especially the case in hot, humid country's such as India.

ML can also be used to predict chemical reactions so in the case of ammonia which is used in fertilisers ML could be used to develop cleaner ammonia production through the electrochemical analysis of lower temperatures for its production.[4]

Agriculture and Forestry

Both industrial scale agricultural and livestock are contributing at least a third of carbon emissions and the latter even more so with the production of methane gases. While destructive agricultural practices such as draining peat bogs and wetlands, which hold vast amounts of carbon, mean that excessive carbon is released into the atmosphere, methane is even a greater emitter of greenhouse gases. Agriculture with the use of ML can serve to lower carbon emissions: reversal of these tendencies can mitigate the release of carbon. This means restoring wetlands, peat bogs and stopping deforestation for agriculture and any livestock production.

ML can be used effectively to produce a form of precision agriculture which could stop carbon release from the soil and greater crop yield thereby mitigating the need for deforestation. ML can predict the risk of fire, monitor emissions and the health of forests. There are robotic tools such as RIPPA which is under development at the University of Sydney, Australia, that is equipped with a hyperspectral camera and can carry out mechanical weeding, vacuuming of pests and targeted pesticide application. It can cover 5 acres per day and bring in large datasets while running on solar energy. Other smart robotic devices are intelligent irrigation systems that decrease water usage and prevent water borne pests. ML can also assist in disease and pest detection and soil sensing. ML through prediction can be used to decide what crops to plant, crop yield and models that can predict crop demand to reduce wastage and better target consumer choice. Unmanned Aerial Vehicles (UAVs) with hyperspectral cameras can be used for all these tasks.

ML has been applied through remote sensing data estimations of the thickness of peat and assess the carbon stock of tropical peatlands. Peatland mapping can be furthered through satellite applications and with low-cost precise monitoring tools which could also predict the risk of fire.

An example from rural Africa demonstrates how effective AI apps can be to small-scale farmers. In Zambia, there are over 22,000 small landowning farmers who use an AI-backed mobile application (app) called AgriPredict to obtain instant information concerning weather patterns and plant diseases as well as selling their produce on the platform. The farmers with these platforms and hitherto unobtainable expert information from agriculturists and meteorologists, now on their affordable mobiles have been able to run their farms more efficiently and at reduced cost.

Mobile phones are available cheaply and are the main source of telecommunications in rural areas in Africa and India which have improved the chances of rural smallholders to succeed.

Prior to this, agricultural experts had to visit remote rural sites to advise for example on the problems with crop production. It was costly, rare and hard to access so AI technology has improved the chances of small-scale rural farmers to succeed, feeding themselves and local communities with nutritious plant-based food without migrating to overcrowded urban areas where they do not often possess the skills to succeed.[5]

Forests

Trees store carbon in above-ground biomass so heights and types of trees provide a good indication of amount of carbon stock. As many areas of forest are closed to UAVs, ML through satellite imagery can be used as predictors or learned estimators of carbon stock in forests globally. Automating afforestation Long-term Uncertain Impact Planting trees which is termed afforestation, the opposite of the destructive deforestation could be used as a means of sequestering CO_2 for the long-term. There is scope for up to 0.9 billion hectares of extra forest cover on the planet. However, mass tree planting must be done with care so not to obliterate peat bogs and wetlands which also act as carbon sinks.

The logging industry is particularly destructive especially when it is done as clearcutting which refers to indiscriminate felling of tress rather carefully and selectively doing so.

Through sensory imaging ML can differentiate between clearcutting and selective tree felling.

Old smartphones powered by solar panels can be used to install in forests to detect through reinforced ML the sound of chainsaws to alert law enforcers that illegal logging is taking place. ML tools are also becoming increasingly used by foresters to determine where to harvest, fertilise, build roads and fire breaks.[6]

Tracking Carbon – a UN goal

A non-profit think tank based in the City of London that makes finance recommendations for companies to transition from fossil fuels to sustainable energy, named Carbon Tracker is using ML through satellite imagery to find the sources of carbon emitting power plants that are contributing to air pollution. With a grant from Google, Carbon Tracker, the first of its kind, will use AI technologies to detect carbon emitting power plants globally and provide the results to the public so power plants can be held accountable for their emissions. In collaboration with WattTime and the World Resource Institute (WRI) organisations which have experience in using AI techniques to transition towards clean energy, will use the most advanced image processing algorithms to detect emissions from space which can track power plant emissions globally. Data from a variety of different sensors operating at different wavelengths and using algorithms will cross-validate a variety of indicators of power plant emissions from thermal infrared signalling heat near smoke stacks and cooling water intake. Visual spectrum recognition will also be used to confirm that a power plant is emitting smoke. Carbon Tracker can be used ultimately to make those companies which are emitting the most carbon to take responsibility for it through for example extra fines and taxes.[7]

Locust Tracking using AI Apps

AI apps can not only assist with carbon tracking but devastating pest invasions that ruin smallholding farmers livelihoods and can cause famine. In rural regions of India, it is difficult enough sometimes surviving with little if any outside support and being isolated in remote areas. This is becoming increasingly the case with the effects of climate change meaning that rainy seasons, such as monsoons in India, which are vital for crop success do not arrive in time, or conditions of drought mean that unexpected pests increase their numbers with devastating consequences.

A recent example that swept East Africa involved huge amounts of locust. The apps developed to deal with this crisis can be transferred to other regions in the world that are suffering from climate change induced local agricultural disasters.

AI Combats Locust Swarm

In 2020, billions of locusts descended on a number of East Africa nations. The intensity of the locust attack had not been seen since the fifties and this time the size of the swarms were being blamed on unusually warm weather brought about by cyclonic cycle climate change. Nineteen million farmers had their livelihoods affected in Kenya, Ethiopia and Somalia.

The outcome of the locust attack could have been much greater if a ground breaking technology driven operation had not been employed. It was a collective effort that created a locust data base as a simple smartphone app which replaced an earlier tablet-based locust tracker app that was on a tablet which is no longer manufactured. The other problem was that even if the original tracker programme that operated through satellite imagery being transmitted to agricultural experts who recommend strategies to combat such locust swarms, Kenya and the other affected countries did not have enough agricultural experts.

PlantVillage and Climate Change Technology

PlantVillage which is a Kenyan non-profit organisation that assists farmers deal technologically with climate change induced agricultural-based disasters was in the forefront of lessening the impact of the 2020 locust swarms. The potential of the 2020 locust swarms were so potentially damaging as to interfere with food security in the region that it drew in an interdisciplinary group of experts from around the world. Dr. David Hughes, an entomologist from United States Penn State University thought it would be a waste of experience not to find solutions that would make it possible to deal with future locust swarms and other pest outbreaks around the world. He noted that the magnitude of locusts could be directly linked to climate change in the increase in cyclonic activity.

Working with Mr. Keith Cressman, a senior locust forecasting officer at the United Nations Food and Agriculture Organization (UNFAO) thought it would be more effective to create a mobile smartphone app for all to collect locust data than to return to creating software for new tablets. He asked David Hughes who already had created a smartphone app with UNFAO to combat an influx of the destructive armyworm crop pests which Hughes implemented through PlantVillage, the organisation he created.

Given the fact that such a large swarm of locust can consume the equivalent in food of 13,000 people, producing a tracking app was an urgent task. The PlantVillage app uses both AI and ML to assist farmers with their crop production in over 60 countries. Using this as a blueprint Dr. Hughes and his colleagues created a new app named eLocust3m, within a month. The app is useful because it shows photos of locusts at different stages in their life cycles which assists the diagnosis of users. GPS coordinates are automatically recorded and AI algorithms are used to double check on all photos entered. Garmin International, a well-known GPS provider, also supported another programme that was able to work on satellite-transmitting devices. "The app is really easy to use," said Ms. Melodine Jeptoo of PlantVillage. She recruits scouts who are trained to track locust swarms and noted that the apps used were readily learned by elders in the community who had little understanding of new technology.[8]

Perils of Lightning Strikes

The morbidity rate from lightning strikes in a largely rural, agriculture based county such as India is very high and is in need of an AI solution to increase protection as often traditional models are ineffective.

More than 100,000 Indians lost their lives to lightning strikes between 1967nand 2019. This has increased to over 2,500 lives lost per annum with more than 18 million such strikes being recorded officially between April 2020 and March 2021 which was a 34% increase from the previous year. This accounts for more than a third of fatalities from natural hazards in the country. Those who survive experience weakness, memory loss and dizziness for prolonged periods.

Mobile apps have been developed recently to track flashes with India's meteorological office forecasting lightning strikes from 3 years ago. At that time an initiative was started called Lightning India Resilient Campaign which also works to raise awareness of the deadly nature of lightning strikes to lightning – prone villages. Villagers can be alerted through mobile apps, radio, TV and by volunteers who give warning through megaphones.

Although lightning can strike anywhere in India, 3 states experience over 70% of them which are Odisha, West Bengal and Jharkhand. Those most vulnerable are males working on farms.

The Indian Institute of Tropical Meteorology through satellite data points to a rapid increase in lightning strikes between 1995 and 2014.[9] This time period matches scientists warning about the effects of climate change globally.

References

1. 'Causes and Effects of Climate Change', Christina Nunez, *National Geographic*, (22 January 2019).
2. Ruth Taplin *Cyber Risk Intellectual Property Theft and Cyberwarfare, Asia, Europe and the USA*, (Abingdon; Routledge, 2021).
3. 'Tackling Climate Change with Machine Learning', 'Electric Systems', Priya L. Donti (5 November 2019). This is based on a paper from an AI conference in June 2019 which had a workshop organised by a postdoctoral student David Rolnick of the University of Pennsylvania. The paper that resulted was supported by; The authors gratefully acknowledge support from National Science Foundation grant 1803547, the Center for Climate and Energy Decision Making through a cooperative agreement between the National Science Foundation and Carnegie Mellon University (SES-00949710), US Department of Energy contract DEFG02-97ER25308, the Natural Sciences and Engineering Research Council of Canada, and the MIT Media Lab Consortium.
4. *ibid 2019* 'Industry', Anna Waldman Brown.
5. 'How AI is helping Rural African Farmers', *BBC Online* (1 December 2020).
6. ibid 2019 'Agriculture and Forestry', Alexandre Lacoste.
7. 'Carbon Tracker to Measure World's Power Plant Emissions from Space with Support from Google.org', Press Release from Stephano Ambrogi of Carbon Tracker, (8 May 2019).
8. 'As Locust Swarmed East Africa, This Tech Helped Squash Them', Rachel Nuwer, *BBC Online*, (8 April 2021).
9. 'Lightning in India: A bolt from the blue that kills thousands', Soutik Biswas, India Correspondent, *BBC Online* (14 February 2022).

RESILIENCE AS A SUSTAINABILITY STRATEGY FOR BUSINESESS IN THE POST-COVID ERA

Mario B. Curatolo

Introduction

Although resilience is not a new concept, its importance and relevance in the business world has been growing in the last couple of years as a result of the Covid Pandemic. This event, was supposed to act as a *"wake-up call"* for businesses *to think out of the box* and take consciousness about the impossibility to postpone any longer the way they allocated human and physical resources. Despite the economic and social impact of the pandemic, only few companies changed the way they operated and used resilience to sustainably survive and thrive in the new normal. As most firms failed to develop and foster their resilience capabilities to a much greater level than before, they became unable to withstand the unpredictable market changes generated by the pandemic, failing to prevail in the new normal post-covid market context.

Resilience has to do with the capacity of firms to adjust and adapt to rapid market changes creatively reorganising and transforming the way they conduct their activities. The Covid Pandemic marked a turning point where it was no longer possible for firms to continue to ignore the need for change, thinking *"we will cross that bridge when we will get there"*. The imminence of the needed change was determined by the fact that firms had already reached *the bridge* with no strategy or in the best of cases ill prepared to "*cross the bridge*". Resilience, therefore is not so much about planning but *anticipating* and *responding*. Anticipating has to do with the ability of firms to predict future relevant scenarios that can help identify "surprise gaps" to foresee potential industry wide disruptions. This anticipation however must be complemented with a practical Response to these future relevant scenarios as a cultural realization by firms that, although not all potential disruptions can be anticipated, procrastination is not the answer. Therefore, a poor and indecisive Response can seriously compromise a firm's sustainability strategy. Only firms that respond early, can drive superior performance in the next normal. In this sense, today, more than ever before, resilience needs to be imbedded in the business culture of modern firms as they can no longer rely on the outdated strategies of business continuity plans that, not only, do not work, but do not respond to the potential new threats, modern firms need to adjust and adapt to.

The concept of resilience is not new to business, since already during the financial crisis of the 1980s, financial institutions were forced to test their resilience through stress-tests which measured their liquidity levels in extreme market scenarios to guarantee their financial solvency. These stress-tests became normal practice in the financial market as financial assurances were required by corporate, private and institutional clients particularly during highly volatile market conditions. Other sectors like the perfume industry were forced to test their resilience to adjust and adapt their products and services during the covid pandemic reinventing themselves as sanitary-gel producers to respond to an increased sense of business social responsibility.

If more "resilience" is needed by modern firms to survive, then the question is, in what way can resilience be developed to help organisations withstand unpredictable change. In this respect, resilience is developed in different ways. Firms will develop operational resilience to flexibly meet changes in demand and remain stable in the face of operational disruptions without sacrificing total quality. Firms must also become technologically resilient to secure and flexibly manage cyber-attacks and avoid technological breakdowns. This will help firms maintain a robust business continuity and an effective disaster-recovery capability. Last but not least, modern firms will be required to develop an organisational resilience that can foster the development and maintenance of a diverse labour force capable of being upskilled and reskilled rendering it flexible and adaptable. Only then, will firms be able to withstand unpredictable changes and prevail in the new normal.

As the covid pandemic unfolds, catastrophic events will grow not only more frequent but more unpredictable. In these circumstances developing resilience capabilities will require firms to engage in practice-drills that simulate future market scenarios to test not only how resilient firms are, but identify the nature and degree of the resilience they need and where they need it.

Although these exercises will end up building resilience as part of the business culture of the firm, resilience as a sustainability strategy could only be reached if companies understand and build resilience from the outset.

When thinking about developing resilience as a sustainability strategy for business, the question arises as to whether developing resilience is easier said than done given the fact that different companies have different cultural ways to approach resilience. This is what renders resilience a very difficult concept to grasp because resilience is about how an organisation is able to maintain its basic functions and therefore its ability to withstand disruption. It is a firm's resilience that allows it to adapt and change becoming fit to survive into the future.

Resilience therefore cannot be understood as a static concept (*Passive Resilience*) circumscribed to the idea that change must take place before the cost of not changing becomes too great, but understood as a dynamic concept (*Active Resilience*) where innovation, readiness and preparedness constitute the cultural business pillars that allow the firm to identify and respond to new opportunities that may arise and therefore adjust and adapt. Change is not a physical planned act, but the cultural reaction of the firm to the identification of surprise gaps. This cultural resilience ends up turning itself into a strength for firms to respond in a more flexible and agile way to future unexpected market changes. If Stress tests can develop resilience *as practice makes perfect*, resilience itself has to do with the cultural *preparedness* (being prepared) that creates long term *businesses herd-immunity*.

The question is then... can resilience be turned into a sustainability strategy that allows firms to withstand unpredictable changes? Given resilience strong cultural component, organizations can create resilience through the adoption of socio-cultural business patterns like:

- Discussing failure and how failure helps firms avoid complacency
- Discussing the impact environmental, human, social and financial capital have on the firm's capacity to survive
- Focus firms' discussion on service outcomes (like the importance of delivering to clients regardless of market circumstances) as their top business strategic priority
- Focus discussion on the tolerance/threshold impact level firms should operate on rather than on the risk management level firms can sustain
- Discussions about how to manage tensions resulting from firms confronting risks, innovation and creativity options
- Run Stress tests on future market scenarios to develop resiliency options
- Discussion on how to test leadership resilience

These sets of practical steps aimed at helping firms develop a culture of resilience are necessary but no sufficient to develop resilience as a sustainability strategy for firms since resilience is intimately related to the way people think and act and therefore subject to their own cultural business prejudices. As we end up focusing on what we are used to, what we have seen before and what we can imagine, we develop basic assumption that confirm how we seek to control business situations and how we sort them out. In other words, we become self-assured about what we do and how we do the things we do. This context only helps create in us a fixed illusion that the solution is at hand if we follow firm's business continuity plans (*protocols*). However, the question is how imaginative have these continuity plans been conceived to account for unpredictable change and thus how prepared is the firm to face the unexpected. Resilience is in this sense is important because it helps firms think out the box by seeking to *know the unknowns' unknowns*.

Consequently, resilience is not about the pessimism associated with the impossibility to anticipate and react to the unexpected, but with a *realism* that helps firms see new business options as challenges that can optimistically be reached. It is in this sense that resilience is not so much about a realistic pessimism but about a *realism with a bit of optimism*. This is how firms can realise new opportunities as reachable options that can help them emerge stronger. The operational effectiveness of a sustainability strategy then will depend on implementing resilience with a *realistic optimism*.

Although business failure manifest itself as an unpredictable and inevitable disruption to firms' business activity, resilience, as part of the firm sustainability strategy, can still help firms adjust and adapt, by helping them deliver solutions (*generating outcomes*) despite the level of disruption faced. By helping firms place more emphasis on the tolerance threshold level they can operate on, rather than on the impact size of the disruption level faced, resilience helps firms transform the way firms withstand unpredictable change to emerge stronger in the new normal market context. The effectiveness of a sustainability strategy to capture business opportunities will depend solely on it being able to operate in a resilient way.

Measuring resilience implies identifying the preparedness level of firms to face the unexpected. This requires firms: to have a *plan in place*, *conduct regular practice drill scenarios* (to develop resilience instruments) and_have a strategy (to follow through the learnings from the practice drills). These three elements should be part of the embedded resilience of the firms' sustainability strategy needed to guarantee a business process in which *planning* will respond to the firm's risk awareness, *testing* will help firms develop new ideas and *delivering* will make sure resilience is culturally embedded.

If resilience is to help firms withstand unpredictable change to emerge stronger in the new normal, decision makers cannot continue to follow short-term development strategies that do not work anymore postponing indefinitely their need *to think out of the box* to tackle the more frequent and less predictable catastrophic events generated by the Covid Pandemic. As firms rapidly implement technology to anticipate and solve these problems, they have had to come to terms with a new generation of employees and consumers for whom another way of working, producing and consuming is possible. This has altered the risk profile returns of firms forcing them to become more resilient to face the changing climate of their companies.Furthermore, as globalisation consolidates itself, more firms operate as global enterprises. This, rather than helping them become stronger, had rendered them increasingly more vulnerable as the supply chain disruptions generated by the pandemic affect their performance. In this context decision makers recall resilience as part of their firms' sustainability strategy to be able to understand how to adjust and adapt to the new supply chain disruption generated by the profound inequalities of a globalised economy. The need therefore to grow beyond the firms' sustainable short-term performance has led decision makers to re-conceive the use of resilience to boost growth in the medium and long term as part of a new sustainability transformation strategy.

The question at this point is not so much if firms need to be resilient to withstand unpredictable change but, what kind of resilience modern firms need in order to withstand unpredictable change. A financial resilience, for example, is important if firms are to handle flexibly the risk management necessary not to lose new business opportunities. In this sense, financial resilience becomes critical as it allows firms to re-assess the financing of new business priorities without compromising their financial survival. Thus, by helping firms control the risk-return trade-offs of new opportunities, financial resilience culturally guides firms to operate in a new normal context. The importance and relevance of financial resilience however should not be overstated as financial resilience is only one aspect of the firm sustainability strategy. If firms are to be resilient to withstand unpredictable change, they need to be operationally resilient too. This means relying on resilience to strengthen their supply chains and delivery mechanism would render more robust their production capacity and flexibility to meet changes in demand without sacrificing quality. Of course, as modern firms heavily invest in technological infrastructures to boost their future growth and development, reliance on technological resilience becomes even more critical as firms need to flexibly manage threats arising from cyber-attacks and unpredictable technological breakdowns. Furthermore, as the need to maintain and make an efficient use of high-quality data become more necessary to guide the sustainable technological transformation of firms in the new normal, this renders technological resilience even more crucial for firms not only in the Information Technology sector but in all sectors of a modern economy. Consequently, one could say that the importance and relevance of technological resilience lies not only on its capacity to protect firms from the side-effects of excessive technological dependence, but on helping firms re-assess the way they use the data generated by their own technology, to transform the way they work. Perhaps one of the most important forms of resilience modern firms need to develop and promote is organisational resilience. Withstanding unpredictable change requires not only financial, operational and technological resilience but an organisational resilience that can help firms reinvent themselves. Organisational resilience can turn firms into *learning organisations* capable of using the diverse experience of a multicultural and international labour force, to become more agile as they unlearn past experiences by facing and solving unpredictable new challenges in an original way. Since organisational resilience is about *inclusion* this transformation in the business culture of firms will lead each and every employee to maximise their best performing capacity, making *inclusion* the engine of sustainable growth. As organisational resilience nurtures a shift from an individualistic to a collectivist business culture, firms can easily unlearn the traditional organisational relationships structures that limited their growth potential to embrace the design and construction of new relationships modes allowing firms to reinvent themselves to operate more effectively in a new normal market context.

As firms' transformation is driven by resilience in its different forms, reputational resilience has become ever more important for the management of modern firms as new firms have to align their values, as socially responsible enterprises, with their actions. This new social relevance and visibility of modern firms has led their sustainability strategy increasingly resort to reputational resilience in the new normal market context. At no other time in history have firms been at the centre of their clients' concerns and subjected to their cultural prejudices. Reputational resilience is about understanding and dealing not only with how final consumers but stakeholders make companies socially accountable to their brand promises and their business commitment to environmental, social and governance issues. As firms become more social units of production, than production units, the pressure on modern firms to balance their business objective with an ethical behaviour forces them to conform to a new socioeconomic paradigm. This has led decision makers to develop reputational resilience business strategies to coherently integrate business mission, value and purposes to address societal expectation while responding to behavioural criticisms.

If firms are to withstand unpredictable changes all different types of resilience must be integrated in a sustainable business model strategy that can help firms adapt, change and transform themselves in line with significant shifts in customer demands, competitive landscape, technology and regulatory norms. However, for this strategy to generate the desired adjustment and changes, it must be based on a business plan resilience that can help firms maintain an innovation portfolio capacity necessary to anticipate and respond to unpredictable changes. Resilience, then, becomes critical as it helps firms understand and predict *(anticipate)* future relevant scenarios through the identification of *surprise gaps* that consent firms *(respond)* develop a *sustainability roadmap* necessary to navigate industry-wide disruptions.

The effectiveness of a sustainability strategy will depend then on resilience being imbedded in the firm's business culture so that firms no longer are tempted to use business continuity plans to respond to potential threats. As the culture of resilience becomes imbedded in the business culture of modern firms, resilience will help transform the way firms understand their business and deal with unexpected threats allowing them to work better in a *new-normal market context.*

At this point, the question is how can firms increase the use of their resilience? Although, increasing resilience capacity by resorting to Buffering Strategies is a preferred method used by many firms to guarantee business continuity, in practice, using buffering strategies that rely on "predictable" planned short and medium-term scenarios, is not advisable particularly in long-term unpredictable market contexts like those many firms face now with the *Covid Pandemic*. In this new unpredictable context, stocking up emergency supplies to respond to short and medium-term predictable supply breakdowns, will not represent a viable solution to keep operational continuity if what firms now face are unpredictable long-term supply chain disruptions. Thus, firms will need to develop a new form of operational resilience to flexibly meet changes in demand to remain stable in the face of operational disruption without sacrificing quality. Consequently, relying exclusively on a buffer stock sustainability strategy would be ill-advised if not complemented with the use of a broader operational resilience.

As modern firms seek to withstand unpredictable changes in the market, this has led their decision makers to find solutions to render their firms increasingly flexible. This flexibility has been sought through balancing a trade-off strategy between different instruments like capital buffers, stocks of goods, over-staffed call-centres etc. that could bring short and/or medium-term stability to their firms. However, the unpredictability of the present market scenario renders the applicability of a trade-off resilient strategy more important and at the same time more difficult as firms' decision makers need to balance the level of risks, they want their firms to operate on with the need to re-tune their company's competitiveness. To achieve these two objectives, firms must resort to a Bake-in resilience strategy to use the diversity of their internal skills and experiences to foster innovation and creative problem solving to help firms reach peak performance levels. The more global the activities of firms become, the more Bake-in resilience strategies are needd to foster quick innovative collaborative adaptation solutions for firms to thrive in this new normal market context. When relying on this add-on strategies it is important to remember that an effective use of resilience depends on understanding how to target add-ons to reduce trade-offs between surprise-gaps to improve firms' ability to emerge stronger in the new post-covid context.

Conclusion

If resilience is to be promoted as a sustainability strategy for the transformation of businesses during the Covid era, complacency will need to be avoided to embed business values like agility and flexibility into the modern firm's resilience culture. At the same time, *resilience by design* will need to be imbedded too as part of the board social business culture of the modern firm. This will make new cooperative and collective challenging strategic trade off choices easier helping the future survival and transformation of modernm firms.

However, since developing resilience is easier said than done, a practical way to render resilience part of a sustainability strategy for businesses in the post covid era is to engage firms into determining how resilient they really are, the degree and nature of the resilience they will need in future and how to design a roadmap to build and maintain the resilience they need to operate in a new normal context

In the end only companies that understand the importance of resilience will prevail

Bibliography

1. Blau Andrew et al., "The world remade by COVID-19: Planning scenarios for resilient leaders", Deloitte April 6, 2020.
2. Bjornkov Christian, "How does social trust affect economic growth", *Southern Economic Journal*, 78, no.4, April 2012, pp. 1346-68.
3. Crouch Andy, Keilhacker and Dave Blanchard, "Leading beyond the blizzard: Why every organization is now a start-up", *The Praxis Journal*, March 20, 2020.
4. Finzi Benjamin, Lipton Mark and Firth Vincent, Can CEOs be un-disruptable? Why oday's best leaders are flexible not steadfast", *Deloitte Insights*, October 17, 2017.
5. Finzi Benjamin, Lipton Mark and Firth Vincent, ambidextrous leadership: Keystone of the un-disruptable CEO, *Deloitte Insights*, October 18, 2018.
6. Finzi Benjamin et al., Disruptive *jiu-jitsu*: The foresight and courage to disrupt the disruptors, *Deloite Insights*, May 1, 2019.
7. Finzi Benjamin et al., Emotional fortitude: he inner work of the CEO, *Deloitte Insights*, July 9, 2020.
8. Gerdeman Dina, "How he coronavirus is already rewriting the future of business", *Harvard Business School*, March 16, 2020.
9. Guterres Antonio, "The recovery form the COVID-19 crisis must lead to a different economy", United Nations, March 31, 2020.
10. Kissinger Henry. A., "The coronavirus pandemicwill forever alter the world order", The *Wall Sreet Journal*, April 3, 2020.
11. Knack Stephen, "Trust, associational life and economic performance", in John F. Helliwell (Ed), *The contribution of Human and Social Capital to Sustained Economic Growth and Well-Being*, (OECD and Human Resources Development, Canada, January 2001).
12. Lee Jennifer et al., Embedding trust into COVID-19 recovery: Four dimensions of stakeholder trust Covid-19, *Deloitte Insights*, April 23, 2020.
13. Renjen Punit, The heart of resilient leadership: Responding to COVID-19, *Deloitte Insights*, March 16, 2020.
14. Renjen Punit, The essence of Resilient leadership: Business Recovery from COVID-19, *Deloitte Insights*, April 22, 2020.
15. Renjen Punit, Industry 4.0: At the intersection of readiness and responsibility, Deloitte Global Annual Survey on business preparedness for a connected era, *Deloitte Insights*, January 20, 2020.
16. Renjen Punit, The heart of resilient leadership: Responding to COVID-19: A guide for senior executives, *Deloitte Insights*, March 16, 2020.
17. Renjen Punit, The essence of Resilient leadership: Business recovery from COVID-19: Building recovery on a foundation of trust, *Deloitte Insights*, April 22, 2020.
18. Redman Russell, "Nielsen: Corona virus has CPG shoppers chaning their ways", *Supermarket News*, March 11, 2020.
19. United Nations , "Sustainable Development Goals" August 3, 2020.

TERRITORIAL RESILIENCE OF THE *BLACKCURRANT ACTORS* IN BURGUNDY/FRANCE IN THE FACE OF THE IMPACTS OF CLIMATE CHANGE

Cornelia Caseau[1]

Introduction

Climate change, which until now has been particularly harmful in areas with extreme temperatures, is increasingly affecting countries with a formerly moderate climate, such as France. Thus, the abnormally violent climatic incidents of the last five years in Burgundy-Franche-Comté have compromised the successive harvests of blackcurrants, a small red fruit emblematic of the region and a flagship product of its agri-food economy. In the medium term, it is the survival of the orchards and the sustainability of an entire industry that is in danger.

The Burgundy-Franche-Comté region is, after the Pays de la Loire and the Plateaux de l'Oise, the third largest producer of blackcurrants (1,800 tonnes in 2021)[2], but the largest in France (900 tonnes in 2021)[3] for the variety Noir de Bourgogne. Some sixty farms supply fruit mainly to the Dijon and Burgundy liqueur makers, which produce 12 million bottles of crème de cassis (blackcurrant cream) annually. Since its appearance in Burgundy in the middle of the 18th century, blackcurrants have occupied, alongside the wines of the Côte de Nuits and Beaune, "a place that is sometimes discreet, sometimes essential to the local economy" (Augustin, 2012)[4], but it was particularly during the phylloxera period that it revealed its full importance. On the one hand, it was necessary to meet the increasing needs of the liqueur industry, and on the other hand, it was a substitute crop for the grapevines, which were destroyed by the disease. Since the beginning of the 20th century, it "has become an important production in the region's activity thanks to the know-how of the producers, the liquorists, restaurant owners and pastry chefs" (Augustin, 2012)[5].

The present article focuses on the preservation of the blackcurrant industry in Burgundy-Franche-Comté and on resilience, particularly in its agri-food dimension. It reflects upon the assets of the *Association des Acteurs du Cassis de Bourgogne-Franche-Comté* (referred to in this article as *Blackcurrant Actors*) and their commitment to territorial resilience in the face of the impacts of climate change.

---

[1] Many thanks to Jean-Dominique Caseau, CEO of L'Héritier-Guyot and Lejay Lagoute, Dijon, France, for the broad and precious information about the blackcurrant sector

[2] Source 'Acteurs du Cassis' (Agricultural Chamber Côte-d'Or)

[3] Ibid.

[4] Augustin, M. La Route du Cassis entre Dijon et Mâcon. eVous, 06/08/2012

[5] Ibid.

Theoretical Framework

"Territoire" Territory

The term "territoire" appeared in the French language in the 13th century, but it was not widely applied until the 18th century. In Anglo-Saxon geographical studies, the terms "place" or "space" are more frequently used to designate a territory (Batat, 2016; 12). The meaning of the word can be completed by "an area on which a human group lives" or "a socialised space" that a human community "develops according to its needs"[6] (Paquot, 2011; 23).

For Villar and David (2014; 3) a territory is more than "the sum of its structural, geographical, social, economic and other components". Aspects that make up a territory including history, culture and territorial identity should also be taken into consideration. Roncayolo associates the material side of an area with "a subjective dimension, linked to feelings of belonging, but also to practices and perceptions that are neither strictly individual nor entirely collective" (quoted by Ingallina, 2007; 10). "The "territoire" is both a support and a relationship" where past and anticipation are "continuously associated [...] as much in material aspects (urban heritage, monuments, sites with a strong symbolic dimension) as in immaterial components (traditions, local productions...) (Ingallina, 2007; 10)".

Resilience

While for several decades *sustainable development* has been synonymous with protecting the planet and our prosperity (for current and future generations), as advocated by the United Nations in the 17 Sustainable Development Goals to be achieved by 2030[7], the notion of *resilience* is now "the buzz", to the extent that it risks "overshadowing sustainable development" (Villar & David, 2014; 2)[8]. Resilience applies to "territories, organisations, individuals, ecosystems" in contexts such as "disasters, economic and social crises, and disruptions of all kinds and forms" (Villar & David, 2014; 2).

The Food and Agriculture Organization (FAO) defines *resilience* as:

"The ability to prevent disasters and crises as well as to anticipate, absorb, accommodate or recover from them in a timely, efficient and sustainable manner. This includes protecting, restoring and improving livelihoods systems in the face of threats that impact agriculture, nutrition, food security and food safety.[9]"

Villar and David distinguish between two types of territorial resilience: "a 'cindynic' resilience, linked to the occurrence of sudden local events (industrial accident, flooding, factory closure), and a 'global' resilience, linked to slow and large-scale phenomena (climate change, global economic crisis, demographic decline)" (Villar & David, 2014; 3). They highlight a number of factors that could improve the resilience capacities of a territory, as facilitating the "inclusion in the territorial texture (history, culture)", "links and trust between actors", "the meaning given to action", "the social capital", "the development of

[6] L'Encyclopédie de la géographie de 1992, quoted by Batat, 2016 ; 12-16.

[7] www.un.org/sustainabledevelopment/

[8] To facilitate reading, the French quotations in the article are all translated by the author

[9] https://www.fao.org/emergencies/how-we-work/resilience/en/

skills", "innovation," etc. They also draw attention to the social dimension of resilience and the necessity to mobilise the resources of the territory and the resilience capacities of human society (Villar & David, 2014; 3, 7). A settlement or community is resilient, "if it knows and can find the necessary capacities for its adaptation in the face of hazards that threaten it" (ibid.). Resilience is not static and may therefore be described as "a setting in motion, a perpetual search for a dynamic balance between paradoxical characteristics and contrary processes: short term and long term, local scale and globalisation, redundancy and efficiency, tailor-made and ready-made, autonomy and dependence..." (Villar & David, 2014; 2).

The notion of *resilience* is closely linked to *territories* ("territoires") and their persistence to climate threats. Farmers and rural communities are on the front line of most climate disasters worldwide (Gioia, 2018; Ephstein et al., 2018), and climate change has already reduced agricultural production in many parts of the world (Michler et al., 2019). Strategies responding to crises affecting agricultural spaces are often related to the development of certain food sectors (Villar & David, 2014; 3; Michel-Villarreal et al., 2019). For the long-term sustainable development of human populations, it is imperative, to identify factors that contribute to the resilience of food systems (Tendall et al., 2015; Seekell et al., 2017; Alcon et al., 2020). In this context, Meyer studied the behaviour of farmers in low- and middle-income countries in the face of global climate change, and draws the attention to the need for further research on societal transformations and demographic trends, as well as changes in consumption patterns (Meyer 2020; 7). Scholars have to "determine the impact of environmental drivers" on food systems' resilience. Neither the bidirectionality between food systems and the environment, nor the linkages between environmental and social systems have been sufficiently addressed (ibid.).

Governments and development agencies have promoted climate-smart agricultural technologies to increase productivity, and at the same time build resilience to climate shocks and externalities (Michler et al., 2019; 149). Associations and communities often provide more relevant solutions than isolated initiatives (Goworek et al., 2018). For example, some companies in South Africa have developed social-ecological community resilience systems, which bring together place-based community capacities and efficiencies "to enhance and maintain its members' livelihoods in the face of both gradual and sudden social-ecological changes" (Hamann et al., 2018; 835).

Other initiatives have emerged, such as the one of farming communities in New Zealand which, through their engagement, have demonstrated the effectiveness of resilience through their relationships within local rural communities. Researchers have noted that "farmer relationships [...] are more influential than relationships with scientists, regulators or even local nonfarmers such as farm equipment salespeople" (Tisch, D. & Galbreath, J., 2018; 1203). Tisch and Galbreath recall the need for "sensemaking" for these farmers in search of organisational resilience, and introduce the term "community sensegiving" to create resilience by local members of rural communities in places that are familiar to them. It is substantial to foster "community sensegiving" by establishing and maintaining "rural meeting places such as town halls, research farms and pubs" (Tisch & Galbreath 2018; 1206).

Methodology

The present paper is a case study in line with the recommendations of Eisenhardt (1989), Eisenhardt et al. (2016) and Yin (2017). The data collection follows a narrative thematic approach, focussing on the territorial and environmental challenges of the sector, and dealing with the question, how the association of the *Blackcurrant Actors* faces the challenges of territorial resilience.

The research questions are:

1. What are the territorial and environmental challenges the blackcurrant sector in Burgundy-Franche-Comté (France) has to face?
2. What are the assets of the *Blackcurrant Actors* to build territorial resilience?

To answer the research questions, a qualitative study was carried out in September 2021 with three main groups of stakeholders in the blackcurrant industry. Blackcurrant producers (fruit and buds) belonging to two Burgundy cooperatives, processors (of blackcurrant cream), and researchers from the National Scientific Research Center (CNRS)[10] and Agro Sup (at the University of Burgundy) and in two local biological laboratories, and the blackcurrant technician of the Côte-d'Or Chamber of Agriculture. Some of these *Blackcurrant Actors* have been working in the sector for a very long time, others only for a few years, which allows for different visions, contributing to a great representativeness of the sample of interviewees.

The 16 interviews, conducted via the Teams platform or by telephone, lasted between 45 minutes and two hours, and were all recorded and transcribed. This qualitative study was enriched by email exchanges before and after the interviews. The interviewees provided documents internal to the blackcurrant sector or to their specialisation, newsletters, results of biological research, presentation slides, documents supporting the application for project funding from the Burgundy-Franche-Comté Regional Council. The study of websites and press articles completed the empirical research.

The results of the interviews were classified according to the three professional groups. The identity of the interviewees is anonymised and encrypted, to ensure the confidentiality of the testimonies.

Table 1: Interviewees of the semi-structured interviews

Producers	*Date and Length of Interviews*
Independent producer	I 1: 23.9. (120 min.)
Producer 1 belonging to cooperative 1	I 2: 22.9. (60 min.)
Producer 2 belonging to cooperative 1	I 3: 24.9. (60 min.)
Producer 1 belonging to cooperative 2	I 4: 28.9. (60 min.)
Producer 2 belonging to cooperative 2	I 5: 27.9. (90 min.)
Processors	
Processor 1	I 6: 29.9. (60 min.)
Processor 2	I 7: 27.9. (60 min.)

[10]Centre National de Recherche Scientifique: French term translated by the author

Producers	*Date and Length of Interviews*
Processor 3	I 8: 22.9. (60 min.)
Processor 4	I 9: 29.9. (120 min.)
Processor 5	I 10: (exchange of e-mails and provision of photos)
Researcher/Technician	
Researcher 1 University	I 11: 27.9. (60 min.)
Researcher 2 University	I 12: 21.9. (60 min.)
Researcher 3 Laboratory 1	I 13: 30.9. (45 min.)
Researcher 4 Laboratory 1	I 14: 30.9. (75 min.)
Researcher 5 Laboratory 2	I 15: 30.9. (60 min.)
Researcher 6 Laboratory 2	I 16: 30.9. (60 min.)
Technician	I 17: 24.9. (60 min.)

Findings

Territorial and Environmental Challenges for the Blackcurrant Sector in Burgundy-Franche-Comté

Climate Change

Blackcurrant is a "northern plant" that does not tolerate temperatures above 30°C (I 4). That's why the "climatic incidents of recent years" (I 5, I 17), ("each year two major climatic events"; I 5) with a "general increase in temperature" (I 4), "periods of heatwaves" (I 5), "great drought", or "post-harvest drought" (I 4), "frost during flowering" or "hail" (I 5), or "the presence of pests or diseases" (I 15), have jeopardised a large part of the cultivation of this small fruit. Extreme climatic phenomena lead to a "reduction or even loss of harvests" (I 15), which means that the Burgundy-Franche-Comté region "might no longer be suitable for planting blackcurrants" (I 15).

Diseases and Pests

Climate change fosters the spreading of diseases and pests like "powdery mildew, downy mildew or bacteria at plant roots" (I 15). With the "mild winters, diseases and pests survive and attack and destroy the orchards" (I 5). Furthermore, the "blackcurrant plants become degenerated", because producers often cut the same plants, and transmit these diseases (I 1, I 13, I 17).

Restructuring of the Land

We observe a "loss of balance between grasslands, forests and arable land" (I 7). Human intervention in the "restructuring of the land" (I 3, I 11), or the suppression of hedges (20 years ago), meadows and forests which "deprives pollinating insects of their food resources and their habitat" (I 11), and causes their "disappearance". Ninety-nine percent of pollinating insects have thus disappeared, compared to the 1980s (I 11, I 15, I 13). Insecticides and neo-nicotinoids "reduce insect biodiversity" (I 11, I 13), soils are "impoverished" (I 7) and become "unusable for planting" (I 15). Farmers abandon plots because the soil is no longer suitable (I 7).

Blackcurrant Actors and Territorial Resilience

In their struggle for the survival of their industry, the blackcurrant stakeholders do not operate individually, but as a community. At the national level, they are assembled in the French interprofessional association of fruit and vegetables for multiple destinations[11] (AFIDEM), made up equally of producers and processors (liqueur industry) (Agreste, 2019). On the local scale, the *Blackcurrant Actors*, are responsible for defending the interests of their members and developing what is now a regional agri-food industry. This association was founded in 2017 to replace the CICD (blackcurrant inter-branch organisation)[12], established in 1955.

The industry approach for the defence of blackcurrant is part of a strategy[13], defined by the French government in 2017 and 2021 (EGalim 1 and 2), relayed by the Regional Council of Burgundy-Franche-Comté and supported by the European Union (Rural Development Programme[14], PEI[15], FEADER[16]) on the one hand, and in support of the FilFruits Transfo[17] project initiated by AFIDEM, and financed by France AgriMer[18] on the other (I 9).

The Mobilisation of Territorial Resources

In addition to the traditional collaboration (since the end of the nineteenth century) between the two branches of the blackcurrant sector, i.e. production and processing (I 5), since 2017 the *Blackcurrant Actors* have included local researchers, laboratories and a technician, to better develop their resilience measures. There is also a close cooperation with regional institutions such as the Regional Council of Burgundy-Franche-Comté and the Agricultural Chamber of Côte-d'Or.

For all those involved, the "territorial anchorage" (I 16) and "a strong attachment to the local product, crème de cassis" (I 17) a "high quality product" (I 5), is essential and makes them "feel affected" (I 16). Production and processing are in a "50-km radius" (I 4), so that the "geographic proximity" (I 4) facilitates interaction and allows them to propose "highly adapted solutions" (I 7). Regularly, members and partners "gather around a table to discuss" these issues (I 4), "find solutions and implement projects" (I 4), and "everyone is

---

[11]"Association Française Interprofessionnelle des Fruits et Légumes à Destinations Multiples" French interprofessional association of fruit and vegetables for multiple destinations (French term translated by the authors)

[12]Comité Interprofessionnel du Cassis de Dijon

[13]"Stratégie et le plan de la filière des fruits et légumes transformés" Strategy and plan for the processed fruit and vegetable industry (French term translated by the authors)

[14]Agriculture et foresterie productive et durable

[15]Partenariat Européen d'Innovation

[16]Fonds Européen agricole pour le développement rural

[17]Filière française de *transformation* de fruits

[18]Établissement national des produits de l'agriculture et de la mer

going in the same direction" (I 8). The close collaboration and the "plurality of knowledge" (I 17) makes it possible to "better define the needs" and "react very quickly" (I 17).

Close Connections between the Local Actors

Each of the actors contributes through a common passion for the profession, ("When it's in your blood, in your DNA, it becomes a *religion*") (I 1). "Human interaction" ("Nothing could replace the human contact") (I 4), "better mutual knowledge" (I 5), "relationships" (I 14), "good communication" (I 13), "dynamism" (I 15), and "team spirit" (I 12) are emphasized by the interlocutors. "We need each other", comments one of the processors (I 6). Without the researchers, we "would not be able to find solutions" (I 6), because we "don't have the skills to help producers solve their problems" (I 8). For the researchers and biologists, it is inspiring to work together with the whole blackcurrant sector, and to be "close to the producers" (I 11) in the field.

Sensegiving through a Strong Interdependence

As the blackcurrant production is a "niche market", and "big companies are not interested in small crops," (I 15) local *researchers* have to find their own, tailor-made answers to improve "local plants" (I 13) and make them more resistant. It gives sense to them, to provide "support to the local farmers", to "motivate them" (I 15), and to show them that they are "no longer alone" (I 15). Researchers and the technician "feel useful" in providing an "applicable response and technical support to the producers" and in furnishing "more systematic joint solutions" (I 13, I 17). It "gives them energy" to observe that the cultivators are "willing to change their working practices" and "apply the advice" (I 17) given.

Without the support of the researchers and the technician, the blackcurrant community would find itself "on the edge of the precipice" (I 7) and might eventually risk "disappearing" (I 16). The *producers* need the protection of the community to survive (I 16), and the collective approach "reassures" them (I 6), "gives them hope" and "visibility for the future" (I 4).

It is a concern for the *processors*, to "give confidence and security to the producers" (I 7). Whereas in former times, the sales price for blackcurrant was decided by the "Stock Exchange" (I 5), since 2017, "multi-annual contracts" between producers and processors have been established, to offer "guaranteed prices" to the farmers over the years (I 16). Producers have to "ensure volumes" (I 8) for the processors, to enable the continuity of the production of the crème de cassis. For the preservation of the organoleptic qualities, required for the preservation of the Geographical Indication of 'Cassis de Dijon' and 'Cassis de Bourgogne', processors rely on the help of the researchers.

The Power of a Collective Approach

As individual initiatives would not be efficient, a collective approach is a better way to find solutions for territorial resilience. The *Blackcurrant Actors* "form a unit" (I 4), and together they are "stronger facing the market and large-scale distribution" and collectively fight against "an unbalanced power relationship" (I 4). The community gives "added strength and credibility despite the small size" (I 7) and allows the organization to be "more heard by clients and politicians" (I 7).

The initial FEADER project of the *Blackcurrant Actors* for territorial resilience, presented to the Regional Council of Bourgogne-France-Comté and the European authorities in 2017, was accepted and funded for a period from 2018 to 2021. A second request, retained in December 2021 (I 9), makes it possible to continue the work over the next three years. This second grant definitely rewards the quality, meaningfulness and transferability of the initiatives of the blackcurrant community, and reflects the European authorities' awareness of the urgency of the situation.

Table 1: Territorial Resilience Assets of the Blackcurrant Actors

The mobilisation of territorial resources	Sensegiving through a strong interdependence
• between production, processing and partners (researchers, institutions) • joint search for solutions to climate change, pests and diseases • plurality of knowledge • territorial anchorage • geographical proximity • highly adapted solutions • rapid reactivity	• mutual support between members, concerned with each other's problems and needs • researchers provide applicable response and technical support to producers • the collective approach reassures farmers, gives them hope and visibility for the future • processors give confidence and security to the producers (multi-annual contracts, guaranteed prices) • producers secure volumes of blackcurrants for the processors • the perpetuation of organoleptic qualities for the Geographical Indication (IG) for all parties involved
Close connections between the local actors	The power of a collective approach
• common passion for the profession • human interaction • good mutual knowledge • close relationships • good communication • dynamism • team spirit	• global defence of the sector → strength, credibility → • market/clients • large-scale distribution • politicians • local/national institutions • European authorities (FEADER project)

Discussion

This study's objective was to better understand the territorial and environmental challenges of the blackcurrant sector in Burgundy-Franche-Comté, and to highlight the assets of the *Blackcurrant Actors* for building territorial resilience. Like for Villar and David (2014; 2), for whom resilience is "a perpetual search for dynamic equilibrium" between "opposing processes", climate change is a large-scale, global phenomenon, whereas *Blackcurrant Actors* operate on a small-scale within the territorially bounded Burgundy-Franche-Comté region (Hamann et al. 2020; see also Berrone et al., 2016; 1941).

In the field of resilience, there is an observable dichotomy between "short term and long term" (Villar & David, 2014; 2): resilience procedures had to be taken by the *Blackcurrant Actors* "in a hurry" (I 17), because producers did not see the climate and biodiversity problems coming, and suddenly found themselves "up against the wall" (I 17), surprised by the acceleration of climate change-related problems. As blackcurrant is a plant that takes three years to bear fruit, a lot of patience is required from producers and researchers, before they can assess the effectiveness of their actions (Michel-Villarreal et al. 2019). Concerning the disparity between "tailor-made" and "ready-made" (Villar & David, 2014; 2), for the small blackcurrant sector "ready-made" remedies do not exist, so that local researchers and biologists have to experiment with innovative, "tailor-made" solutions.

We agree with Villar and David's assertion about the importance of the "social dimension" for territorial resilience, and the mobilisation of local resources in the commitment against the impacts of climate change. Adherence to the community facilitates the "involvement" of the stakeholders (Villar & David 2014; 3). The enrolment of the *Blackcurrant Actors* in their association and the social interaction between members and partners are rather strong, and present a solid basis for developing resilience strategies.

Our article demonstrates that small local associations may have a certain external power, when they exhibit a strong internal cohesion and solidarity. The *Blackcurrant Actors* function without any competitive spirit or political notion (I 9), and can, in spite (or because?) of their small size, indirectly cooperate and develop resilience strategies with the government. In the context of the General Assembly of Food[19] for example, they have contributed to the elaboration of the AFIDEM's propositions to the French government, and to the draft laws EGalim 1 (2017) and EGalim 2 (2021). Whereas Hamann et al. (2018) emphasise the efficiency of the "placed-based community" model in South Africa over the growing inability of the states to deal with great challenges, the model of the *Blackcurrant Actors* demonstrates, that an effective collaboration between local associations and national institutions is possible.

The tripartite model of cooperation of the *Blackcurrant Actors* proves, that in the field of territorial resilience, the close connections between professional branches can be quite rewarding. We affirm therefore, in opposition to Tisch and Galbreath (2018), who maintain, that the relationships within farmers of local rural communities in New Zealand are more influential than those with other professional branches in the region, that professional groups in the blackcurrant sector are complementary and represent a sort of mutual enrichment. "Sensegiving" for its members, as defined by Tisch and Galbreath (2018) (see also Whiteman & Cooper, 2011), and a strong interdependence between the stakeholders, facilitate the search for adapted answers.

Lastly, Meyer (2020) deplores the lack of research about the impact of environmental drivers on food systems' resilience, and on the bidirectionality of food systems and the environment. Our article contributes partly to filling the gap, in presenting a case where this bidirectionality exists.

Conclusion

The article presents a rather positive picture of the association. Nevertheless, it should be noted that not all solutions exist today (I 16), and that further action will be required (I 13).

[19] Etats Généraux de l'Alimentation

The *Blackcurrant Actors* do not have sufficient means to self-finance their research projects. Without external financial support, the scientific research may not continue in the medium or long term (I 11), which would have a negative effect on any potential future progress, and a significant part of the efforts undertaken so far could be shuttered. Burgundy has certainly become a forerunner in the field of territorial resilience (I 12), but it is still necessary to have a broader vision and seek international cooperation (I 7).

Beyond the immediate need for securing fruit production despite the effects of climate change, the key role of the blackcurrant processors, and their capacity to adapt to the consumer demand and new trends, and to create new sales opportunities, should also be considered (Meyer, 2020). The market for crème de cassis has been declining for several years (-3.5% in 2020) (I 9), due to a structural drop in consumption (I 4) and the rather traditional image of this product (I 12). In addition, blackcurrant liqueur encounters competition from other spirits (rum, white spirits, modern liqueurs and whisky), and the internationalisation of the supply (1 9).

The limitation of this article is that it is focused on the cooperation of the *Blackcurrant Actors* facing the effects of climate change. Since the processors are not involved on the agricultural side, their role in the process has been slightly overlooked in this article. In forthcoming research it would be interesting to deepen the question, and examine, how the processors can reinforce the resilience of this sector.

Bibliography

Academic Articles

1. Alcon, F., Marín-Minano, C., Zabala, J.A. and de Miguel, M.D. (2020). Valuing diversification benefits through intercropping in Mediterranean agroecosystems: A choice experiment approach. *Ecological Economics* 171: 1-10. https://doi.org/10.1016/j.ecolecon.2020.106593.
2. Berrone, P. et al. (2016). Understanding community dynamics in the study of grand challenges: How nonprofits, institutional actors, and the community fabric interact to influence income inequality. *Academy of Management Journal, 59*(6), 1940-1964.
3. Eisenhardt, K. M. (1989). Building Theories from Case Study Research. *The Academy of Management Review*. Vol. 14, No. 4 (Oct.): 532-550.
4. Eisenhardt, K. M., Graebner, M. E. and Sonenshein, S. (2016). Grand Challenges and Inductive Methods: Rigor without Rigor Mortis. *Academy of Management Journal,* Vol. 59, n° 4. https://doi.org/10.5465/amj.2016.4004
5. Epshtein, D., Curtiss, J., Gagalyuk, T. and Unay Gailhard, I. (2018). The Factors of Resilience of Agricultural Enterprises against External Shocks. *Problems of Economic Transition.* 60/12: 883-906. DOI/ https://doi.org/10.1080/10611991.2018.1672476.
6. Gioia, P. (2018). Pathway to resilience: hands and hearts for peasant livelihoods and fair relations between humans and nature. *Third World Quarterly.* 39/7: 1403-1410. DOI: https://doi.org/10.1080/01436597.2017.1350820.
7. Goworek, H., Land, C., Burt, G., Zundel, M., Saren, M., Parker, M. and Lambe, B. (2018). Scaling Sustainability: Regulation and Resilience in Managerial Responses to Climate Change. *British Journal of Management, 29:* 209-219. DOI: 10.1111/1467-8551.12295.

8. Hamann, R., Makaula, L., Zievogel, G., Shearing C. and Zhang, A. (2020). Strategic Responses to Grand Challenges: Why and How Corporations Build Community Resilience. *J Bus Ethics* 161: 835–853 (2020). https://doi.org/10.1007/s10551-019-04345-y.
9. Meyer, M. A. (2020). The role of resilience in food systems in low- and middle-income countries. *Global Food Security 24:* 1-9.
10. Michel-Villarreal, R., Vilalta-Perdomo, E., Hingley, M. and Canavari, M. (2019). Evaluating economic resilience for sustainable agri-food systems: The case of Mexico. *Strategic Change* 28: 279-288. DOI: 10.1002/jsc.2270.
11. Michler, J.D., Baylis, K., Arends-Kuenning, M. and Mazvimavi, K. (2019). Conservation agriculture and climate resilience. *Journal of Environmental Economics and Management 93:* 148-169. DOI: 10.1016/j.jeem.2018.11.008.
12. Pagès-Hélary, S., Dujourdy, l. and Cayot, N. (2020). Flavour compounds in blackcurrant berries: Multivariate analysis of datasets obtained with natural variability and various experimental parameters. *LWT Food Science and Technology.* https://doiorg. 10.1016/j.ltw.2021:112425.
13. Paquot, T. (2011). Qu'est-ce qu'un territoire ? In : *Vie Sociale* 2011/2 (N° 2): 23 - 32.
14. Seekell, D., Carr, J., Dell'Angelo, J., D'Odorico, P., Fader, M., Gephart, J....Tavoni, A. (2017). Resilience in the global food system. *Environmental Research Letters,* 12, 025010. http://doi.org/10.1088/1748-9326/aa5730.
15. Tendall, D.M., Joerin, J., Kopainski, B., Edwards, P., Shreck, A., Le, Q.B. ...Six, J. (2015). Food system resilience: Defining the concept. *Global Food Security,* 6: 17-23. http://doi.org/10.1016/j.gfs.2015.08.001.
16. Tisch, D. and Galbreath, J. (2018). Building organizational resilience through sensemaking: The case of climate change and extreme weather events. *Business Strategy & the Environment 27/:.* 1197-1208. DOI: https://doi.org/10.1002/bse.2062.
17. Whiteman, G. and Cooper, W. (2011). Ecological sensemaking. *Academy of Management Journal, 54*(5), 889-911.

Other Publications

18. Batat, W. (2016). Marketing territorial expérientiel. Bassins de vie, Branding, Digital, Expérientiel : toutes les facettes du nouveau marketing territorial. Ellipse
19. Bonescu, M., and Caseau, C. (2020). Les produits locaux au service de la marque territoriale. Le cas de la "Crème de cassis de Dijon". In: Bayet-Robert, P., Stengel, K. (coord.). *Le marketing culinaire et alimentaire face aux défis du XXIe siècle*, Tours: L'Harmattan: 55-76.
20. FAO. Food and Agriculture Organization of the United Nations
21. https://www.fao.org/emergencies/how-we-work/resilience/en/
22. Humbert, F. (2021). La filière des vins et spiritueux, de plus en plus responsable. *Décision Achats* (3 mai). https://www.decision-achats.fr/Thematique/strategie-achats-1236/rse-achats-durables-2258/Breves/filiere-vins-spiritueux-plus-plus-responsable-360107.htm#
23. Ingallina, P. (2007). L'attractivité des territoires, in : Actes des séminaires fév.-juill. éd. Blais, J.P., Ingallina, P. et Vernie, M. 2009. Ministère de l'Ecologie, de l'Energie, du Développement Durable et de l'Aménagement du Territoire : 9-18.
24. Villar, C. and David, M. (2014). La résilience, un outil pour les territoires ? Manuscrit auteur, publié lors du séminaire IT-GO Rosko. Roscoff, 22-23 Mai.
25. Yin, R. K. (2017). Case Study Research and Applications. Design and Methods. Sage Publications Ltd.

26. Documents related to the blackcurrant sector
27. Agreste Bourgogne-Franche-Comté (2019). Le Cassis en Bourgogne-Franche-Comté : deux filières spécifiques. N° 54.
28. https://draaf.bourgogne-franche-comte.agriculture.gouv.fr/Le-Cassis-en-Bourgogne-Franche
29. Anstett, M.C., Denis, C., Duchet-Annez, M., Golotte, A., Nars-Chasseray, M. and Pagès-Hélary, S. (2020), *Newsletter Cassis*, 27.09.2020
30. Bertin, A.L. (2016). Comment pérenniser le cassis Noir de Bourgogne ? *Le Bien Public,* 10.09.2021
31. Laboratoires Spiral (2006). Valorisation de la filière cassis et fruits rouges en Bourgogne. Rapport d'étude.
32. Nars Chasseray, M. (2021). *Formulaire de Dépôt* PEI Cassis 2021.
33. Nars Chasseray, M. (2020). Projet FEADER 2018-2020. Pérennité et développement de la filière Cassis en Bourgogne. Journée d'échange avec les groupes organisationnels allemands, le 28 novembre 2019.
34. Pagès-Hélary, S. and Cayot, N. L'arôme du cassis. Poster.
35. Statuts (2017) : Filière Régionale des Acteurs du Cassis en Bourgogne Franche-Comté. Breteniére.

INNOVATION, INDUSTRY AND INFRASTRUCTURE WITHIN SUSTAINABLE DEVELOPMENT GOALS: ANALYSIS OF EMERGING ASIAN ECONOMIES

Swati Mehta

Abstract

United Nations Sustainable Development Goals gives a promising roadmap for inclusive and sustainable growth. Firms, industries, sectors and economies are all striving for long-run growth, which becomes more strategic following a particular roadmap. Industrialization is largely assumed as the engine of growth that has pulled the other inter-related sectors across economies. But delving deep in to the factors that lead to successful industrialization, innovation assumes the prominent position mainly after the growth of endogenous growth models and evolutionary growth models of early 1980s that were substantiated with empirical evidences. In the highly competitive world and with fragmented production processes, it becomes necessary to identify the distinguishing factors that have the potential of growth. In this context, the aim of the paper is to explore the innovation capability of different Asian economies to understand the emerging economies of the East and South-East Asia.

Keywords: *Innovation Capability, Sustainable Development Goals, Asian Economies, and Manufacturing Hubs*

Introduction

Industrialization was instrumental in transforming the economies of now developed economies from Global North from West to East. England, USA, Germany, Italy, Japan, Russia and South Korea etc. all concentrated on building innovation capabilities leading to industrial revolutions at different times. First industrial revolution happened in England and North-Western Europe that made their economies climb the development ladder, that were followed by the Second Industrial revolution that transformed the economies of Germany and USA. The Third Industrial Revolution was the age of advances in electronics, Information and Communication Technologies (ICT) that lead to the success story of East Asian countries like South Korea and Taiwan. Now, the world is in the midst of the fourth industrial revolution that is an age of artificial intelligence, robotics, Internet of things etc. The countries with advances in these upcoming technologies would be at the helm of technological wars. The trade war, which is more of a technological war between USA and China in 2018-19 was the testimony of the growing competition backed with technological advances (The Economist, 2019). The emergence and growth of 'Factory Asia' is changing the global production systems with the greater fragmented production processes and growing transport facilities and ICT. China has emerged as the 'game changer' with becoming the 'manufacturing hub' that not only concentrated in the production of low-tech manufacturing like textiles, footwear, food processing etc. but also emerged forcibly in the manufacturing of electronics, automobiles, pharmaceuticals, biotech, etc. China also has several 'spikes' to the neighboring countries in South and South-East Asia including South Korea, Taiwan, Singapore, Hong Kong to the new emerging economies like India, Vietnam, Philippines, Malaysia, Cambodia etc. In this context, it is imperative to examine the overall 'innovative capabilities' that these Asian economies are accumulating to understand the long-term prospective growth scenario. The idea is to examine the 'innovative capabilities' from the broader perspectives of United Nations advocated Sustainable Development Goals.

The structure of the Chapter is as follows. In Section II, the relationship of Innovation and Economic Growth within the paradigm of Sustainable Development Goals is discussed. Section III concentrates on different Sustainable Development Goals for long-term inclusive and sustainable growth of the economies. Section IV focuses upon the chosen Asian economies to understand the nature of their innovation capability to understand their long-term growth prospects. In Section V, the various Targets, Goals and Prospects concerning SDG9 were examined for the chosen Asian economies. Section VI concludes the Chapter.

Innovation, Economic Growth and Sustainable Development Goals

The importance of technical change was implicit in the Classical theories starting with Adam Smith in his 'Wealth of Nations'. The precision in work that enhances with 'division of work' becomes the norm in the production process. But the economic growth models of late twentieth century with the contribution of neo-classical economist, mainly Solow (1956) treated 'technological change' as exogenous variable estimated as 'residual' of factors contributing to economic growth after controlling labor and capital inputs. Abramovitz (1956) called the estimated 'residual' as the 'measure of our ignorance' as it may also include many growth enhancing/contracting factors. A year later, post-Keynesian economist, Kaldor (1957) introduced 'technical progress function' in a way to make the complex factor of production endogenous (Verspagen, 2005). But a real breakthrough happened in the early 1980s. Two divergent schools of thoughts: Neoclassical and Neo-Schumpeterian deciphered the process of generating 'technologies' that can be transformed to 'innovation' leading to 'knowledge accumulation' over time. Romer (1986,1990); Grossman and Helpman (1991) modeled the process of Research and Development (R&D) that may lead to 'horizontal' and 'vertical' differentiation of goods. The 'weak uncertainty' entails the cost-benefit analysis of R&D spending (Verspagen, 2005). On the other hand, the Neo-Schumpeterian school of thoughts captured the greater complexity of innovation process with the publication by Nelson and Winter (1982). The evolutionary approach assumes the process of innovation as holistic, time consuming and evolving with many actors, organizations and institutions working together in an interactive manner building close inter-related systems. This connotes that growth and sustainability of nations states necessitates the transformations within numerous inter-related sectors. In simple words, the inclusive and sustainable economic growth is necessitated for different economies at different levels of their development. According to the World Poverty Clock, there were almost 750 million people living on less than \$1.90 a day (The Economist, 2021). The Food and Agriculture Organization of the United Nations (FAO) projected that nearly 8 percent of the world population can be undernourished in 2030[1]. It further found that conflict being the primary driver of hunger apart from the major cause of child moralities and malnutrition. Climate change is the challenge that the whole world economies are facing. It affects production, productivity, geopolitics, migration patterns, demographic structures etc. As of 2022, "*the world has eight years to halves greenhouse-gas (GHG) emissions relative to 2010 levels*"[2]. Innovation is increasingly needed to balance the carbon footprint and economic growth. Therefore, to meet the numerous challenges for the mankind United Nations Member States recognized the need to end poverty and other deprivations along with improving health and education facilities that can reduce inequalities along the path of economic growth, while systematically tackling climate change and preserve natural resources. The *2030 Agenda for Sustainable Development* with a clear road map for achieving the identified 17 Sustainable Development Goals were adopted in 2015.

Sustainable Development Goals: Inter-relationship for Mutual, Inclusive and Sustainable Growth

Seventeen inter-related 'Global Goals' adopted as 'Sustainable Development Goals' by United Nations member states in 2015 for the economic, social and environmental sustainability of the world nations. As the focus of the paper is to examine the 'innovation capability' of the nations for sustainable socio-economic-environmental growth, it is Sustainable Development Goal 9 on '*Industry, Innovation and Infrastructure*' that specifically address these issues. Figure 1 portrays the framework of inter-relationship between different SDGs that needs to be developed holistically for sustainable growth. Stating the importance of *Quality Education* under SDG4, it develops not only the critical thinking but also infuses the desire for learning for building stronger human capital with different skill-intensity over the years. The digital age with technological sophistication of Third and Fourth Industrial Revolution pushing forward the boundaries of advanced teaching-learning process. Economic Growth is the most focused area for policymakers across nations. The focus on SDG9 on *Decent Work and Economic Growth* draws roadmap to achieve long-run sustainable economic growth with gainful employment opportunities that plays a predominantly important role in *Reducing Inequality*- the focus of SDG10. SDG9 (Industry, Innovation and Infrastructure) and SDG11 (Sustainable cities and communities) also complement each other with the growing need of green and clean technologies for future sustainable growth. Advancing technologies increasingly becoming greener for wider acceptability and future advancements. SDG12 that focus on Responsible consumption *and Production* takes into concentration the future generations along with the present ones for the optimal utilization of resources. However, different SGDs need to create an environment that provides opportunities to achieve the targets. In this context, the importance of *SDG16: Peace, Justice and Strong Institutions* is manifested. Stronger Institutional mechanism infuses the sense of confidence for investing

[1] These projections take into consideration the Covid-19 pandemic. Accessed from https://www.globalhungerindex.org/trends.html.

[2] https://www.economist.com/graphic-detail/2022/02/18/are-climate-goals-compatible-with-reducing-poverty.

and taking challenges for future growth and sustainability. Peace within and outside the nation states plays a predominant role for the morale of the people across trades.

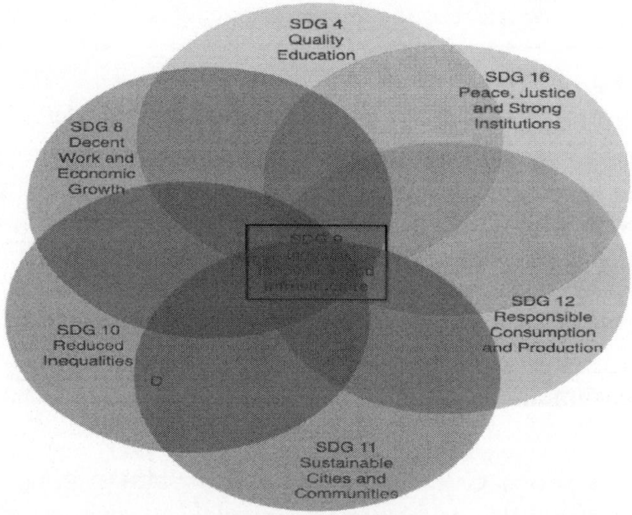

Figure 1: Interrelated Sustainable Development Goals
Source: Author elaboration

Innovation Capability in Asian Economies

To build resilient infrastructure, promote inclusive and sustainable industrialization and foster innovation is *Goal 9* of Sustainable Development Goals. In simple terms, the focus on SDG9 is upon the building infrastructure for industrialization with innovation. This emphasis on 3Is of infrastructure, industrialization and innovation is the testimony of the theoretical strand of literature discussed in the Section II. To reiterate, innovation assume the dominant position in determining the major source of growth, as was witnessed during the four industrial revolutions that has transformed many countries of the world. The structural transformation in the Global North-West, in America and parts of Europe is the testimony of the power of innovation and benefits of harassing its prowess. From Global East, the beacon was held high by Japan that was later shared by Asian Tigers. South Korea, Taiwan, Hong Kong and Singapore grew exorbitantly with export of their manufactured goods leading to increasing their contribution in world production system in certain short-cycle technological goods. Likewise, the growth of Chinese manufacturing sector along with other Asian economies like India, Viet Nam, Philippines, Malaysia, Indonesia and Thailand are indicating a shift in the global production system to Asia. UK based Centre for Economic and Business Research (CEBR) forecasted that "*China will overtake USA to become the world's largest economy by 2028 and India will become the third largest economy by 2030*"[3]. The

[3] BBC News (Dec 26th 2020) Chinese economy to overtake US 'by 2028' due to Covid accessed from: https://www.bbc.com/news/world-asia-china-55454146.

growing importance of Asia is projected in many research works. Amsden (2001) identified 12 countries from 'The Rest' including seven from Asia namely China, India, Indonesia, Malaysia, S Korea, Taiwan, and Thailand that can become instrumental in converging with 'The West'. Nayyar (2013) included Turkey in the Amsden's "the Rest" list to make the total count 'eight' from Asia that are expected to play a dominant role amongst 'The Next-14'. Asia surpassed all other continents in GDP in 2010 (Figure 2). China becomes the world's largest economy in purchasing power parity terms in 2014. China's global share of GDP is around 16 percent in 2018 (McKinsey Institute Report, 2019)[4]. Therefore, Asian economies can be classified in to three generations depicting the timings of their growth and catching-up period. Japan graduated from middle-income country to high-income country in the period from 1950s to 1970s that accompany structural transformation to high-value added sectors and products (Okazaki, 2019). 1960s was era of Four Asian Tigers, South Korea, Singapore, Hong Kong and Taiwan. They showed exorbitant growth and rapid structural transformations through exports of manufactured goods. Indonesia joined the World Bank category[5] of upper-middle income status in July 2020, only to loose it during the pandemic[6]. The other upper-middle income countries from Asian are China, Malaysia and Thailand. The world is looking with all hopes to other Asian countries, mainly to India, Philippines, and Viet Nam that are still in the lower-middle income bracket. The Asian countries, mainly in the upper-middle income and lower-middle income groups aspire to transform into higher income brackets. Figure 3 shows the GDP per capita at purchasing power parity at constant dollar 2017. Singapore has the highest per capita income followed by Hong Kong, Japan and South Korea. China and India with high population have the lower GDP per capita. The high per-capita income along with inclusivity and sustainability ensures the future growth prospects with concentration on building 'innovation capability'. In this context, the focus of the Chapter is on the Twelve Asian economies namely Japan, Hong Kong, S Korea, Singapore, Taiwan[7], China, Indonesia, Malaysia, Thailand, India, Philippines and Vietnam with respect to the One of the Seventeen Sustainable Development Goals; viz, SDG9 that emphasized upon building *resilient infrastructure, promote sustainable industrialization and foster innovation.*

---

[4] McKinsey Report (2019), 'China and the World, Inside the dynamic of a changing relationship', downloaded from https://www.mckinsey.com/~/media/mckinsey/featured%20insights/china/china%20and%20the%20world%20inside%20the%20dynamics%20of%20a%20changing%20relationship/mgi-china-and-the-world-executive-summary-feb-2020-en.pdf.

[5] World Bank classifies countries into four groups according to the income levels. For the 2022 fiscal year, low-income economies are defined as those having a GNI per capita of $1045 or less in 2020; lower middle income economies between $1046 and $4095; upper-middle income as those with GNI per capita between $4095 and $12695; high income economies as with GNI per capita of $12696 or more.

[6] https://www.bloomberg.com/news/articles/2021-07-08/indonesia-loses-prized-upper-middle-income-status-amid-pandemic.

[7] The data for Taiwan is not available for the indicators used in the Chapter. But, given the exorbitant progress, the inclusion of Taiwan as an important Asian Tiger is imperative.

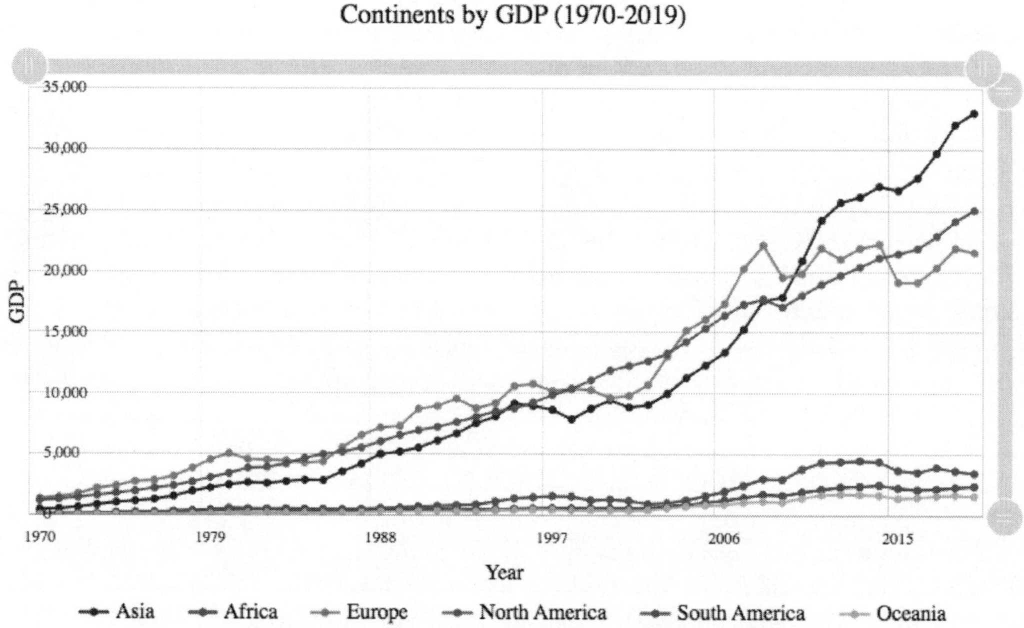

Figure 2: Share of Different Continents in GDP

Source: https://statisticstimes.com/economy/continents-by-gdp.php

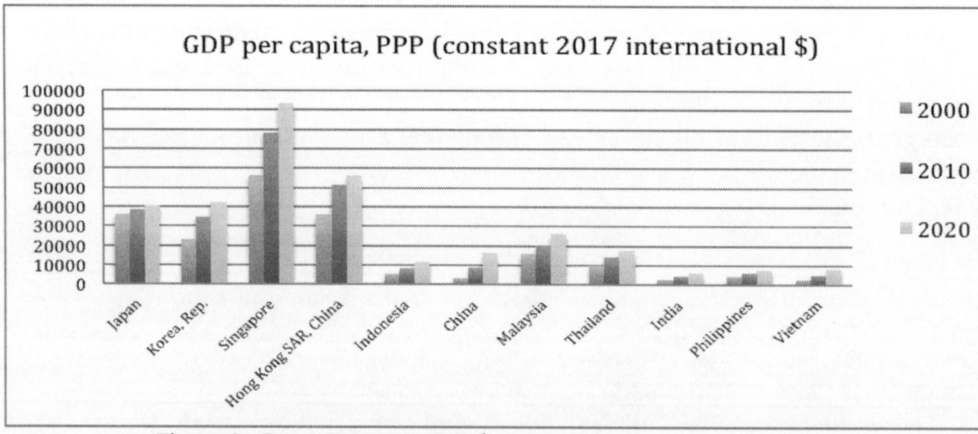

Figure 3: *Gross Domestic Product Per Capita – Asian Economies*
Source: World Development Indicators

SDG9: Targets, Goals and Prospects

In this section, targets of Sustainable Development Goal 9 on Industry, Innovation and Infrastructure are examined for the chosen 12 Asian economies. United Nations has set 8 Targets and 12 indicators for SDG9 as shown in Table 1.

Table 1: SDG9: Targets

Target	*UN Definition*
9.1	"Develop quality, reliable, sustainable and resilient infrastructure, including regional and trans border infrastructure, to support economic development and human well-being, with a focus in affordable and equitable access for all."
9.1.1	"Proportion of the rural population who live within 2 km of an all-reason road."
9.1.2	"Passenger and freight volumes, by mode of transport"
9.2	"Promote inclusive and sustainable industrialization and by, 2030, significantly raise industry's share of employment and gross domestic product, in line with national circumstances, and double its share in least developed countries."
9.2.1	"Manufacturing value added as a proportion of GDP and per capita."
9.2.2	"Manufacturing employment as a proportion of total employment."
9.3	"Increase the access of small-scale industrial and other enterprises, in particular in developing countries, to financial services, including affordable credit, and their integration into value chains and markets."
9.3.1	"Proportion of small-scale in total industry value added."
9.3.2	"Proportion of small-scale industries with a loan or line of credit."
9.4	"By 2030, upgrade infrastructure and retrofit industries to make them sustainable, with increased resource-use efficiency and greater adoption of clean and environmentally sound technologies and industrial processes, with all countries taking action in accordance with their respective capabilities."
9.4.1	"CO2 emissions per unit of value added."
9.5	"Enhance scientific research, upgrade the technological capabilities of industrial sectors in all countries, in particular developing countries, including, by 2030, encouraging innovation and substantially increasing the number of research and development workers per 1 million people and public and private research and development spending."
9.5.1	"research and development expenditure as a proportion of GDP."
9.5.2	"Researchers (in full-time equivalent) per million inhabitants."
9.A	"Facilitate sustainable and resilient infrastructure development in developing countries through enhanced financial, technological and technical support to African countries, least developed countries, landlocked developing countries and small island developing States."
9.A.1	"total official international support (official development assistance plus other official flows) to infrastructure."
9.B	"Support domestic technology development, research and innovation in developing countries, including by ensuring a conducive policy environment for, inter alia, industrial diversification and value addition to commodities."
9.B.1	"Proportion of medium and high-tech industry value added in total value added."
9.C	"Significantly increase access to information and communications technology and strive to provide universal and affordable access to the internet in least developed countries by 2020."
9.C.1	"Proportion of population covered by a mobile network, by technology."

Source: Complied, https://sdg-tracker.org/infrastructure-industrialization#targets

The Eight Targets under the broad Sustainable Development Goal 9 gives the benchmark for different countries of the world to achieve. With the focus of the Chapter on the Twelve Asian economies, we examined their respective pattern.

The first major Target of SDG9 is 9.1 emphasized upon the development of quality, reliable and resilient infrastructure. As development of infrastructure has a very broad scope, the target 9.1.1 emphasized upon the 'proportion of rural population who live within 2 km of an all weather road'. Another target 9.2.2 focuses upon the 'passenger and freight volumes, by mode of transport'. Air transport and railways are prominent modes of transport apart form the roadways.

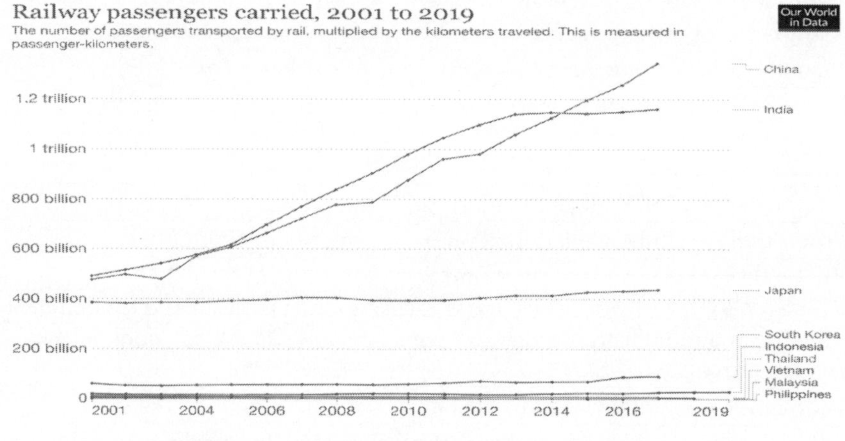

Figure 4: Railways Transport: Asian Countries

Source: https://sdg-tracker.org/infrastructure-industrialization#targets

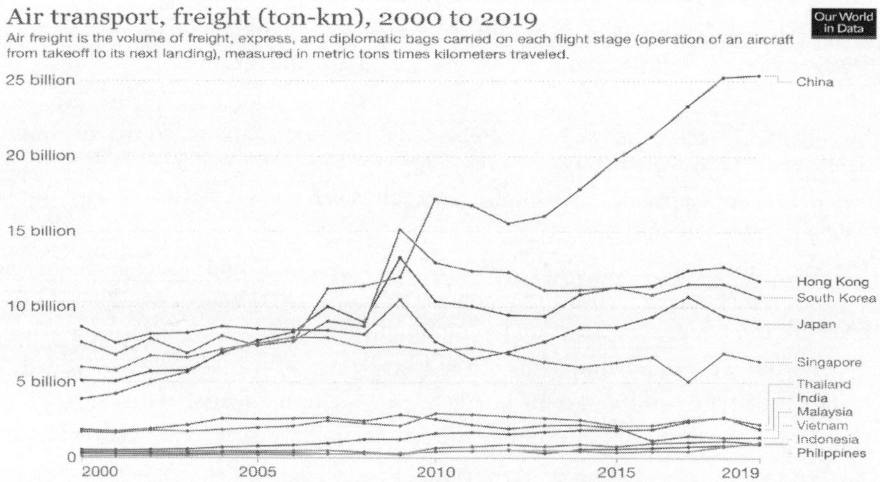

Figure 5: Air Transport: Asian Economies

Source: https://sdg-tracker.org/infrastructure-industrialization#targets

Figure 4 shows that in Railways transportation system China and India leads in Asian economies with China surpassing India in 2014. Japan is another Asian country with the number of Railway passengers carried were around 400 billion during the period 2001 to 2020. Further Figure 5 shows the Air transport freight for Asian economies. It shows that China has the highest freight ton-km of about 25 billion followed by Hong Kong, South Korea, Singapore. On the other hand, the air transport in terms of freight was less than 5 billion for Thailand, India, Malaysia, Vietnam, Indonesia and Philippines. Therefore, for the target 9.1, China is leading in both railways and air transport, while the countries in the upper-income bracket were leading in Air transport as compared to those in the lower-middle income bracket, mainly India, Philippines and Vietnam.

Target 9.2 emphasized upon the promoting inclusive and sustainable industrialization. Its two indicators 9.2.1 and 9.2.2 focused upon 'Manufacturing value added as a proportion of GDP and per capita' and 'Manufacturing employment as a proportion of total employment'. Figure 6 shows the Manufacturing value added to GDP from the period 2000 to 2020 for the chosen Asian economies. The manufacturing value added to GDP for China was more than 30 percent in 2005 that fell to about 26 percent in 2020. Manufacturing value added to GDP remained around 25 percent for Thailand and South Korea. Importantly, the share of manufacturing value added to GDP for Vietnam surpassed India during 2017 to reach at more than 15 percent. Hong Kong is the only Asian Tiger whose manufacturing value added to GDP remained less than 5 percent as it greatly relied on international business an trade.

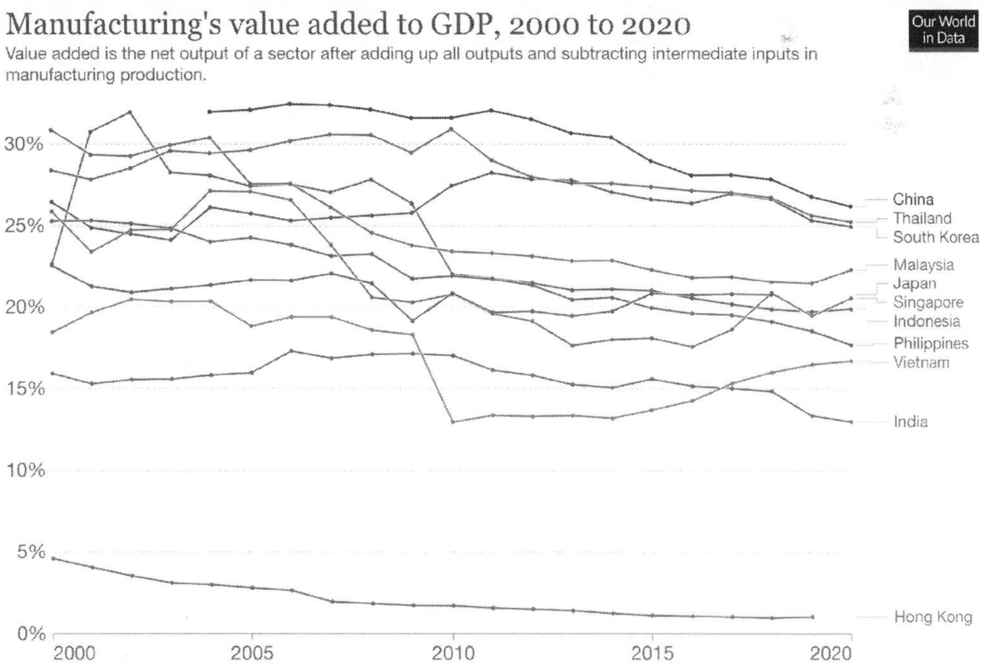

Figure 6: Manufacturing Value Added to GDP: Asian Economies

Source: https://sdg-tracker.org/infrastructure-industrialization#targets

Another indicator under the target 9.2 is of 'manufacturing value added per capita'. Figure 7 shows the pattern of 'manufacturing value added per capita' for the chosen Asian economies and it was found that for Singapore, South Korea and Japan, the variable was high and is increasing, abet the Covid 19 pandemic period of 2020. India, Indonesia and Vietnam have the lowest share amongst the group of chosen Asian countries.

These results of indicator 9.2.1 shows that countries, mainly India, Indonesia, Vietnam have to put greater emphasis on increasing the manufacturing value added per capita to comply with the targets fixed by United Nations to be achieved by 2030.

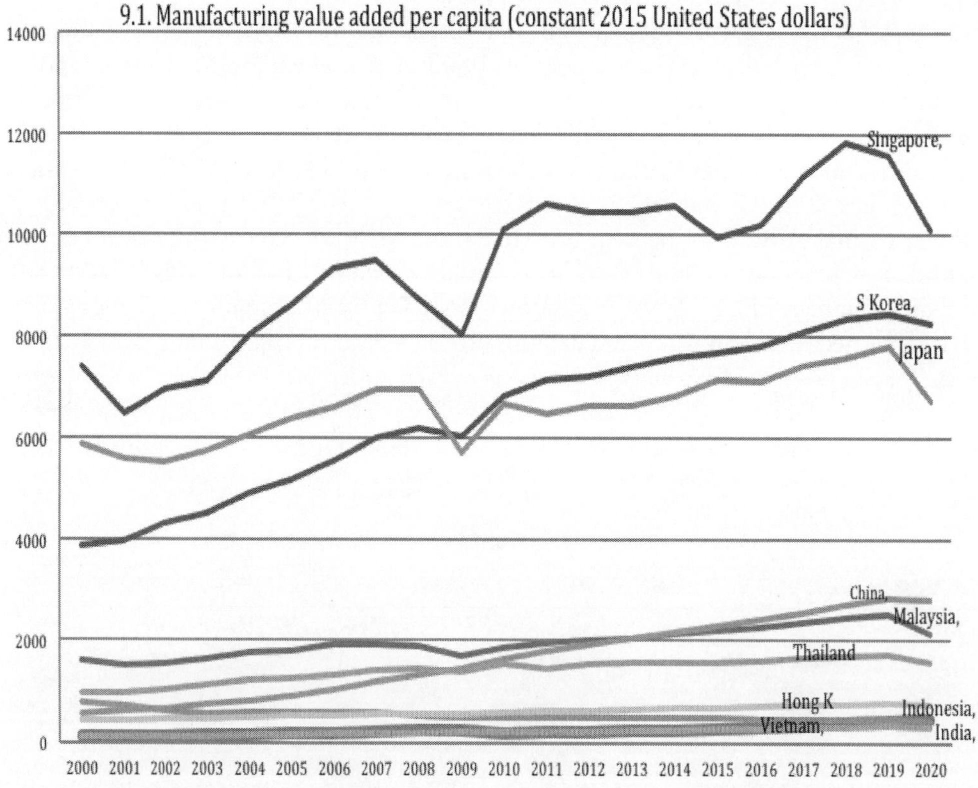

Figure 7: Manufacturing Value Added per Capita: Asian Economies

Source: Sustainable Development Goals Database, Department of Economic and Social Affairs, United Nations. Downloaded from https://unstats.un.org/sdgs/UNSDG/CompareTrendsOneSeries

Figure 8 shows the share of different Asian countries in Industrial employment for the period 2000 to 2017. It was found that the industrial employment showed a general trend of converging, with the share of countries like Malaysia, Japan, Singapore, Hong Kong, South Korea falling whereas the share of China, India, Vietnam, Thailand increasing over time.

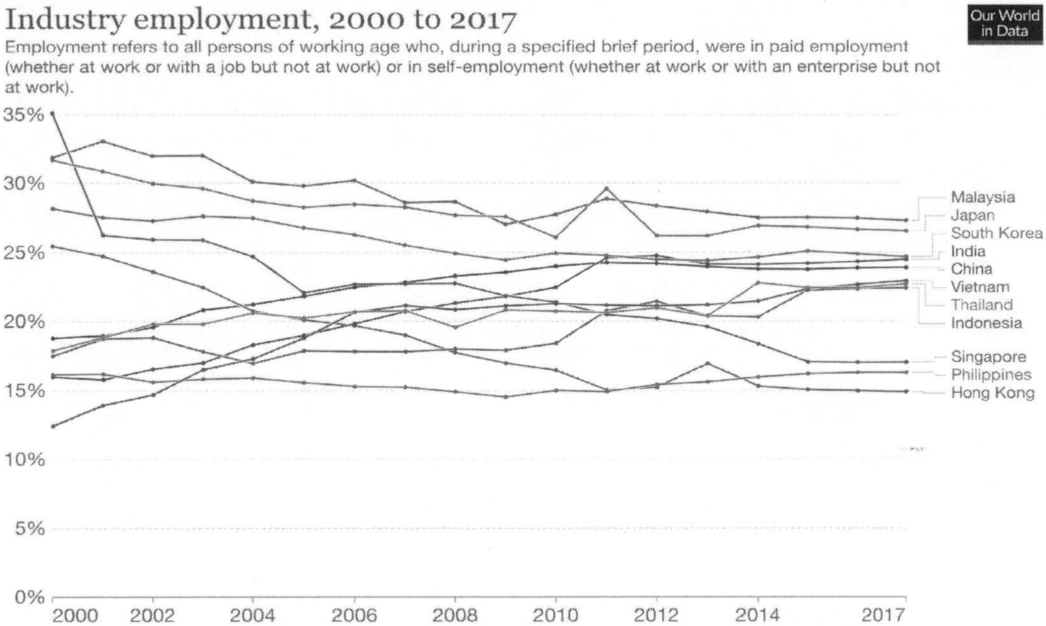

Figure 8: Industry Employment: Asian Economies
Source: https://sdg-tracker.org/infrastructure-industrialization#targets

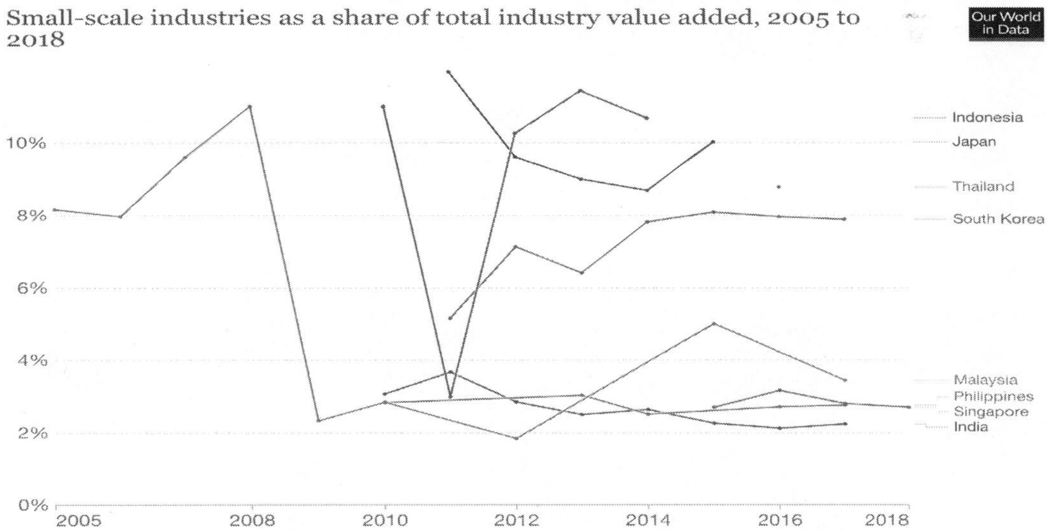

Figure 9: Small-scale industries: Asian economies
Source: https://sdg-tracker.org/infrastructure-industrialization#targets

Target 9.3 postulates to increase the access of small-scale industries and other enterprises mainly in developing countries for inclusive manufacturing sector. 9.3.1 focuses upon the proportion of small-scale in total industry value added. The result for the Asian countries, for which the data was available, is presented in Figure 9. It shows that the share of small-scale industries fell for Malaysia, Japan while it increased for South Korea for the period 2005 to 2018. Overall, the share of small-scale industries as a share of total industry value added remained less than 10 percent with a very low level of (less than 4 percent) for India, Singapore and Philippines.

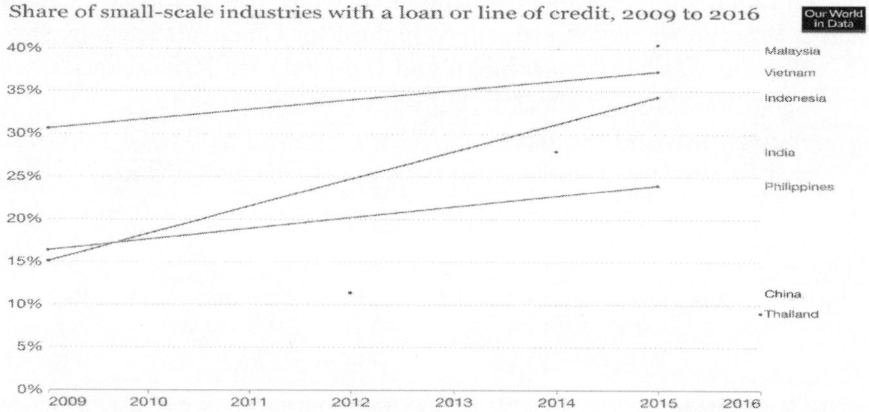

Figure 10: Proportion of Small-scale Industries with a Loan and Line of Credit

Source: https://sdg-tracker.org/infrastructure-industrialization#targets

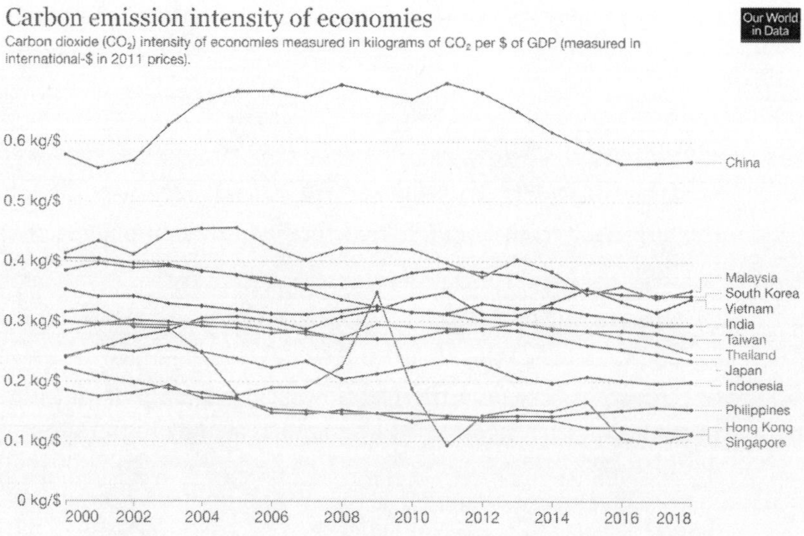

Figure 11: Carbon Dioxide Intensity: Asian Economies

Source: https://sdg-tracker.org/infrastructure-industrialization#targets

For the indicator 9.3.2: 'proportion of small-scale industries with a loan and line of credit', the data was available for seven countries as shown in Figure 10. The dot for Malaysia,

India, China and Thailand indicates that the data is available for one year only. But for the others like Vietnam, Indonesia and Philippines the lines depicts that the proportion of small-scale industries with loan or line of credits increase in these countries over the reference period, based upon the data availability.

By 2030, increased resource-use efficiency and greater adoption of clean and environmentally sound technologies and industrial processes are needed to make the sustainable growth possible. Figure 11 shows the Carbon emission intensity for the chosen 12 Asian economies. It was found that carbon emission intensity is highest for China, although its rate is falling since 2012. India, Taiwan, Thailand, Japan and Indonesia fell into the bracket of 0.2-0.3 kg per dollar of carbon emission intensity. Singapore, Philippines and Hong Kong decreases carbon emission intensity over the years.

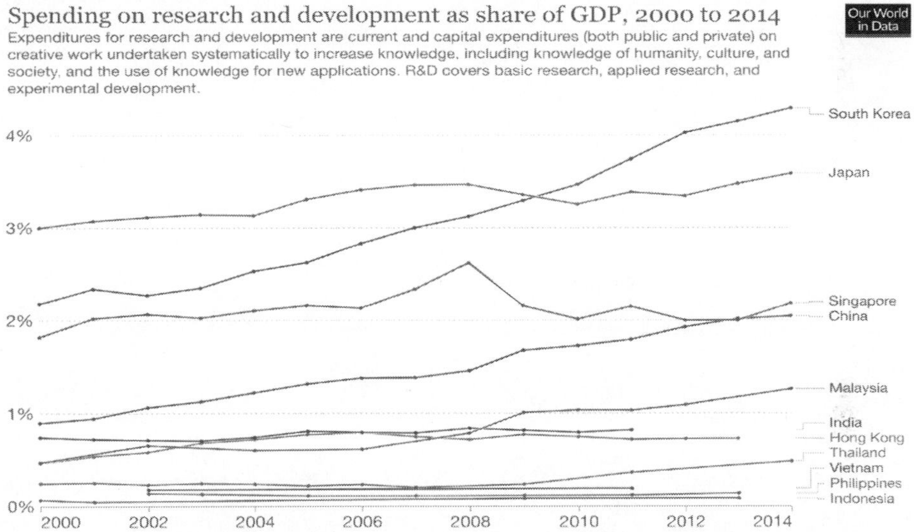

Figure 12: R&D as a Share of GDP: Asian Economies

Source: https://sdg-tracker.org/infrastructure-industrialization#targets

Figures 12 and 13 show 'Research and Development expenditure as a proportion of GDP' and 'Researchers per million inhabitants' for the Asian countries to comply with the indicators 9.5.1 and 9.5.2, respectively. Target 9.5 with its two indicators gives importance to 'enhance scientific research, upgrade the technological capabilities of industrial sectors in all countries'. It was found that R&D spending is increasingly high for South Korea and Japan. China too doubled its R&D spending from 1 to 2 percent from 2000 to 2014. But for countries like India, Hong Kong, Thailand, Vietnam, Philippines and Indonesia, the R&D share of GDP remained less than 1 percent. Hence, it is very important for the countries to increase their R&D spending to sustain the competitive and fast changing technological paradigms.

Figure 12 shows that 'Researchers in R&D per million people' increases in South Korea, Singapore, Japan, Hong Kong, Malaysia and Thailand. For India, Vietnam and Indonesia, Researchers in R&D per million people is very less. In nutshell, target 9.5 demands that both

R&D expenditure as a proportion of GDP and Researchers per million people should be increased, mainly in India, Indonesia, Vietnam and Indonesia.

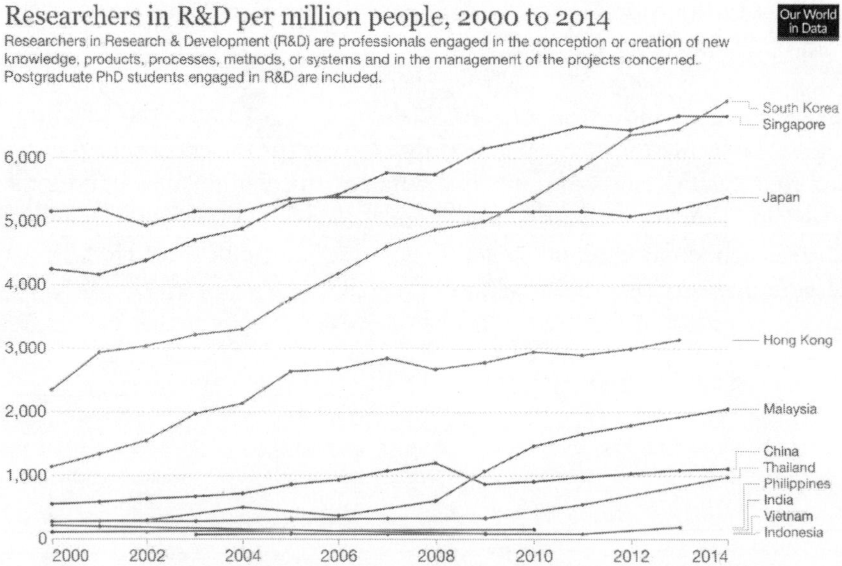

Figure 13: Researchers in R&D: Asian Economies

Source: https://sdg-tracker.org/infrastructure-industrialization#targets

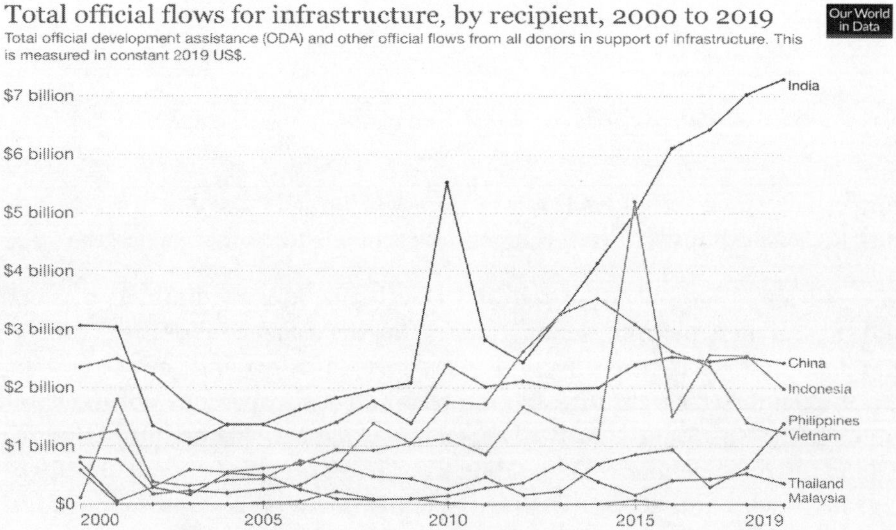

Figure 14: Flow for Infrastructure: Asian Economies

Source: https://sdg-tracker.org/infrastructure-industrialization#targets

Under indicator 9.A.1, the total international support for infrastructure is measured. Figure 14 show that India received the highest support (about more than $7 billion) in

2019 from all donors in support of infrastructure. Malaysia and Thailand received the least official support for infrastructure development amongst those whose data is available.

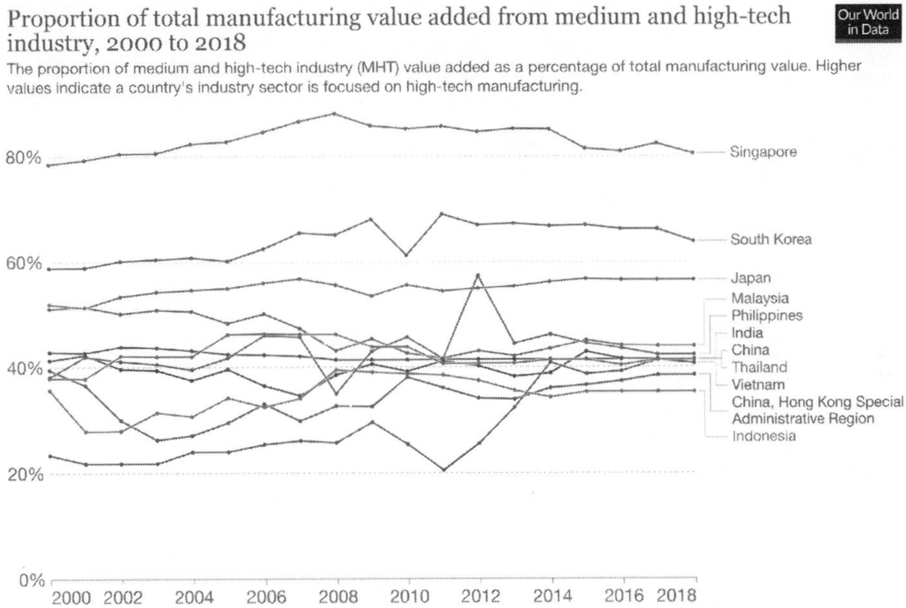

Figure 15: Medium and High Tech Industry: Asian Economies

Source: https://sdg-tracker.org/infrastructure-industrialization#targets

The indicator 9.B.1, 'Proportion of medium and high-tech industry value-added in total value-added' depicts the support to domestic technology development, research and innovation for industrial diversification and value-addition. Figure 15 shows that proportion of medium and high-tech industries is highest in Singapore followed by South Korea and Japan from chosen Asian economies. Vietnam almost doubled its share of medium and high-tech industries from the period 2000 to 2018. China, India, Malaysia, Philippines, Thailand, Vietnam has about 40 percent of their industrial value-added contributed by medium and high tech industries for the year 2018.

9.C focus upon 'significantly increase access to information and communication technology and strives to provide universal and affordable access to the Internet. 9.C.1 is the indicator to examine the proportion of population covered by a mobile network. Mobile cellular subscriptions and Internet access as a proportion of population are important variables depicting the progress made in context of target 9.C.

Figure 16 and 17 shows the Mobile cellular subscriptions, measured as a number per 100 people; and 'share of population using Internet', respectively. It was found that for all the chosen Asian countries, both the variables showed an upward trend for the period 2000 to 2019. South Korea, Hong Kong, Japan, Singapore, Malaysia have more than 80 percent of their population using Internet.

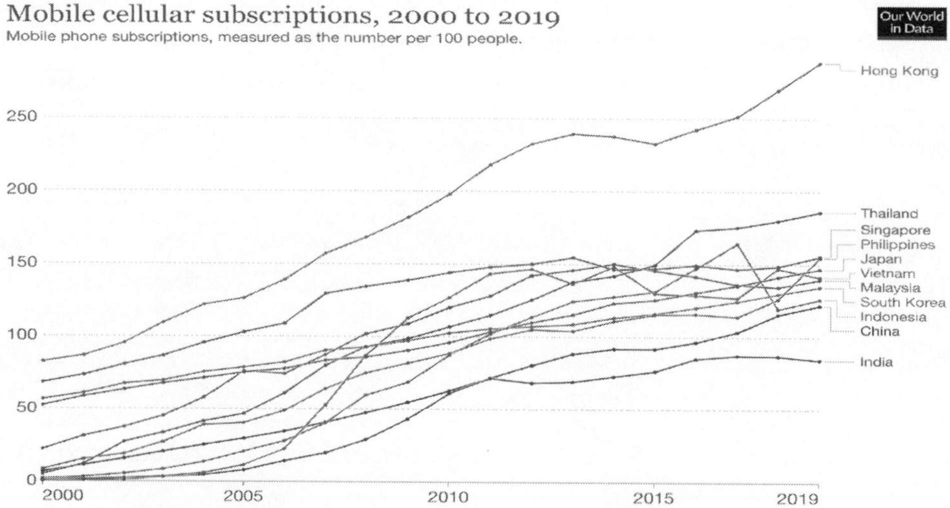

Figure 16: Mobile cellular subscriptions: Asian Economies

Source: https://sdg-tracker.org/infrastructure-industrialization#targets

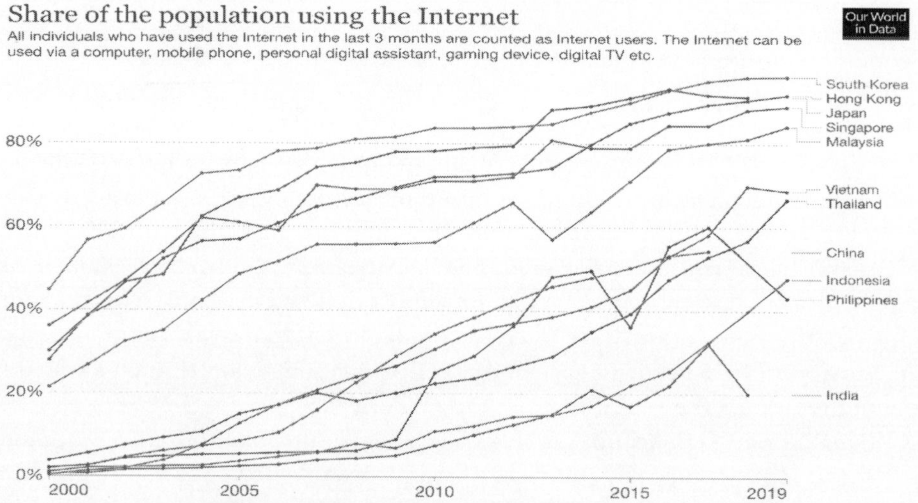

Figure 17: Population using Internet: Asian Economies

Source: https://sdg-tracker.org/infrastructure-industrialization#targets

Conclusion

United Nations Sustainable Development Goals (SDGs) have seventeen components that have lots of complementarity along with the stronger individual importance. These SDGs are adopted for developing the national economies holistically with components of inclusiveness and sustainability. The focus of the chapter is on SDG 9, which spotlights upon 3Is, Infrastructure, Industries and Innovation. Theoretical and empirical literature starting from Adam Smith to the Marxist, Classical, Neoclassical, Neo-Schumpeterian school acknowledged 'innovation' and power of 'knowledge' as the important source of growth. Industrialization backed with innovation and stronger infrastructure played a prominent role in the process of now developed economies. But the world is witnessing changes. Asia is found to be growing fast. In this context, the Chapter examines the chosen Twelve Asian economies with respect to the goals earmarked under the SDG 9. Of the 8 targets with different indicators, Asian economies presented an optimistic picture. China is growing fast, but others are also following. The in-debt analysis based on the descriptive examination of the various important variables shows that Asian countries have to strategically transform their economies to high value added activities and sectors following the goals set by the United Nations under the various SDGs. Innovation and advanced infrastructure can be instrumental in building 'technological capabilities' for gainful, inclusive and sustainable industrialization.

References

1. Abramovitz M.A. (1956) Resources and Output trends on the United States since 1870s, *American Economic Review*, 46: 5-23.
2. Amsden, A. H. (2001) The Rise of the Rest: Challenges to the West from Late Industrializing Economies, New York: Oxford University press.
3. Grossman G.M and E. Helpman (1991) Innovation and Growth in the Global Economy, Cambridge, Mass.:MIT Press.
4. Nayyar, D. (2013) Catch Up: Developing countries in the World Economy, Oxford: Oxford University Press.
5. Nelson, R.R and S. Winter (1982) An Evolutionary Theory of Economic Change, Cambridg, Mass: Harvard University Press.
6. Romer, P. (1986) Increasing Returns and Long run Growth, *Journal of Political Economy*, 94: 1002-1037.
7. Romer, P. (1990) Endogenous Technological Change, *Journal of Political Economy*, 98: S71-S102.
8. Solow R.M. (1956) A contribution to the theory of Economic Growth, *Quarterly Journal of Economics*, 70: 65-94.
9. The Economist (2019) The ceasefire in the trade war between America and China is fragile, downloaded on 13 Feb' 2022 from https://www.economist.com/finance-and-economics/2019/12/18/the-ceasefire-in-the-trade-war-between-america-and-china-is-fragile.
10. The Economist (2021) The number of people in extreme poverty is falling again, downloaded on 26th Feb' 2022 from https://www.economist.com/the-world-ahead/2021/11/08/the-number-of-people-in-extreme-poverty-is-falling-again.
11. Verspagen, B. (2005) Innovation and Economic Growth in Fagerberg, J. Mowery, D.C and R.R. Nelson (eds) *The Oxford Handbook of Innovation*, 487-513; Oxford University Press.

RETHINKING AND REVITALISING OUR PATHWAYS TO SUSTAINABLE HUMAN WELFARE AND SAFE PLANET

V. Rengarajan

Premise

The knowledge on the etymology of the current crisis on sustainability in the development pathways merits an attention of the policy makers and the researchers as well as it would be useful to consider ethical characterization of human activities in their reactive process to the governance while conceiving any alternate pathways towards challenging the present crisis. The historical fact on the causative factors for the said crisis, could be traced from the distinctive development approaches adopted and also from the outcome of responsive human activities motivated by such ideological imperatives in the pathways. For the purpose of investigating the root cause for the sustainability issues, which are more linked to the consequential functioning of the human activities driven by the ancient economic thinking, a close perusal on these activities through Amartya Sen's lens would be useful one. According to Amartya Sen the economics is related to ultimately to **the study of ethics** and **that of politics** (Amartya Sen, 1999, p. 3). While the ethical approach focused on **social achievement of the ultimate** goal of the economic model, the latter 'engineering' approach is primarily concerned with logistics issues rather than with the ultimate end (human development). Here he brings two concepts the ultimate goal of social achievement and the logistics or the implementation process (engineering) more from governance perspectives towards reaching the ultimate goal. The latter is invariably involved with the dynamic human activities. Logically the successful achievement of ultimate goals depends on the ethical execution of the activities by the individual human beings collectively for the achieving common end (social achievements).

Looking from Sen's perception, it is understood that the ancient economies, right from 18th century, have been able to perform the task related to social development but mainly helped in solving the logistics in the pathways but failed to attain the desired goal ultimately at the end. In this context it merits quoting A Sens' remark "The ends are taken as fairly straight forwardly given, and the object of exercise is to find the appropriate means to serve them. Human behavior is typically seen as being based on simple and easily charecterizable motives" (A. Sen, 1999, p. 4). Over a period of time, the implication of non-ethical character of human activity and of human behavior, motivated or corrupted by the respective political ideologies, have further worsened to ensure desired level of social impact at the end. To quote evidently, after the advent of French physiocrates and their Laissez-faire policy (free trade) the life style has a metamorphic changes knowingly or unknowingly at environment cost. On social front, during 1990-91 India witnessed a free trade policy embedded in LPG ideology (liberalisation privitation, globalisation). The imperatives of these liberals which fuelled 'animal spirit' of wealth creator, had motivated the human behaviour more speculatively in the market only for, promoting unethical competition for self- interest maximisation and profiteering in the process of resource utilization. Eventually the outcome of the demoralised human activities has led to harmful implication on the equitable growth and on earth's climatic condition. Seemingly in India according to Oxfam reports, 73% of wealth generated in 2017 went to the richest 1%. The gap between the rich and poor is reportedly widening persistently. Anthropogenic greenhouse gas emissions are rapidly increasing giving rise to global warming. According to the Intergovernmental Panel on Climate Change between 1880 to 2012 global mean temperatures have risen by about 1.1 degree centigrade (Gauri Shankar Gupta, 2019). Ultimately the unethical behaviour and the attitude of human beings paved the way for Anthropocene era from 2000 thereby creating a delusion on the history of human development and on the safe eco system.

Three discernible inferences from the above economic thought process and its implications on the human development scanned through Sen's lens merit attention from sustainability perspectives. **First**, the ethical human behaviour with rationality behind is recklessly assumed for every responding activities to ensure the sustainability in the pathways. That is to emphasise the imperative need to promote primarily the values of the ethical economics and behavioural economics followed by environmental economics, ecological economics since the former shape the nature of outcome of the latter one. **Second,** the past learning outcome of the so called 'economics' modelling, discernibly indicates the prevalence of enough damages on both humanity in terms of widening social inequality & deepening poverty and on the earth in terms of ecological destruction as well. **Third** in view of the above facts, as a pre-condition for shifting paradigm from economic to earthonomics commandingly necessitate **the recalibrating of the glory of ethics as the mother of economics,** followed by promoting ethical economics, behavioural economics, environmental ethics, inclusive development ethics, financial inclusion ethics, etc.

The Specific Objectives

Given the perspectives on the conjectures related to sustainability as discussed above, the specific objectives of the paper is to investigate them with the following queries:

1. What were the values of **ancient indigenous knowledge** on human activities towards establishing sustainability to human welfare and on safe planet earth?
2. Why have our **social inclusive development** pathways, experimented since planning era not ushered in sustainability in social sector?
3. How could **green finance** facilitate as a means of strengthening the process of ushering in sustainability in the inclusive development pathway?
4. Whether digitalization-based technology as a medium for inclusive social development, is a bane or boon in the pathway to sustainability in all the sector?
5. What are the alternate strategies for transition to socially sustainable inclusive development on priority among other SDGs goals s in modern time in India?

Methodology

Descriptive analysis is made using secondary data from government. Evaluation study reports, the literature reading and the respective web sites. Critical Assessment on the sustainability of selected social development programmes has been done using Theory of Change (TOC) framework.

The analysis and the findings are presented under five heads, viz., (1) Ancient indigenous knowledge and sustainability, (2) Social development pathways-paradigm shift, (3) Green finance – facilitator for establishing sustainability, (4) Innovation & Technology – a boon or bane in the development pathway, and (5) Alternate pathways to sustainability.

Ancient Indigenous Knowledge and Sustainability

The values of ancient wisdom can help in designing more sustainable infrastructure without much harming to the nature. The stock of ancient indigenous knowledge could be perceived under two categories distinctly as it would enable us to emulate or integrate where ever possible in the modern livelihood space.

Livelihood practices for sustainability and 32 Religious rituals in unisons with the nature.

Livelihood Practices for Sustainability

Over time, the ancient people have developed a way in which to manage and use their resources that ensures their conservation into the future. Such traditional societies are interested more in preserving their own social, cultural and environmental stability and integrity than in maximizing material production. The tribal community per example, live in secluded place in hilly regions with the limited population and also share the livelihood activities together with the obedience to the integrated common living norms linked with the nature like forest, hill, water, animals etc in the earth. Consequently, there is no 'exploitation' of nature—which they do not consider as a collection of commodities—in the interaction between humans and natural milieu. On the contrary, their way of life is based on a strong sense of interconnection and interdependence. Activities in traditional societies often include a strong symbolic dimension in which every action is highly ritualized, and allow humans to participate in the preservation of the natural order. "Of course these rituals differ between cultures, as each society has freedom to own its belief systems, which determine its cultural identity and type of technology" (Berkes et al., 2000). Modern science and ancient knowledge constitute different paths to knowledge, but they are rooted in the same reality. For example, **food habits are an integral part of cultural practices**. Choice of food – not only what is consumed every day by the household but also what is cultivated – has a direct impact on the health of our local ecosystem and on the planet. The UN Food and Agriculture Organization website states that, the global meat industry is a disproportionate user of water, energy and one of the largest emitters of greenhouse gases. In this context the tradition of vegetarian diet in India proves to be most ecologically sound and the least violent against other species of life. Obviously, the concept of vegetarianism and non-violence in Indian traditions is based on sound ecological wisdom of harmonious living with nature. In a recent report of the Intergovernmental Panel on Climate Change (IPCC) has advised people to shift to plant-based diet to reduce CO_2 emissions. Contemporary analogy of 'ahimsa' in western science is 'environmental ethics'. Both having non-anthropocentric logics, they seem to have something in common. Both the philosophies suggest something more than human existence as a highest aim of life.

Ancient indigenous knowledge on earthonomics and its sustainability could be also traced more from the primitive people's religious practices and the individual's spiritual belief adopted in their way of life. Many researchers have attempted to establish the linkages between religion and ecology in India and other countries. The Russian researchers emphasized that "It is very important to study how people perceive the concept of religious consciousness in general and in applying to ecological issues in particular." In their concluding remarks reveal "Freedom of expression in religion may include different worships and unite all life forms equally valuable into the whole universe, but it is not similar to physical universe and it is above it, as well as it is beyond human understanding. Religious understanding of ecology is theocentric, while environmental ethics is biocentric" (Daniil E. Krapchunov et al., 2021).

An Interesting feature merit attention is that traditional society, **being a small one and sparsely spread** and remain disconnected enjoyed **with freedom** for performing any religious activities which helped in balancing the sustainability to ecology in their respective habitations. According to Nelson, "**Freedom** to worship what you want to worship, to combine contradictory factors like scientific and technical development with religious rituals" (Nelson, 2010). During the Vedic period (1750–500 BCE), trees were referred to as 'vansapati' or lord of the forest and have been invoked as deities, just as rivers, lakes, birds and certain animals. As per Vedic **traditions, planting of trees and living in forests are considered as great virtues.**

In sum, the historical brief on. Ancient indigenous knowledge, discussed above reveals that anthropogenic activity was very much ethically tuned regardless of types of spirituality at individual level, They had integrity in following normative principles in their livelihood activities and also in their religious and spiritual activities both at community and individual levels in ancient times. The attributable reason for the ethical behaviour to eco system is due to more freedom enjoyed by them to treat the nature such as sun, rivers, forest, mountain as god in their respective places/habitations. This kind of life style and livelihood activities with more freedom for religious activities indicates the prevalence of an sanctified bondage between human development and ecology without much harming the pathway to sustainability.

Social Development Pathways – Policy Paradigm

An attempt has been made to overview on the vision and impact of the past socio economic development programmes historically since 1950 as it would reveal the capability and the wisdom of policy makers in India in planning for inclusive development from the most under developed status embedded in acute poverty hunger and high level of inequality. By and large this slew of development programmes are also very much concerned towards contributing its share to achieve UN sustainable Development Goals (SDGs) related to **'no poverty'**, **'zero hunger'** and **'gender equality'**.

Multi Institutions, Multi Sectoral Programmes and Target Oriented Social Inclusion

A plethora of socio-economic development programmes having a common goal of poverty cure no hunger and gender equity, have been implemented but with varying degree of logistics to achieve the goal. For better appreciation on the focus of various dimension of development programmes covering the poor, unemployed and other marginalised section of the community, a prudential dissection has been broadly done for grouping these interventions in social sector. into five categories, viz., (1) Wage employment programmes, (2) Self-employment programmes, (3) Food security programmes, (4) Social security programmes, and (5) poverty alleviation programmes. Among these programmes, many of them like Integrated Rural Development Programme (IRDP), Self-Employment Unemployed Youth (SEEUY), Self-Employment Programme for Urban Poor (SEPUP), Scheme of Urban Micro Enterprises (SUME,) Rashtrya Mahila Kosh (RMK), and Swarnajayanti Gram Swarozgar Yojana (SGSY) were linked with subsidy and bank credit.

Democratic Inclusive Planning Process

Meticulous planning and governance on the logistics of these socially inclusive concerned programmes focusing poverty sector assume importance from sustainability outlook. These aspects, could be witnessed from the following observations on the past happenings. Towards percolation of development benefits at village level, the potential credit outlays, required for various economic activities under these inclusion programmes, intended for the poor and women, have been prepared annually. These credit outlays were dovetailed into the comprehensive District Annual Credit plans (DCP) prepared by the respective lead banks for the district concerned. These bankable activities by and large fall under the category of micro credit programmes for women, Self-Help Groups (SHG) weaker sections and Differential interest Rate (DIR) under priority sector advance portfolio. So, to say both district level credit planning dovetailed with inclusive social development planning for the district have come to stay for socio economic development at the district level. This apart, under service area approach village credit plans were also prepared by the serving bank branch at bottom level while village panchayat development (VDP) plan also has come to stay for strengthening the inclusive development in rural areas. Here it may be noted that the social welfare programmes related to road, power, health, sanitation, education drinking water etc being non bankable schemes are directly executed by the respective government departments at distract level

Risks and Shifts in the Development Pathway

Although a well-designed logistics and governance, as described above, are available, the sustainability goal concerned with poverty, hunger and gender equality remains elusive in the pathways. The inequity gap between the rich and the poor widens persistently. As a corollary, the implementation process and the attitude of the participants becomes debatable as could be observed from the overall findings of the evaluation studies conducted on these programmes from sustainability perspectives. For appreciating the insights of shocks/risk and shifts that crop up in the development pathway, some of the key evaluative findings of three selected interventions from Programme Evaluation Organisations reports of Planning Commission (PEO, 1980 & 1985), given in Annexure-2 and 3 merit attention.

Awareness on the Risks in the Development Pathway

Although the conventional evaluation reports, conducted after the project completion, brings out some facts on the convolutions that hindered the achievement of desired goal, a prudential perception on the various kinds of risk shifts in the implementation process itself, has become necessary one for taking remedial action concurrently. In this regard it may be noted that the transition to sustainability requires not only an understanding of the risks that society is facing but also making a shift towards sustainability. Such risks include not only 'resources and global warming but also established economic models and social ethics and values' (Carole Boyle et al. 2013). For better appreciation on the nature and the kind of risks occurring in the pathways and the mode of identification these risks in the result chain under the theory of change (ToC) framework, illustrations are made in Fig. 1 and Fig. 2 respectively.

Figure 1 reveals that there are various kinds of risks right from the planning model till reaching the goals. These risks could be classified broadly under three risk associated groups, viz., governance, social and environment. **Governance risks** include no design fault model in targeting and product designing, political interference from supply side, human behaviour and their activity responses. **Social risks** refer to lack of demand pull, lack of accountability of the beneficiary, etc. **Environmental** risks represent flood, drought, famine, hurricane, epidemic, wildfire, etc.

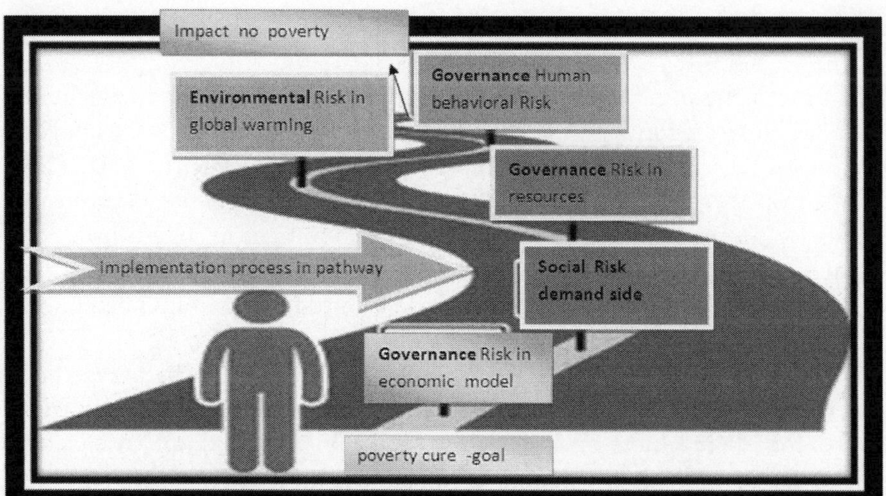

Figure 1: Kinds of risk/shocks in Development Pathway

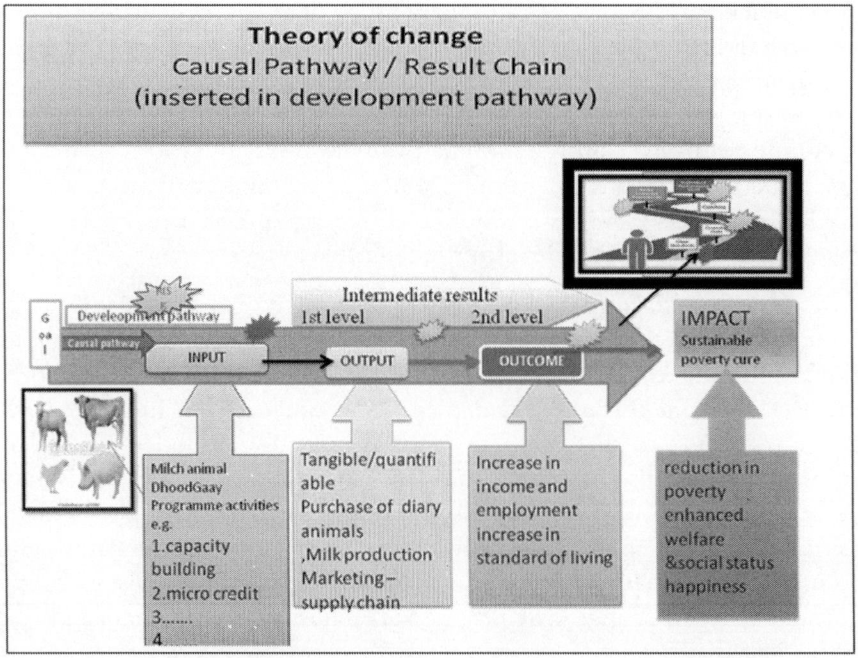

Figure 2: Identification These Risks in the Result Chain Under the Theory of Change (ToC) Framework

Figure 2 portrays the interlinkages of these risks which occur in various stages in different magnitude under each and every activities undertaken in the implementation process ultimately affecting the sustainability in the pathway. Administration of theory of change (TOC) framework for conduct concurrent monitoring and evaluation has become therefore an imperative one need to identify the risks in the pathway as illustrated in Figure 2.

Risk Assessment on Sustainable Social Inclusiveness

Having highlighted the need to consider the risk/shock factors that affect the pathway to sustainability as illustrated in Figures 1 and 2, an attempt has been made to make two kinds of assessments on the risks in the development pathway experimented, viz., (a) an overall risk assessment on the outcomes of social development programmes juxtaposing with the present status on poverty, inequality and gender development at macro level would reveal following facts on the risks that are blocking the sustainability in the pathway; and (b) a critical risk assessment under TOC framework on selected programmes using the data from PEOs report.

The overall assessment reveals that In the **first governance risks** being the major one among others, were found in the form of economic top down modelling, target oriented, 'one size fits' for all products and services politically pushed from supply side, lack of infrastructure support for producing functioning of the activity financed, and unethical human behaviour, absence of concurrent evaluation and monitoring. **The social risks** include principally lack of demand-oriented product and services, lack of social participation and auditing, **The environment risks** remain disconnected to the social development programmes and poses a great challenge to sustainability of whatever gained in pathways.

The critical assessment on the risks factors using ToC components indicates the following risks by and large coming under governance category:

1. Evaluation has been carried out at the end of the project – useful for knowing the impact but is useful for lessons learning on risks only. Mid-course correction to remove these risks becomes difficult in the absence of concurrent M&E.
2. Inadequacy of quantitative output indicators do not reflect the real impact sustainability of the project goal as envisaged.
3. There is no validation of the assumptions on **RISKS** concerned with the project activities in the development pathway, paralyses the sustainability.
4. The risks associated to human behaviour and the social values have the greatest influence over the flow of benefits in the development pathway. But non consideration of these risks is impeding the sustainability of project goal.
5. The prevalence of unethical human behaviour in the free market economy (indiscriminate multiple lending and haphazard multiple borrowing) remain ignored in pathway.
6. Political galvanization of implementation process in the form of corruption, nepotism and red taps, freebees, write off loans, etc.

Policy Paradigm – Development Perspectives

From development perspectives, there is therefore an imperative need for policy paradigm to the task of removing the harmful risks related to **governance** in the pathways. For the said task, new paradigm need to consider the following facts, viz., convergence of alike schemes and robust assumptions are needed in the economic models in the context of multidimensional poverty and SGDs. Poor implementation process aided with enfeebled M&E system without midcourse correction need to be replaced with a diligent M&E under TOC framework to remove these risks and shocks in every stage under each activities in the development pathway. Human behavior which plays a crucial role in the pathway need to ethically nurtured to establish that the **individual rights and duties are meaningful only in conjuncture.** In the development process, environmental risks which affects heavily the social inclusion process are hardly taken into account as an integral component of these social intervention programmes. All the risks are assumed but are neither validated nor controlled in the pathway.

Green Finance – Challenges as a Facilitator for Establishing Sustainability

Policy Climate

Climate change has been on the G20 agenda ever since its first summit in 2008, though more recently the focus has been on Circular Carbon Economy (CCE) to deal with harmful emissions. The companies operating in these countries, which are leaders in recognising the Environmental, Social and Governance (ESG) principles into their financing aspects. These indices are aimed at guiding investors who are interested in investing in green activities for improving their stock performance (RBI 2021). India has started emphasising on green finance as early as 2007. Since then, there have been several fiscal and financial incentives at work in India. These incentives are in line with India's commitments under the 2015 Paris Agreement to reduce greenhouse gas emission intensity by 33 to 35 per cent below 2005 levels, and to achieve 40 per cent of installed electric power capacity from non-fossil sources by 2030 (RBI 2021).

Strategies

Despite such concerted measures to push the **Indian economy** and infrastructure towards a clear embrace of green finance, the incorporation of environmental, social and governance (**ESG**) **factors** across corporate India **still remains at a nascent stage** – a gap highlighted by the Covid-19 pandemic (India Global Business, Aug. 2020). Therefore, the key areas of focus in this sector in India include (a) Support public sector for creating enabling environment, (b) promoting public -private partnership on financing mechanism such as green bonds, and (c) capacity building of community enterprises on micro finance activities

Within the conceptual framework this section attempts to **define the term green finance** along with the types of **green financial products and services** in Indian banking sector context and highlight **the challenges** in meeting the green financial resources to utilize it as effective medium for strengthening the pathways to establish environmental and social inclusion sustainability as well.

Green Finance and the Green Financial Products and Services

In Indian context, green finance stands for increasing the level of financial flows (from banking sector through, micro credit, insurance, and from capital market through bonds & investment) from public and private and non-profit sectors to sustainable development. A key part of it is better manage environmental and social risk take up the opportunity that brings both a decent rate of return and environmental benefit and deliver greater accountability (India Global Business, Aug. 2020). Besides policy support, participatory approach is also encouraged as an essential part of governance over the human activities so as to ensure accountability of the local community to preserve the eco system in and around their respective habitation.

From sustainability perspectives, the activities related to green financial services and products of banking sector are presented illustratively under three categories, viz., environment, social and governance for better understanding the role of green finance at micro level.

Table 1: Green Bank Financial Products and Services

Sustainability Arena	*Purpose*	*GreenBank Financial Services (Examples)*	
		Green Deposit Product	*Green Loan Product*
Environmentally inclusive finance	Climate change mitigation	Social forestry Deposit scheme (IOB)to promote preserve the forest called VenketeswaraVarabbhivirichi scheme	Bank loan product for solar equipments (for start-up co. and for purchase of solar products. Similarly, for biogas plants, social forestry, effluent treatment plants, renewable energy equipments, appliances, houses, and vehicles
Sociallyinclusive finance	No poverty and hunger	Prop poor micro-finance products (micro savings, micro credit, micro insurance, micro pension,money transfer)	Priority sector credit support to subsidy linkedpro poor inclusive development program s like SGSY,SHG, MSMEs, MUDRA Micro credit for income generating activities like dairy, sheep/goat rearing, piggery, fisheries, poultry,tailoring, etc. **Tree Patta loan** scheme(IOB) Micro credit is given for cultivation of coconut in the canal/road bund allottedwith theright to enjoy the usufructof the trees
Green Finance Governance Over Anthropogenic Process			
SustainabilityArea	*Purpose*	*GovernanceOver Anthropogenic Process*	*Participatory Approach*
Sustainability ofGreen finance	Policyparadigm: For Green finance planning implementation integrated with district credit planningmonitoring and evaluationunderTOC framework	Connected to following green financing Groundwater abstraction loanschemeslike, 1. ground water pumping - bore pumps, deepening well. electric motor operated pumps with clearance fromthe authority 2. surface mining, urbanization and subsurface construction (tunneling). 3. subsurface mining,vegetation removal, chemical explosions and infrastructure (loading)adoption of eligibility criteria, withoutcorruption andclandestine extraction	Eco development committee like joint forestmanagement(for creation ofharmony between forest department and local communityentrustingland tenure and forest rights of participatory communitywith green finance)

Table 1 shows various kinds of green financial services and product in the market that encourage the activities to establish sustainable development in banking sector. However, among others there are unique green deposit and loan products like Venketeswar Varaabhiviirti deposit and Tree Patta loan scheme, provided by the banking sector that promotes social forestry on one hand and income generation to the marginalised poor & landless poor on the other hand. These innovative green finance products facilitate for achieving sustainability for social inclusion of marginalised & the landless poor with the enhanced capacity for income generating activity to come out of poverty and also for the protection of forest cover thereby facilitating sustainable eco system.

However, there are concerns related to governance in this green financing arena. Reportedly, there is a massive non-compliance of the norms, stipulated for utilization of green finance products for the purposes of ground water extraction, mining, afforestation, hinders sustainability of eco system. This kind of unethical attitude of the implementing authorities in coalition with the beneficiaries, poses a great risk in the pathways to development to sustainability. The sustainability of both the environment and social inclusion, enabled by green finance also, largely depends on the effective governance on the implementation of the green finance products as per the stipulated norms in the pathway. But there are many challenges to face in this regard.

Challenges of Green Finance in India

Green finance in India is still in its embryonic stage. Apparently, the progress reveals that Green bonds constituted only 0.7 per cent of all the bonds issued in India since 2018, and bank lending to the non-conventional energy constituted about 7.9 per cent of outstanding bank credit to the power sector, as on March 2020 (RBI Jan 2021). According government estimate to achieve green financing target, India needs to mobilise a total of $2.5 trillion by 2030, according to government estimates. Another estimate suggests that $4.5 trillion is needed to achieve India's goals for urban sustainability and renewable energy by 2040 (India Global Business, Aug. 2020). Given the quality of governance on inclusive green finance as discussed above, the data on the past performance and future requirement of green finance is threatening. What are the challenges to face in the process of reaching the above target under green finance more effectively in the pathways to sustainability?

1. **Improvements in general awareness:** There is no systematic monitoring and evaluation system for monitoring green finance although many green finance products and services are available in the financial market. Even the available one is inadequate for diligent assessment on sustainability There is a paucity of related data for assessing the awareness regarding green finance and sustainable development from conventional sources.
2. **Effective Green lending by the banking system:** There is a lack of integrated credit planning with poor MIS on green finance at state/district levels. As already referred to earlier District Annual Credit plans (DCP) are being prepared by the respective lead banks at district level besides credit allocation to the banks' own micro credit programmes for women, Self Help Groups (SHG) weaker sections and Differential

interest Rate (DIR) under priority sector advance portfolio. Although some of green finance products are found here and there under these bank loan category, they remain isolated without its functional linkage from sustainability perspectives. It merits the attention of Reserve Bank of India/NABARD for taking appropriate policy initiatives to promote the values of and the preparation of separate inclusive green finance plan at state/district/block, village levels through the lead Banks in the country.

3. The cost of **issuing green bonds** has generally remained higher than the other bonds in India (RBI 2021), which discourages the participation of private investors in this venture capital market. Governments need to offer an enabling environment and business eco system for ease of doing business such as capital subsidy, interest subvention and low tension power tariff subsidy towards facilitating more inclusion of participants in this green sector.

Last, the banks are more than financial intermediaries but are now expected to play in diverting private capital to more on the green finance activities For effective participation. the banks need to assume a more direct role in confronting and incorporating climate change through implementation of an integrated green financial plan (Figure 3) at ground level as it would a long way to ensure not only the sustainability to the green project/activities financed by them but also to sustainable green finance that enabled the emergence of green projects in terms of good recovery.

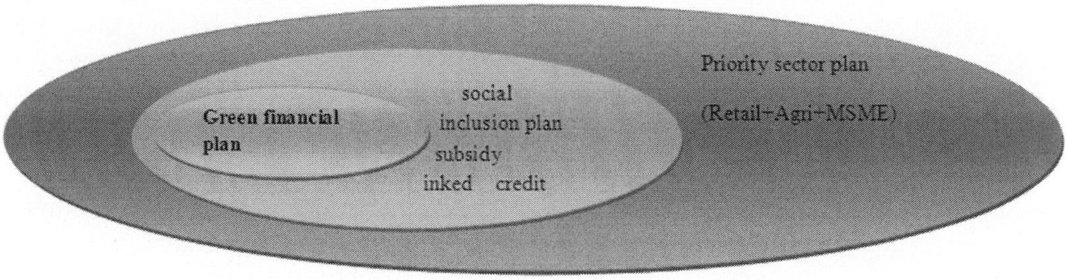

Figure 3: Integrated Green Financial Plan

Innovation & Technology – A Bane or Boon in the Development Pathway

Innovation & Technology as a Boon to Sustainability

As a consequence of globalization, liberalization and privatization in the global economy since 20th century as referred to earlier, the contour of business domain in competitive market system, emboldened by innovations & technology based business analytics, is widening horizontally and deepening vertically across the planet with the inevitable eventualities such as social exclusion, digital divide, cybercrime, climate change concerns. However, India has also committed to strive to reach net-zero emissions by 2070. To go forward in this task, these anxieties demand a clear appreciation on the **eventualities** of progress made by the technology and innovation in two broader sectors areas, viz., green industrialisation and communication from sustainability perspectives:

- First one is pertaining to green industrialisation technology focusing on innovative decarbonisation modelling pointing out the significant role for battery, green hydrogen, carbon capture, and storage technologies to decarbonise. Second one is related to communication technology based on digitalization either for communication or financial transaction or both in the nook and corner of the nation facilitating inclusive development
- A quick perusal over on the technological development in the given demographic scenario in India, would reveal some positive eventualities and negative ones as well.

Positive Eventualities

- **First one is related to governance.** Patronized by high level policy support to deploy renewal energy a number of domestic manufacturing of renewable energy technology components (solar/biogas energy) increased providing employment and income to unemployed poor segment.
- **Second one pertains to social inclusion.** In the case of urban area, the consumers, and particularly Generation C, are already fully adapted to the digital environment. They naturally expect to be always connected, are willing to share personal data, and are more likely to trust referrals from their closest friends than well-known brands. During corona period online teaching method have protected the student's community from learning losses. In rural areas, financial inclusion policy, supported by government scheme like Prime Minister Jan Dhan Yojana, has enabled a significant number of hither too excluded poor and women have been included in formal banking system there by benefiting for their wage payment transfer (as in the case of MGNREGA) and other government financial support (PM-Kissan Yojana Rs 6000 per annum to small and marginal farmers) without delay and middle men's interference as well. All these events facilitate socially inclusive development benefiting the marginalised poor and women.
- **Last one pertains to Technology push:** As an indispensable innovative input, digital technology continues to expand its influence in bringing affordable broadband to many industrialists and billions of consumers as well. In parallel, low-cost connected devices are being deployed in every industry, and cloud computing, and the vast information-processing machinery it requires, is developing quickly. Every household has a mobile device linked with Aadhaar and bank account thereby enabling faster communication and quicker transfer of funds. These development ensures a kind of conducive tech based eco-system for productive functioning of the investment and loan made to green industrialisation in the process of sustainable development.

However, there are **some issues impeding** the sustainability in the pathway. The phenomenon of occurrence of exclusion and also the exclusion after inclusion particularly in informal sector where majority of the poor live, leads to some anxiety. 'The exclusion anywhere is a threat to inclusion everywhere' (Rengarajan, V., 2018, p. 1). Here shoe pinches to declare whether technology is a boon due to following issues.

- **In the first, Social acceptance by the poor community for digital inclusion causes hurdles in informal sector –** Most of the excluded community live in informal setting influenced by multi disciplinary demographic characteristics which do not provide a conducive eco system for socially acceptable digitalization. Palpably, the gap of digital divide is significant between the rural and urban India. India is ranked 127 among 201 countries in terms of internet penetration. With the second largest number of internet users in the world, its internet penetration rate is only 13.5% (Digital divide 2020).
- **Second, one is concerned with digital illiteracy in poverty sector.** Given the level of capability of the poor, the process digitalization appears to be too fast to get adopted by the unbanked poor. Most of the poor in informal sector don't remember their date of birth. It is too difficult to recollect smartly and also confidentially their password, one time password, and decode the symbols used for digital operations in the devices like phone or PC or POS etc. These poor segments cannot be expected to be too smart to counter the needs of innovative diagnostics application. in day today operation. It is therefore strongly asserted to create **a preparedness for digitalization process** in the demand side on a priority basis through suitable capability building programmes for financial numeracy financial literacy followed by digital literacy for these poor unbanked poor.
- **Third,** in the context of wider prevalence of fraudulent practices and cybercrime, the poor people are victimized at large. Evidently in the case of MGNREGA payment system, Aadhaar Payment Bridge System (APBS) has given rise to litany of complicated problems like **misdirected payments** and **payment failure** due **to erroneous aadhaar mapping** with the payment software (*The Hindu*, Nov. 6, 2021). On similar vein, in the case PMFBY misuse of password by vested group in rural area has resulted payments of insurance claims to the ineligible farmers. If both the examples are of any indication, the poor people in the informal sector has to live with technological risk with no hope of sustainable inclusion in development pathway.
- **Fourth,** the tech based devices like Personal computer, lap tab, mobile, POS, ATM, make the poor people to depends on the immediate accessibility to the dependable services and repair units/personal, at the door step for the customer in the last mile. In the case of Mobile mode financial transaction which has come to stay in rural areas, ironically we have more number of mobile phones than toilets at household level. In this context, the establishment of a mobile service unit or kiosk or individual skilled entrepreneur in this services at every panchayat level has become an imperative one for sustainable social inclusion in the last mile.
- **Last issue** but not the least, the task of successful deepening of the digital based financial services in the rural area and sustainable financial inclusion in the informal economy depends on adequate provision of infrastructure that is related to last mile uninterrupted connectivity and tele-communication facility in the rural areas. Apparently with the pandemic making digital teaching norms, children in rural area, who have little access to gadgets and network connectivity have been pushed into

deeper marginalisation. This kind of digital divide paralyses the sustainable social inclusion in the development path way.

In fine aligning existing Research and development (R&D) investments pertaining to the technologies & innovation is imperatively needed for providing enabling eco system to green industrialization & communition activities without hurdles and also to facilitate capacity building of the poor for easy digital adaptation in the informal sector as this issue assumes crucial to sustainable inclusive development. Otherwise any further irrational digital push in social sector is like **'putting the cart before the horse'...**

Alternate Pathway to Sustainability

Taking cognizance of the cultural values of ancient indigenous knowledge on sustainability on one hand and of the prevailing challenges in the process of removing the risks in the pathway to environmental and social inclusion sustainability, an alternate pathway for integrated socially inclusive green finance development plan to be initiated at state. distinct, block and village levels, is illustrated in Figure 4.

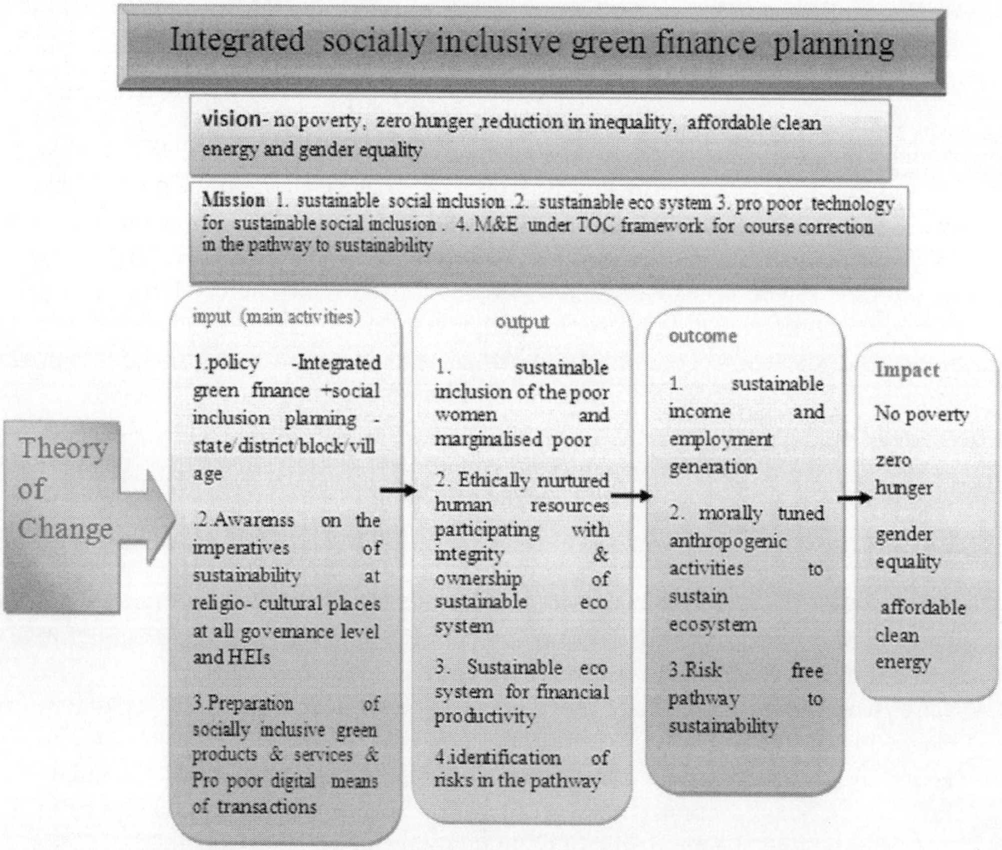

Figure 4: Integrated Alternate Pathway to Sustainability (Illustration)

Three main features of alternate pathway to sustainability:

1. This pathway is designed based on Environment Social Governance (ESG) principles
2. This pathway is an integrated model with the vision towards ensuring sustainability to multiple SDGs, viz., no poverty, zero hunger, reduction in inequality, affordable clean energy and gender equality
3. The pathway is sketched in built with the concurrent evaluation and monitoring system under TOC framework towards removing the harmful multi dimensional risks hindering sustainability

References

1. Amartya Sen (1999, p. 2). 'On ethics and economics ' Oxford India, paperback, India.
2. Amartya Sen (1999, p. 4). 'On ethics and economics'. Oxford India, paperback, India.
3. Berkes F., Colding J., & Folke C. (2000). Rediscovery of Traditional Ecological Knowledge as Adaptive Management. *Ecological Applications* 10(5): 1251–1262. Ecological Knowledge. Ecological Society of America. [pdf] Available at: http://onlinelibrary.wiley.com/doi/10.1890/105 10761(2000)010%5b1251:ROTEKA%5d2.0.CO %3b2/epdf [Accessed on 17 July 2017]
4. Bas Fransen – 2021. Eco matcher 'Revisiting Ancient Innovations for Modern Environmental Problems'. Eco Matcher https://www.ecomatcher.com/revisiting-ancient-innovations-for-modern-environmental-problems/
5. Daniil E. Krapchunov et al. (2021). 'Freedom of belief and ecological consciousness', *India European Proceedings of Social and Behavioral Sciences,* e-ISSN: 2357-1330, DOI: 10.15405/epsbs.2021.12.03.91, https://www.researchgate.net/publication/357383659_Freedom_Of_Belief_And_Ecological_Consciousness_In_India
6. Digital divide (2020). Dimension of digital in India: An extensive study of issues involved Payel Dutta State Aided College Teacher, Asansol Girls' College, Kazi Nazrul University, Asansol, West Bengal, India. E-mail: kutty.dutta2010@gmail.com, Received: May 2020, Revised and accepted: August 2020, https://www.bibliomed.org/mnsfulltext/197/197-1598088012.pdf?1637936917
7. Gauri Shankar Gupta (2019). Sustainable Development and Relevance of Ancient Wisdom, Dissertation submitted to the Doctoral Program in Management https://rgdi.sze.hu/images/RGDI/honlapelemei/fokozatszerzesi_anyagok/Final%20Dissertation_Gauri%20Shankar%20 Gupta.pdf
8. Govt. PEO (1980). Evaluation Report on *Food for Work Programme*, Programme Evaluation Organisation Planning Commission, New Delhi Final report, Nov. 1980, pp. 46-47.
9. Govt. PEO (1985). Evaluation Report on Integrated Rural Development Programme, Programme Evaluation Organisation, New Delhi, May 1985.
10. **India Global Business, Aug. 2020. India Global Business staff** 'Planting the seeds of green money', published on 24 Aug. 2020, 4:29 pm. https://www.indiaglobalbusiness.com/the-big-story/planting-the-seeds-of-green-money
11. Nelson L.E. (2010). Purifying the earthly body of God; Religion and ecology in Hindu, India University of New York press.
12. Renagarajan, V. (2018). *Mystic inclusion: Surgical strikes for inclusive inclusion*, Notion Press India, p. 1.
13. RBI (2021). RBI Bulletin https://rbidocs.rbi.org.in/rdocs/Bulletin/PDFs/04AR_2101202185D9B 6905ADD465CB7DD280B88266F77.PDF
14. The Hindu (2021). Anuradha & R. Narayanan article 'Long road to timely MGNREGA payments', *The Hindu* English newspaper dated November 8th, 2021, Chennai.

Annexures

Annexure 1 List of selected evaluation/research study on social inclusive development programme and the key findings

Sl No	*Sources of Selected Propgrammes*	*Selected Key Evaluative Findings (For the Purpose of the Study*
1.	Evaluation of food for work programme (August – oct 1979) page 46 & 47 Programme evaluation Organization Planning commission Government Of India (GOI) New Delhi Nov 1980	1. Inadeqaucy of depots run by Food Corporation of India (FCI) 2. Misuses/malpractices by the contractors 3. benefits were short term and seasonal 4. benefits due to durable assets will accrue only in upper strata of the village community leading to further income disparities 5. Insufficiency of wage paid- The programme has therefore not fully eradicated hunger but lessened starvation of the poor
2.	Evaluation report on Integrated rural development programme (IRDP)Page 138 Programme Evaluation Organization Planning commission GOI New Delhi May 1985	No uniformity in the selection of target families The families in the lowest income group were required to be covered first. No preparations of shelf of bankable schemes for different areas and not familiar with economics of various schemes No assessment of availability of inputs , assets marketing and potentiality of the area. No follow up for organizing milk producers society Onetime benefit of milch animal did not help the beneficiaries to cross the poverty line Encouraging labor intensive orientation activities with adequate forward and backward linkages
3.	Tamil Nadu corporation for development of women Ltd publication. IFAD Terminal evaluation report 1998 (TCDW website)	1. Targeting: As against the project expectation of at least 60 per cent coverage of special categories, actual coverage was around 30 per cent. The proportion of non-eligible members/ beneficiaries who had already out of the poverty cellar was around one-third of the total members covered under the IFAD project. 2. the position in regard to coverage of SC / ST women in groups had not improved.

Annexure 2: Theory of Change-Log Frame for Selected Social Programme

Programme	*Reported Outcome/ Result*	*Theories of Change*		
		Assumptions	*M&E Indicators*	*Convolution Around TOC*
1. Food for work programme (1977 (Govt. PEO 1980)	1. Inadequacy of depots run by Food Corporation of India. 2. Misuse/malpractices by the contractors. 3. Benefits were short term and seasonal. 4. Benefits due to durable assets will accrue only in upper strata of the village community leading to further income disparities. 5. Insufficiency of wage paid- the programme has therefore not fully eradicated hunger but lessened starvation of the poor.	1. Adequacy of storing facility for handling the food materials. 2. Ethical behavior of actors in the supply side. 3. Sustainable eradication of hunger in the long run. 4. Direct benefit to the persons who live below poverty line with sufficient wage. 5. Eradication of hunger and unemployment	No process monitoring with any result indicators. Periodical monitoring of the achievement of physical target (output) only. Evaluation was done after two years of implementation i.e.1979	1. None of the assumptions have been validated there by annihilating the causal path (input and output) with impaired results. 2. In the log frame, the assumptions are made with more focus on the changes of material input -output management in the causal pathway but vitally the behavioral aspects of the actors in both supply and demand sides that influence the casuistry is ignored or side-lined.

Programme	*Reported Outcome/ Result*	*Theories of Change*		
		Assumptions	*M&E Indicators*	*Convolution Around TOC*
2. Integrated Rural Development Programme (IRDP) – 1978-79 (Govt.PEO 1985)	1. No uniformity in the selection of target families. 2. The families in lowest the income group were required to be covered first. 3. No preparations of shelf of bankable schemes for different areas and not familiar with economics of various schemes 4. No assessment of availability of inputs, assets marketing and potentiality of the area. No follow up for organizing milk producers' society. 5. Onetime benefit of milch animal did not help the beneficiaries to cross the poverty line. Encouraging labour intensive orientation activities with adequate forward and backward linkages.	1. Poorest families are included under IRDP adhering some norms for covering the poorest first. 2. Schemes suitable context situation are prepared considering with economic viability. 3. backward and forward linkages are available for all income generated assets for which loan (+subsidy) is sanctioned. 4. Sustainable graduations of the poorest from the poverty affected family.	No process monitoring with any intermediate result indicators. The programme was launched in 1978-79. After the gap of 5 years evaluation was done in 1983-84. Periodical monitoring of the achievement of physical target (output) only. For studying the impact, Sample beneficiaries' selection done at state, district/block/ cluster and beneficiaries' level. At block level stratified sampling was done. Questionnaires administered for assessing the impact of the programme.	1. most of the assumptions have been nullified there by annihilating the causal path (input and output) with impaired results. 2. In the log frame, the assumptions are made with more focus on the changes of material input -output management in the causal pathway but vitally the behavioural aspects of the actors in both supply and demand sides that influence the casuistry is ignored or side-lined.

Programme	*Reported Outcome/ Result*	*Theories of Change*		
		Assumptions	*M&E Indicators*	*Convolution Around TOC*
3. Tamil Nadu Corporation for Development of women Ltd. (1997) Publication, Terminal IFAD evaluation report 1998 (TCDW website).	1. Project impact Poverty impact According to AFC estimates, 64% of all project beneficiaries crossed the poverty line. Social impact Perhaps the single most striking result of the project can be seen in the remarkable increase in opportunities for disadvantaged women to come out of their homes and enter the public domain. Women have also acquired a new physical mobility and have been able to expand their contacts with banks, NGOs and district authorities.	1. Most of the loans would be used for crop improvement purposes. 2. The assumption that women would generally make wise choices because their expertise and knowledge of local market conditions was sound. 3. Institutional credit: the Indian Bank was responsible for providing credit to village women towards accessing low cost funds.	No process monitoring was done. Evaluation was done at the terminal year of the project. Periodical monitoring was done only on the achievements of physical target (output).	The following facts bearing on the ultimate change has been ignored: 1. Diversification of loan and financial exclusion impacted by banker's attitude. 2. Group Mortality/ defunct, dropouts are witnessed in weak group causing exclusion. This fact has not been captured. All the above said convolution, occurring in the result chain may not facilitate for sustainability of change and reduction in inequity gap among the poor segment.

PART II: ORGANISATIONS AND SUSTAINABILITY

CORPORATEGOVERNANCERATING:AGLOBALSTRATEGY TOWARDS GOOD CORPORATE GOVERNANCE

Sanjay Bhayana and Sapna Arora

The Preamble

Corporate Governance has been attracting a lot of consideration and debate in the last couple of years. Stakeholder particularly media interest in corporate governance issues had increased intensely. Reports of corporate governance failures and related concerns are normally in the news.

In order to improving and strengthen corporate governance, various committee viz. Kumar Manglam, Naresh Chandra have been formed at national level whereas Cadbury committee, Greenbury committee, Hample committee, Blue Ribbon committee, OECD principles have been implemented at international level. In India, recommendations of these committees on good corporate governance have been compulsorily adopted by all the companies listed on the stock exchange through SEBI, but still companies are not able to perform up to mark or coming up-to the expectations of the stakeholders.

Therefore, because of the pressure from the stakeholders to perform well, companies are coming forward to do the rating of their governance practices. The rating process includes an assessment of both confidential and public information, interviews with senior company representatives, including directors of company.

Present State of Indian Companies about Rating

ICRA a rating agency has assigned its first corporate governance rating to Indian Tobacco Company (ITC). The rating agency has assigned CGR2 to the tobacco major on a rating scale of Corporate Governance Rating 1 (CGR) to Corporate Governance Rating 6 (CGR), where CGR1 denotes the highest rating. This is the first corporate governance rating. Similarly, CRISIL another rating agency has rated four companies HDFC, HDFC Bank, Hero Honda and Dabur on the basis of Governance and value creation (GVC) level. Where GVC level 1 rating being assigned to HDFC, HDFC Bank, Hero Honda and GVC level 2 rating has been assigned to Dabur India Limited. Where GVC level 1 rating being the highest and the GVC level 8 rating being the lowest.

Governance Scores; What it Predict?

The basic objective of such scores is to know the level of transparency, fairness, courtesy, quality of disclosure, effectiveness of the board, accountability and responsibility of the organization. These are basically unbiased benchmarks which are basically used to know and evaluate that companies are doing their work properly or not with respect to governance practices.

Corporate Governance Rating; It is Not?

- It is not any exact financial commitment
- It is not the evaluation of capital market
- It also does not show any kind of business competitiveness or performance

More preciously Corporate Governance Rating is not any kind of audit or compulsion for any company.

Position at the Global Level

One famous and renowned international rating agency Governance Metrics International (GMI) during his worldwide survey of 38 countries positioned India at the 19th ranked with 4.91 average score on the basis of various corporate governance variables such as executive remuneration/compensation, accountability of the board, financial disclosures and transparency, rights of the shareholder and internal controls. One of the rating agency has done survey of around 4000 companies and the score was assigned between 1 to 10. County Ireland graded at the top with 7.55 score. Whereas on the other hand Canada, Britain and Australia are still suffering. Immediately after Singapore and Thailand India is at no. 3 in Asia. Further, Belgium Denmark and France having score of 4.09.

Rating Criteria

To evaluate Corporate Governance standards, certain criteria/parameters have been adopted by the rating agencies. The rating criterion for evaluating the companies may varies from one rating agency to another agency. Agencies have adopted some common elements called rating benchmarks. The elements for evaluating the companies are depicted in the Table 1.

Table 1: Showing the Rating Criteria adopted by the Agencies

1.	Ownership structure ▪ Ownership structure transparency ▪ Concentration and influence of ownership
2.	Financial stakeholder relations ▪ Information on shareholder meetings ▪ shareholder meeting procedures and voting related procedure
3.	Financial transparency and information disclosure ▪ Quality and contents of public disclosure ▪ Timing of disclosure to public at large ▪ Independence and standing of company's auditors
4.	Structure of the Board and adopted process ▪ Companies Board structure and their compositions ▪ Board Role and its effectiveness ▪ Outside director's role and their independence

Awards and Appreciations

Currently there are lots of organizations/rating agencies at the worldwide level which are providing the awards on the basis on the rating of corporate governance. The same has been depicted in the table 2.

Table 2: Showing the Various Awards Given by the Agencies

Sr. No.	*Name of the Award*	*Expiation of the award*
1.	CLSA award for Asia-Pacific Markets by Asian Corporate Governance Association	Award given to the 100 large cap companies in 2007 and 2010.
2.	Corporate Governance Asia	Best Asian company has been awarded.
3.	Finance Asia	Award given to best Asia's Companies on the basis on best investor relations and strong dividend policy.
4	Governance Metrics International Inc ("GMI")	Rating to companies on the basis of various securities regulations, stock exchange listing requirements and various corporate governance codes and principles. Rating has been given on the scale of 1.0 to 10.
5	Hang Seng Indexes Company Limited	Award has been given on the basis of high standard of performance in environmental, social and corporate governance aspects.
6	Hong Kong Institute of Certified Public Accountants	The criterion of the award is good disclosure practices, best corporate governance practices and promoting the same practices also.
7	Hong Kong Institute of Directors	Award has been given to the company directors on the basis of their commitment and performance towards their roles and duties.
9	Hong Kong Management Association	The association is giving best annual report award for the publication of outstanding report. It is based on accurate and sufficient information provided to stakeholders.
10	IR Magazine	Such magazine is conducting study of the investors to know the leading companies and the perception of the investors towards the companies.

Source: http://www.hkex.com.hk/eng/exchange/corpgov

Conclusion

To conclude, it can be inferred from the above paragraphs that rating services are highly beneficial and source of motivation for the stakeholders & investors as well as companies. With regard to the investors, it is advising on transparency and disclosure practices whereas CGR help companies in terms of improving image and valuation, stock exchange listing, transactions with creditors and so on. Companies can use/set as a standard for further improvement.

If the outcome/results of the ratings are used proactively then it can lead to enhancement of the long-term shareholder value.

A Bite from Future

Securities and Exchange Board of India (SEBI), apex regulatory body is also thinking to come up with such type of rating mechanism/evaluating pattern/ index. Though these agenda are in pipeline and the basic objective of this rating mechanism would be to check the status of corporate governance of listed companies. In the years to come the benchmark of SEBI will also use by other rating agencies also. These are viz. the quality of wealth management, sharing of wealth with the all stakeholders and level of wealth creation by the corporate.

Bibliography

1. Roy, A. "Just 19 Cos Make Public Corporate Governance Rating in Last 5 Years", The Wall Street Journal, January 8, 2009.
2. Majumdar, S. "Corporate Governance Ratings", The Financial Express, December 18, 2002.
3. www.Computerusers.com
4. http://www.hkex.com.hk/eng/exchange/corpgov
5. http://www.gmiratings.com
6. www.RMRR.com
7. http://www.corporate-eye.com
8. "ICRA Begins Governance Rating With ITC', Rating Update4, A Periodical Update on Credit Rating, September 2002, p.1.
9. "Crisil Rates Four Firms On Governance And Value Creation," Business Standard, 17 January 2003, p.6.

A STUDY ON FACTORS AFFECTING SELF–HELP GROUPS AND THEIR ACTIVITIES IN RURAL COMMUNITY OF HARYANA

Rashmi Tyagi and Jatesh Kathpalia

Abstract

In India, the central government has catalyzed the spread of SHGs since 2011 through the National Rural Livelihood Mission (NRLM). NRLM is India's flagship program to reduce poverty by mobilizing poor rural women into self-help groups and building community institutions of the poor.NRLM's mandate is to enroll one woman from every poor household into an SHG. By May 2019, the program had mobilized nearly 60 million women in close to 6 million SHGs (GOI, 2019) SHGs harness strong social ties between rural women based on shared work, responsibility and because of similar socio economic background. It has now become a vehicle of change for the poor and marginalized and to allievate poverty. Economic empowerment through SHGS provides women the confidence for participation in decision making not only at household–level but community level also. The active involvement of women in SHGS have also build leadership qualities in them thus becoming potential candidates as sarpanch and Panchayat Pradhans. It is perhaps a landmark achievement that due to the involvement of banks for small savings and credit groups today 67 billion women are members of 6 million SHGS. The present study was conducted in Fatehabad and Kurukshetra Districts of Haryana. One block from each district was selected randomly for the purpose of the study. From Fatehabad block three villages namely Mastana, BhodiaKhera, Bighar were selected and from Kurukshetra block village Hathira, Sangor and Ghararsi villages was selected. Sixty farmers were also selected randomly from each block. On the whole, a total of 120 farmers were surveyed with the help of well structured interview schedule. Data was analyzed and tabulated to draw the inferences as per objectives of the study. Regarding family size 37.50 percent farmers had between 5-8 members followed by 35.00 percent farmers who up to 4 members and 27.50 percent farmers who had above 8 members. The analysis revealed that 41.67 percent farmers belonged to general caste 40.83 percent to backward caste and 17.50 percent to scheduled class. Regarding educational qualification 41.67 farmers had education upto secondary school level and 24.17 percent farmersupto middle level. Regarding family size 37.50 percent farmers had between 5-8 members followed by 35.00 percent farmers who up to 4 members and 27.50 percent farmers who had above 8 members.

Regarding the association, farmers 52.60 percent who belonged to age category of upto 35 years of age and farmers 51.20 percent who belonged to nuclear family type had medium level of socio economic empowerment. Further analysis revealed that 47.20 percent farmers who belonged to joint family had low level of socio economic empowerment.

Keywords: *Socio-economic impact, Socio-economic factors, Self-help group, Empowerment, Activities*

Introduction

The SHG Bank Linkage Project launched by NABARD in 1992 has blossomed into the world's largest microfinance project.Today, the SHG-BLP is regarded as the largest micro-finance programme in the world with a total membership of 100.14 lakh groups (covering nearly 12 crore households) across India and having extended collateral-free loans of 87,098 crore to 50.77 lakh SHGs as on March 31, 2019. It is a fact that more than 90 per cent of the SHG members are women). NRLM is India's flagship program to reduce poverty by mobilizing poor rural women into self-help groups and building community institutions of the poor. NRLM's mandate is to enroll one woman from every poor household into an SHG. By May 2019, the program had mobilized nearly 60 million women in close to 6 million SHGs (GOI, 2019). The concept of SHG is based on the underlining principle "for the people, by the people and of the people" SHGs harness strong social ties between rural women based on shared work, responsibility and because of similar socio economic background. It has now become a vehicle of change for the poor and marginalized and to allievate poverty. Pal et al. (2020) also mentioned in his study that group-based micro-credit initiatives, as part of the broader social and solidarity-based finance initiatives, have gained prominence over the past decade, especially in developing economies like India. Lending to the poor, especially women, through micro-credit groups, are significantly associated with the utilization of commons. Economic empowerment through SHGS provides women the confidence for participation in decision making not only at household–level but community level also. The active involvement of women in SHGS have also build leadership qualities in them thus becoming potential candidates as sarpanch and Panchayat Pradhans.In continuation to the efforts to alleviate poverty Government of India, in 1999 introduced Swarn Jayanti Gram SwarozgarYojana (SGSY) to promote self-employment in rural areas through formation and skilling of SHGs. This programmeevolved as a national movement in 2011 and became National Rural Livelihoods Mission (NRLM) – world's largest poverty alleviation programme. These SHGS work as pressure groups in raising their voice against dowry, alcoholism and their participation in governance process also impacts policy decisions. Pal *et al.* (2020) concluded in his study thateconomic empowerment through SHGs, provides women the confidence for participation in decision making affairs at the household-level as well as at the community-level. The most important functions of Self-Help Groups areto encourage and motivate its members to save, to persuade them to make a collective plan for generation of additional income, and to act as a conduit for formal banking services to reach them. Self-help groups as collective strength of women is playing a crucial role in Indian economy and has become a comparative advantage over bringing interventions directly to individuals.Ithas become inseparable part of the developmental infrastructure, embodyingmassive social capital of social mobilization and empowerment of women. With the rapid spread of SHGs over time, the innovations associated with them have also flourished.

C. Nichols (2021) also mentioned in her study that utilizing SHGs as platforms for development programs is attractive to governments and donors for multiple reasons. Foremost, are promises of greater cost-effectiveness and efficiency if information is transmitted to groups rather than individuals. There is also potential for 'economies of scope', where development agencies can deliver multiple programs through one intervention platform (Gugerty et al., 2019)Sangvikar *et al.* (2019) also mentioned in his study that the primary objective of SHGS is to work together, regularly save money, developing a common fund by shared contribution, and exerting reciprocal support for urgent needs. In order to become financially sustainable, the required resources are generated by the members of the group. He also said that the provision of loans is also realised using the common fund developed by all the members of the group and thus bringing the dimension of self-employment for every member of the group and above all the functioning of the group is based on collective decision making and assuring the utilisation of credit and repayments as per time.Narang (2012) also mentioned in her study that as a group-oriented model, SHGs in India is a mechanism for women's development to bring in individual and collective empowerment through improvement in both 'condition' and 'position' of women. Now women in India are mobilized to protest against domestic violence, rising prices, legal discrimination, rape, child marriage, domestic violence etc. In this way, it aims to empower women with various forms of power.

In view of this the present study was designed with following specific objective:

- To examine the activities of self help group in rural areas.
- To assess the impact of self help groups on women empowerment and economic status of family.
- To study the factors affecting the self-help group

Materials and Methods

The study was conducted in Fatehabad and Kurukshetra Districts of Haryana. One block from each district was selected randomly for the purpose of the study. From Fatehabadblock three villages namely Mastana,BhodiaKhera, Bighar were selected and from Kurukshetra block village Hathira, Sangor and Ghararsi villages was selected. Sixty farmers were also selected randomly from each block. On the whole, a total of 120 farmers were surveyed with the help of well structured interview schedule. The collected data were coded, tabulated, analyzed and interpreted according to the objective of the present study with the help of appropriate statistical techniques. The descriptive statistical tools such as frequency, and percentage and chi square test had been adopted to draw the inference from the study. In the end, the collected data from the field was analysed in term of identifying various specific objectives.

Results and Discussion

Contextual Matrix of the Respondents

The analysis revealed that maximum number of farmers i.e. 47.50 percent belonged upto 35 years of age group. Regarding family type maximum number of farmers 70.00 percent belonged to nuclear family and 30.00 percent to joint family. Regarding family size 37.50 percent farmers had between 5-8 members followed by 35.00 percent farmers who up to

4 members and 27.50 percent farmers who had above 8 members. The analysis revealed that 41.67 percent farmers belonged to general caste 40.83 percent to backward caste and 17.50 percent to scheduled class. Regarding educational qualification 41.67 farmers had education upto secondary school level and 24.17 percent farmersupto middle level. The analysis revealed that 16.67 percent farmers had no occupation followed by 18.33 percent who were engaged in labour and only 33.33 and 31.67 percent farmers who were engaged in farming and small scale enter prises and service category respectively. The results revealed that 45.83 percent farmers had income upto 1,00,000 per annum and only 18.33 percent farmers above Rs. 2,00,000. Regarding mass media exposure 48.33 percent farmers had medium level of media exposure.

The analysis revealed that maximum number of farmers i.e. 46.67 percent had membership of one organization in social participation. Regarding socio economic status 44.17 percent farmers had high socio economic status followed by 43.33 percent who had medium level of socio economic status.

Table 1: Contextual Matrix of the Respondents

Variables	*Kurukshetra (N=60)*	*Fatehabad (N=60)*	*Total (N=120)*
Age			
Up to 35 years age group	27(45.00)	30(50.00)	57(47.50)
Between 36-55 years age group	21(35.00)	24(40.00)	45(37.50)
Above 55 years age group	12(20.00)	6(10.00)	18(15.00)
Family Type			
Nuclear	45(75.00)	39(65.00)	84(70.00)
Joint	15(25.00)	21(35.00)	36(30.00)
Family size			
Up to 4 members	24(30.00)	18(30.00)	42(35.00)
5-8 members	21(35.00)	24(40.00)	45(37.50)
Above 8 members	15(25.00)	18(30.00)	33(27.50)
Caste			
General caste	24(40.00)	26(43.33)	50(41.67)
Backward caste	27(45.00)	22(36.67)	49(40.83)
Scheduled caste	09(15.00)	12(20.00)	21(17.50)
Level of Education			
Illiterate	09(15.00)	06(10.00)	15(12.50)
Up to middle	12(20.00)	17(28.33)	29(24.17)
Secondary & senior secondary school level	27(45.00)	23(38.33)	50(41.67)
Graduation and above	12(20.00)	14(23.33)	26(21.66)

Variables	*Kurukshetra (N=60)*	*Fatehabad (N=60)*	*Total (N=120)*
Occupation			
Nil	12(20.00)	08(13.33)	20(16.67)
Labour	08(13.33)	14(23.33)	22(18.33)
Farming	22(36.66)	18(30.00)	40(33.33)
Small scale enterprise and service	18(30.00)	20(33.33)	38(31.67)
Annual Family Income			
Up to Rs. 1,00,000/-	24(40.00)	31(51.66)	55(45.83)
Between Rs. 1,00,000/- 2,00,000/-	26(43.33)	17(28.33)	43(35.84)
Above Rs. 2,00,000/-	10(16.67)	12(20.00)	22(18.33)
Mass media exposure			
Low (up to 9)	06(10.00)	10(16.67)	16(13.33)
Medium (10-17)	26(43.33)	32(53.33)	58(48.33)
High (above17)	28(46.67)	18(30.00)	46(38.33)
Social organization participation			
No membership	05(08.33)	09(15.00)	14(11.66)
Membership of one organization	27(45.00)	29(48.33)	56(46.67)
More than one organization	28(46.67)	22(36.67)	50(41.67)
Socio-economic status			
Low (12-18)	05(08.33)	10(16.67)	15(12.50)
Medium (19-24)	2440.00)	28(46.67)	52(43.33)
High (25-31)	31(51.67)	22(36.66)	53(44.17)

Source: Figures in parentheses denote percentage

Reasons Behind Joining SHGs

Regarding the reasons behind joining SHGs 95.00 percent of the farmers reported the reason as to generate personal income. Easy accessibility of working place was reported as reason by 68.33 percent of farmers .The other reasons like training facilities was reported by 77.50 percent followed by to participate in group functions 57.50 percent, easy availability of loan 80 percent, to work in group 60.00 percent, feeling of security 45.00 percent and development of skill was reported by 71.66 percent of farmers. Regarding utilization of free time as reason to join SHG was reported by 48.33 percent of farmers followed by the reason of unemployment of husband 26.66 percent and to get recognition as reason was reported by 35.00 percent of farmers. Ghosh (2012) also confirmed in his study that theSHG-Bank linkage programme has significantly improved the rural poor's access to formal financial services and had a positive impact on the socio-economic conditions of SHG household and the results also revealed that the average annual net income, assets and savings of the households increased significantly in post-SHG situation

Table 2: Reasons Behind Joining SHGs (N=120)

Sr. No.	*Reasons*	*Frequency*	*Percentage*
1.	To generate personal income	114	95.00
2.	Easy accessibility of working place	82	68.33
3.	Training facilities	93	77.50
4.	To participate in group functions	69	57.50
5.	Easy availability of loan	96	80.00
6.	Work in group	72	60.00
7.	Feeling of security	54	45.00
7.	Development of skill	86	71.66
9.	To develop more contacts	38	31.66
10.	To utilize free time	58	48.33
11.	Unemployment of husband	32	26.66
12.	To get recognition in family	42	35.00

Figures in the parenthesis denote percentage
Responses were multiple

Table 3: Number of Years Spent in Self Help Groups (n = 120)

Year spent	*Frequency*	*Percentage*
Upto 2 years	42	35.00
2 to 4 years	57	47.50
More than 4 years	21	17.50

Analysis clearly revealed in Table 24 that 47.50 percent farmers had been involved in self help groups for 2-4 years followed by 35.00 percent farmers who had been involved upto 2 years and rest of the farmers 17.50 percent were involved for more than 4 years.

Income Generating Activities Undertaken by Farmers in SHGs

Data in Table 25 revealed the type of income generating activities that were undertaken by the farmers. In Kurukshetra district, 75.00 percent of the farmers had taken pot and planter making activities and rest 25.00 percent were making pickles. In Fatehabad district, maximum numbers of farmer 48.33 percent were involved in embroidery, 36.67percent in stitching and 15.00 percent in cooking at their own dhabas. Singh etal (2017) also reported in their study in Haryana that SHG women of 1279 groups were involved in Income generating activities such as Food preservation, Dairy Farming, Vermin Compost, Tie and Dye, Cutting and Tailoring, Embroidery, Kitchen gardening, Beautician, Dari making, Gur patti making and Petty shops etc.

Table 4: Income generating activities undertaken by farmers in SHGs

Sr. No	*Income Generating Activities*	*Kurukshetra (n= 60)*	*Fatehabad (n= 60)*	*Total (N= 120)*
1.	Pot and Planter Making	45(75.00)	-	45(37.50)
2.	Pickle making	15(25.00)	-	15(12.50)
3.	Embroidery	-	29 (48.33)	29(48.33)
4.	Stitching	-	22 (36.67)	22(36.67)
5.	Cooking at own dhaba	-	09(15.00)	09(15.00)

Figures in the parenthesis denote percentage
Responses were multiple

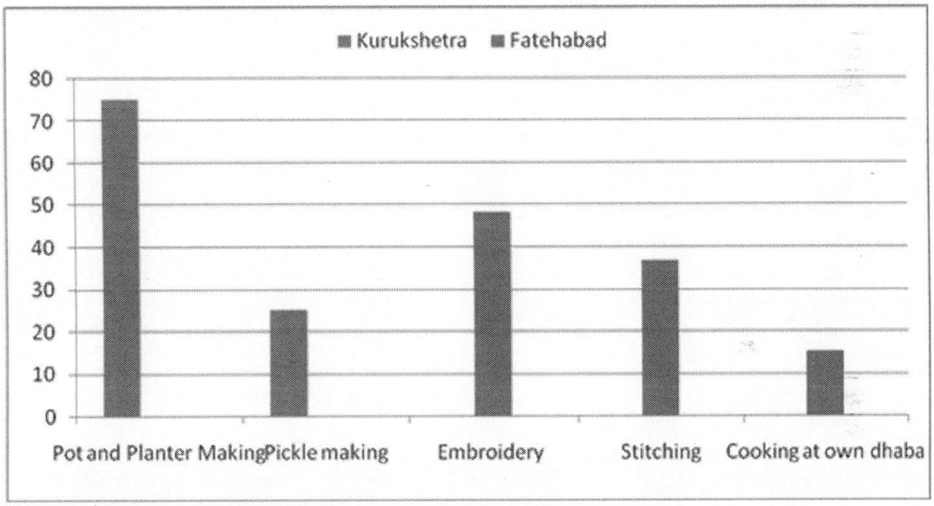

Figure 1: Income Generating Activities Undertaken by Farmers in SHGs

Use of Money Earned by Farmers from SHG Activities

Data analysis revealed that majority of farmers 80.00 percent farmers revealed that they were spending money on quality education of children followed by 77.50 percent farmers that were spending on household items. After that, the money spent on buying jewellery was reported by 43.33 percent of farmers while only 33.33 percent, 21.66 percent and 15.00 percent of farmers were using the money on purchase of dairy animals, purchase of vehicle and contribution in purchase of land respectively. District wise analysis revealed that majority of the farmers was spending money on quality education of children in Kurukshetra and on household items in Fatehabad.Varshaetal (2019) also reported in her study that the long-term association with SHG group helps in building trust among the group members, leaders, and government, and supports societal development. The members avail the loan for specific purposes like children education, bangles selling, pickle and papad manufacturing, broomstick manufacturing, farming, and poultry leads to women entrepreneurship at the micro level. The present study revealed education as a deeplevel attribute has a significant impact on women empowerment.

Table 5: Use of Money Earned by Farmers from SHG Activities

Sr. No	*Investment*	*Kurukshetra (n= 60)*	*Fatehabad (n= 60)*	*Total (n= 120)*
1.	Household items	42(70.00)	51(85.00)	93(77.50)
2.	Quality education of children	54(90.00)	42(70.00)	96(80.00)
3.	Purchase of dairy animals	18(30.00)	22(36.66)	40(33.33)
4.	Jewellery	34(56.66)	18(30.00)	52(43.33)
5.	Purchase of vehicle	14(30.00)	12(20.00)	26(21.66)
6.	Contribution in purchasing of land	11(18.33)	06(10.00)	18(15.00)

Figures in the parenthesis denote percentage
Responses were multiple

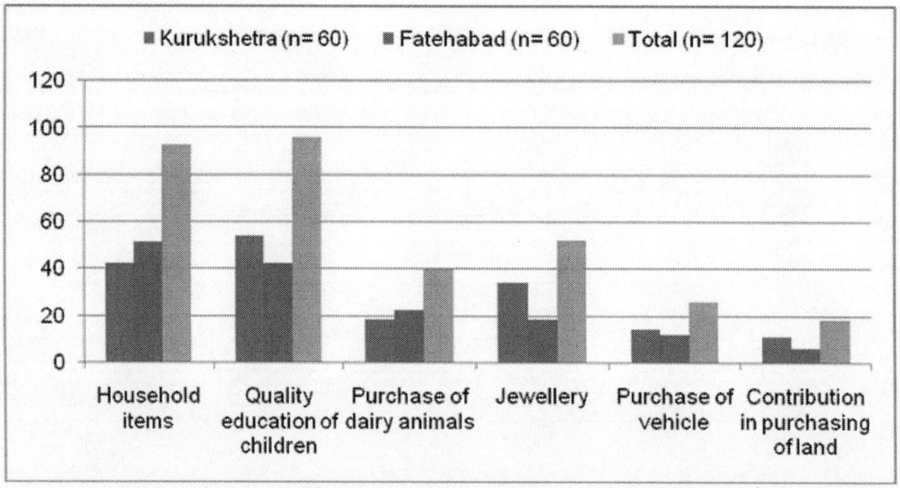

Figure 2: Use of Money Earned by Farmers from SHG Activities

Functioning of SHGs

In Table 27 data revealed that near about 45.00 percent of farmers spent 3-4 hours daily followed by 33.33percent that spent above 4 hours and rest 21.67percent spent up to 2 hours every day.

Regarding monthly individual income 36.66 percent farmers earned uptoRs. 2000 followed by 31.67 percent farmers who earned Rs. 2001 to Rs. 4000 and above Rs. 4000 each respectively.

Considering monthly group income 60.00 percent farmers earned above Rs. 15000 and the rest 40.00 percent farmers who earned up to Rs. 15000.

The data analysis regarding income of farmers before joining SHGs more than half of the farmers had no income and 24.17 percent farmers had earning uptoRs. 2000 followed by 15.00 percent farmers who had income between Rs. 2001-4000 and the rest 7.50 percent farmers had above Rs. 4000.

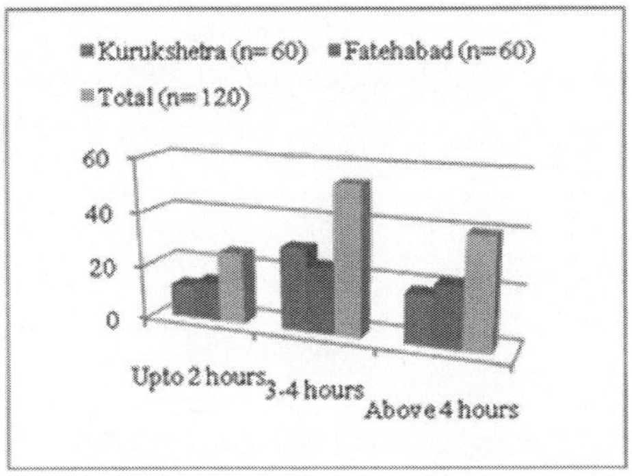

Time spent on economic activities

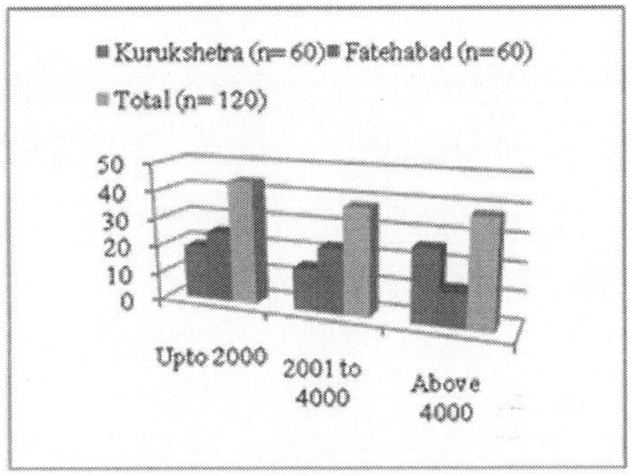

Income from SHGs:

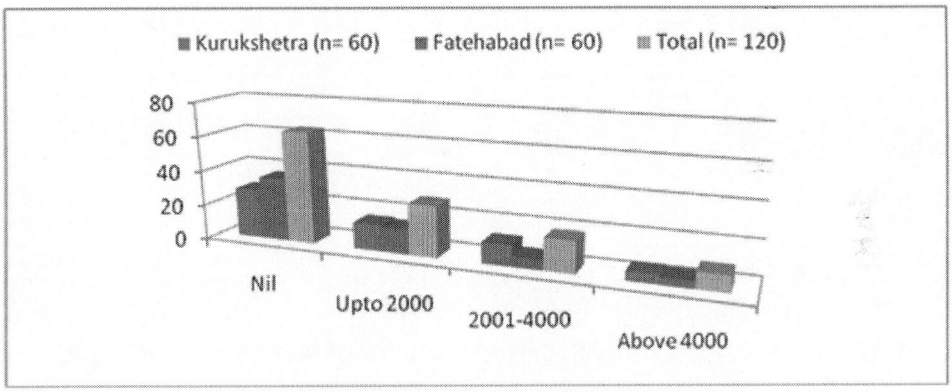

Income of famers before joining SHGs

Figure 3: Functioning of SHGs

Table 6: Functioning of SHGs

Sr. No.	*Variables*	*Kurukshetra (n = 60)*	*Fatehabad (n = 60)*	*Total (n = 120)*
1	Time spent on economic activities :			
	Daily			
	Upto 2 hours	12(20.00)	14(23.33)	26(21.67)
	3-4 hours	30(50.00)	24(40.00)	54(45.00)
	Above 4 hours	18(30.00)	22(36.66)	40(33.33)

Sr. No.	Variables	Kurukshetra (n = 60)	Fatehabad (n = 60)	Total (n = 120)
2	Income from SHGs:			
	Individual income (monthly)			
	Upto 2000	19(31.66)	25 (41.66)	44(36.66)
	2001 to 4000	15(25.00)	23(38.33)	38(31.67)
	Above 4000	26(43.33)	12 (20.00)	38(31.67)
	Group income (monthly)			
	Upto 15000	12(20.00)	36(60.00)	48(40.00)
	Above 15000	48(80.00)	24(40.00)	72(60.00)
3	Monthly income of farmers before joining SHGs:			
	Nil	28(46.66)	36(65.00)	64(53.33)
	Upto 2000	15(25.00)	14(26.66)	29(24.17)
	2001-4000	12(20.00)	06(10.00)	18(15.00)
	Above 4000	05(8.33)	04(3.33)	09(7.50)

Figures in the parenthesis denote percentage

Socio Economic Changes Experienced by Farmers After Becoming Member of SHG in Family

Regarding economic changes experienced by the farmers increase in income was reported by 85.00 percent farmers followed by 15.00 percent farmers as same and none of the farmers reported decrease in income. Regarding expenditure and purchase of assets 79.16 percent and 65.00 percent reported increase in it respectively. There was increase in savings reported by 75.00 percent farmers.

In regards to personal and social changes, majority of the farmers i.e. 75.00 percent and 72.50 percent reported increase in respect to education of children and improvement in social status. Rana etal (2017) also confirmed in their study that Majority of the respondents i.e.64.64 percentage in the groups have reported a positive influence on their share in the family income and 23.23 members state that the situation remained the same; only 12.12 percentage members in these categories respectively say that they cannot say anything. They also revealed that Monthly income of majority of sample respondents has increased after joining SHGs , Monthly expenditure and savings both have gone up after joining SHGs and majority of sample respondents opined that their power has increased in taking decisions after joining SHGs either inside or outside their family. The majority of sample respondents opined that their power has increased in purchase and sale of current assets, domestic animals, and ornaments, purchase of home appliances, purchase of clothes and participation in social activities. Regarding the purchase of land 75.00 percent farmers reported no changes after becoming members of the SHGs. Majority of the farmers i.e. 70.00 percent felt that the greater participation in village power structure remained same as before.

Overwhelming majority of farmers i.e. 68.33 percent revealed that now there was increased better access to health facilities. There was increase in expenditure on social ceremonies and decision making on important family issues reported by farmers 63.33 percent each. Rest 56.66 percent reported well utilization of free time as well.There is a positive influence of SHGs on employability in India. Sangvikaretal(2019) also reported that direct indicators on employability as an effect of self-help groups. The direct indicators are expenditure, annual income, and improvement in economic position.

Table 7: Socio-economic Changes Experienced by Farmers After Becoming Member of SHG in Family (n = 120)

Sr. No.	*Aspects*	*Increase*	*Same*
1.	Economic changes		
	Income	102(85.00)	18(15.00)
	Savings	90(75.00)	30(25.00)
	Expenditure	95(79.16)	25(20.83)
	Purchase of assets	78(65.00)	42(35.00)
2.	Personal and Social changes		
	Support in edu. of children	90(75.00)	30(25.00)
	Purchase the land	12(10.00)	108(75.00)
	Decision making on important family issues	76(63.33)	44(33.33)
	Greater participation in village power structure	36(30.00)	84(70.00)
	Better access to health facilities	82(68.33)	38(31.67)
	Expenditure on social ceremonies	76(63.33)	44(36.66)
	Improvement in social status	87(72.50)	33(27.50)
	Utilization of free time	68(56.66)	52(43.33)

Figures in the parenthesis denote percentage
Responses were multiple

Personal Empowerment of Women Through SHGs

Regarding personal and psychological empowerment attributes Ist rank was given to confidence followed by relatives self respectIInd rank, self esteem which was given IIIrd rank, independence was given IVth rank followed by mutual respect Vth rank, and family acceptance and relatives acceptance as VIth and VIIth rank respectively.Sangvikaretal(2019) also reported in his study that personal gains in regard to shg members included confidence in entrepreneurship, optimistic outlook, facing business challenges, risk-taking, collaboration, and team work and creativity, and innovation.He also said that gains related to the business were product development, business skill development, effective communication, and expertise about the production or service and gains related to development were stability and self-sufficiency, awareness and participation, self-employment, banking procedures, better income, economic independence, and better family life.Maheshwarietal(2016) mentioned in their study that joining a Self Help Group has given them enough confidence to speak, to come forward to be a part in family decision making which is supposedly a male domain, assessing the banks for loans and discussing with the managers without taking their husbands along. Varshaetal (2019) confirmed that SHGs have a positive social impact on women as most of them started participating in decision making which was earlier supposed to be male domain. SHGs have helped in women emancipation. In 53.3% cases more than 75% of the group members participate in decision making when it comes to credit disbursements, getting together for a social cause, or solving some individual problem with the group efforts. Pradeep (2019) reported in his study that The Chi-square value between age of the

Table 8: Personal Empowerment of Women through SHG n = 120

Sr. No.	*Personal and Psychological Empowerment Attribute*	*Level of Empowerment*			*Weighted Score*	*Mean Score*	*Rank*
		High (3)	*Medium (2)*	*Low (1)*			
1.	Confidence	54	48	18	276	2.30	I
2.	Independence	42	52	26	256	2.13	IV
3.	Self-respect	48	56	16	272	2.26	II
4.	Mutual respect	32	68	20	252	2.10	V
5.	Family acceptance	34	62	24	250	2.08	VI
6.	Relatives acceptance	36	45	39	237	1.97	VII
7.	Self esteem	42	63	15	267	2.22	III

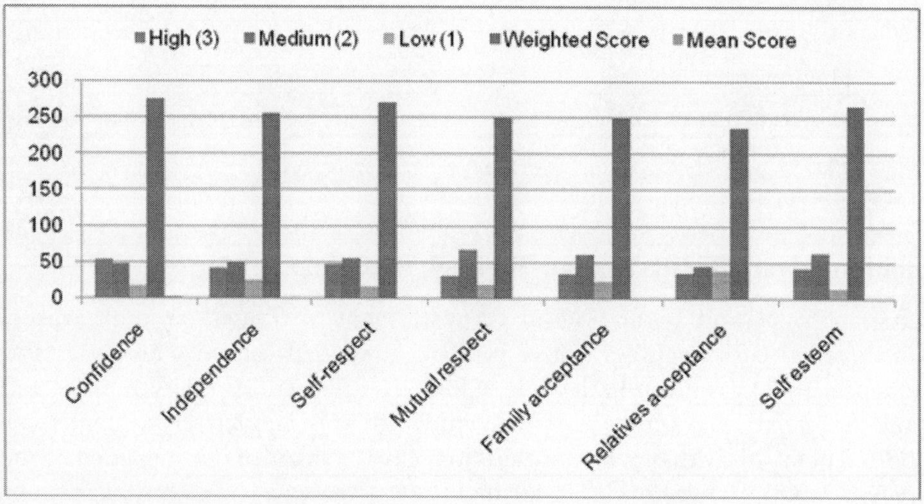

Figure 4: Personal Empowerment of Women Through SHG

respondents and Respected in the society after joining to SHGs is found to be statistically significant indicating that the majority respondents who are between 31-35 years of age reported that they are respected in the society after joining to SHGs and thus the association with Self Help groups will enrich the respect towards women in the society.

Social Empowerment of Women Through SHGs

Regarding social and cultural empowerment attribute group cohesiveness was given Ist rank as perceived by the farmers followed by commitment to educating daughters which is given IInd rank. Similarly IIIrd rank has been given to freedom of movement followed by interactive skills which was given IVth rank, likewise awareness on social problems has been given Vth rank followed by participation in social programmes which was given VIth rank. In the same content organisational skills were given VIIth rank, public speaking and acceptance in society VIIIth rank. Lastly, awareness on rights was given IXth rank

Table 9: Social Empowerment of Women Through SHG n = 120

Sr. No.	*Social and Cultural Empowerment Attribute*	*Level of Empowerment*			*Weighted Score*	*Mean score*	*Rank*
		High (3)	*Medium (2)*	*Low (1)*			
1.	Organisational skills	24	56	40	224	1.86	VII
2.	Group cohesiveness	42	52	26	256	2.13	I
3.	Interactive skills	32	47	41	231	1.92	IV
4.	Public speaking	23	43	54	209	1.74	VIII
5.	Awareness on rights	18	26	76	186	1.55	IX
6.	Acceptance in society	26	37	57	209	1.74	VIII
7.	Awareness on social problems	32	46	42	230	1.91	V
8.	Participation in social programmes	28	52	40	228	1.90	VI
10.	Freedom of movement	36	51	33	243	2.02	III
11.	Commitment to educating daughters	38	57	25	253	2.10	II

Economic Empowerment of Women Through SHGs

Regarding the economic empowerment attributes financial security was given Ist rank, followed by personal belongings which was given IInd rank. Likewise income was given IIIrd rank, entrepreneurial skill IVth rank, and technical skill was given Vth rank. Similarly, economic status was given VIth rank followed by expenditure and savingsVIIth and VIIIth rank respectively. Financial management skills were given IXth rank. Nichols (2021) mentioned in her study that introductory trainings are given to new SHGs so they understand the norms of weekly meetings, savings, and bookkeeping, however, due to wide variation in socio-economic conditions as well as social capital there is considerable variability in how well SHGs are able to follow such norms.

Table 10: Economic Empowerment of Women Through SHG n = 120

Sr. No.	*Economic empowerment attributes*	*Level of empowerment*			*WMS*	*Mean score*	*Rank*
		High (3)	*Moderate (2)*	*Low (1)*			
1.	Technical skill	28	69	23	245	2.04	V
2.	Entrepreneurial skill	42	46	30	248	2.06	IV
3.	Financial security	58	34	28	270	2.25	I
4.	Economic status	45	32	43	242	2.01	VI
5.	Income	42	46	32	250	2.08	III
6.	Savings	27	36	57	210	1.75	VIII
7.	Expenditure	38	44	38	240	2.00	VII
8.	Financial management skills	24	36	60	204	1.70	IX
9.	Personal belongings	40	50	40	260	2.16	II

Association of Socio-economic Empowerment of Farmers with Socio-Economic Variables

Regarding the association, farmers 52.60 percent who belonged to age category of upto 35 years of age and farmers 51.20 percent who belonged to nuclear family type had medium level of socio economic empowerment. Further analysis revealed that 47.20 percent farmers who belonged to joint family had low level of socio economic empowerment.

The data analysis revealed that 46.15 percent farmers who had educational knowledge upto graduation level and above had medium level of socio economic empowerment. Significant association was found between education and socio economic empowerment at chi square 14.43*. Pradeep (2019) reported in their study that the Chi-square value between Educational Qualification and Self Interest to Join SHGs is found to be statistically significant indicating that Self Interest to Join SHGs is influenced by the Educational Qualification of the Respondents. Majority respondents who possess primary and secondary Education have shown the self interest to join the SHGs. Regarding occupation half of the farmers who were engaged in small scale enterprise and service had high level of socio economic empowerment. The data analysis revealed that 54.5 percent farmers who had income between Rs. 100000 and Rs. 200000 had high level of socio economic empowerment. The data analysis revealed that overwhelming majority of farmers 81.30 percent who had low mass media exposure had medium level of socio economic empowerment followed by 54.30 percent farmers who had high level of mass media exposure had high level of socio economic empowerment. High significant association was found between mass media exposure and level of socio economic empowerment.

Social participation was found significantly associated with Level of socio-economic empowerment. Majority of the farmers who had medium level of social participation had high level of socio economic empowerment.

The data analysis revealed that overwhelming majority of the farmers 80.00 percent who had low level of socio-economic status had low level of socio-economic empowerment. Contrary to that majority of the farmers 56.6 percent who had high level of socio-economic status had high socio-economic empowerment. Rana etal (2017) also confirmed in their study that Majority of the respondents i.e.64.64 percentage in the groups have reported a positive influence on their share in the family income and 23.23 members state that the situation remained the same; only 12.12 percentage members in these categories respectively say that they cannot say anything. They also revealed that Monthly income of majority of sample respondents has increased after joining SHGs , Monthly expenditure and savings both have gone up after joining SHGs and majority of sample respondents opined that their power has increased in taking decisions after joining SHGs either inside or outside their family. The majority of sample respondents opined that their power has increased in purchase and sale of current assets, domestic animals, and ornaments, purchase of home appliances, purchase of clothes and participation in social activities. Pradeep (2019) in his study confirmed that the Chi-square value between Occupation and improvement in economic conditions in the family after joining to SHGs is found to be statistically significant indicating that the majority respondents who are house wife responded that there is a improvement in the economic condition of the family after joining to the SHGs.

Table 11: Association of Socio-economic Empowerment of Farmers with Socio-economic Variables

Socio-economic Variables	*Level of Socio-economic Empowerment*			*Total*
	Low (10-14)	*Medium (15-18)*	*High (19-22)*	
Age				
Up to 35 years age group	6(10.5)	30(52.6)	21(36.8)	57(47.50)
Between 36-55 years age group	11(24.4)	20(44.4)	14(31.1)	45(37.50)
Above 55 years age group	16(88.9)	1(5.6)	1(5.6)	18(15.00)
Total	33(27.50)	51(42.50)	36(30.00)	120(100.0)
$\chi 2$= 42.45				
Family Type				
Nuclear	16(19.0)	43(51.2)	25(29.8)	84(70.00)
Joint	17(47.2)	8(22.2)	11(30.6)	36(30.00)
$\chi 2$= 12.58				
Family size				
Up to 4 members	7(16.7)	23(54.8)	12(28.6)	42(35.00)
5-8 members	11(24.4)	21(46.7)	13(28.9)	45(37.50)
Above 8 members	15(45.5)	7(21.2)	11(33.3)	33(27.50)
$\chi 2$= 11.17				
Caste				
General caste	10(20.0)	22(44.0)	18(36.0)	50(41.67)
Backward caste	14(28.57)	20(40.81)	15(30.61)	49(40.83)

Socio-economic Variables	*Level of Socio-economic Empowerment*			*Total*
	Low (10-14)	*Medium (15-18)*	*High (19-22)*	
Scheduled caste	7(33.33)	9(42.85)	5(23.80)	21(17.50)
χ2= 9.72				
Education				
Illiterate	6(40.0)	8(53.3)	1(6.7)	15(12.50)
Up to middle	8(34.8)	9(39.1)	6(26.1)	29(24.17)
Secondary school level	8(14.3)	24(42.9)	24(42.9)	50(41.67)
Senior secondary level and above	11(42.3)	10(38.5)	5(19.2)	26(21.66)
χ2= 14.43*				
Occupation				
Nil	13(65.0)	6(30.0)	1(5.0)	20(16.67)
Labour	2(9.1)	17(77.3)	3(13.6)	22(18.33)
Farming	14(35.0)	13(32.5)	13(32.5)	40(33.33)
Small scale enterprise and service	4(10.5)	15(39.5)	19(50.0)	38(31.67)
χ2= 37.03*				
Annual Family Income				
Up to Rs. 1,00,000/-	17(30.9)	34(61.8)	4(7.3)	55(45.83)
Rs. 1,00,000/- 2,00,000/-	7(16.3)	16(37.2)	20(46.5)	43(35.84)
Above Rs. 2,00,000/-	9(40.9)	1(4.5)	12(54.5)	22(18.33)
χ2= 34.00				
Mass media exposure				
Low (up to 9)	2(12.5)	13(81.3)	1(6.3)	16(13.33)
Medium (10-17)	21(36.2)	27(46.6)	10(17.2)	58(48.33)
High (above17)	10(21.7)	11(23.9)	25(54.3)	46(38.33)
χ2= 28.32*				
Social participation				
Low (up to 6)	5(35.7)	8(57.1)	1(7.1)	14(11.66)
Medium (7-12)	17(30.4)	22(39.28)	17(30.35)	56(46.67)
High (above 12)	11(22.0)	21(42.00)	18(36.00)	50(41.67)
χ2= 6.13*				
Socio-economic status				
Low	12(80.0)	2(13.3)	1(6.7)	15(12.5)
Medium	17(32.7)	30(57.7)	5(9.6)	52(43. 3)
High	4(27.5)	19(35.8)	30(56.6)	53(44.2)
χ2= 52.02**				

Figures in the parenthesis denote percentage
*Significant at 5% level of significant

Constraints Faced by the Farmers While Working in SHGs

Regarding personal constraints 60.00 percent farmers reported lack of family support in household work followed by increased work burden 58.33 percent.

Regarding educational constraints 48.33 percent farmers reported of lack of timely information about govt subsidy for purchase of animals/animal food. Lack of knowledge about facilities provided by govt. was reported by 37.50 percent farmers and 35.00 percent farmers revealed that there was lack of guidance regarding training.

Table 12: Constraints Faced by the Farmers while Working in SHGs

Sr. No.	*Constraints*	*Frequency (N=120)*	*Percentage*
1.	Personal Constraints :		
	Increased work burden	70	58.33
	Non co-operative attitude of husband/in-laws	48	40.00
	Lack of family support in household work	72	60.00
	Control of husband over income	34	28.33
2.	Educational Constraints :		
	Lack of knowledge about facilities provided by govt.	45	37.50
	Lack of guidance regarding training	42	35.00
	Lack of timely information about govt. subsidy (for purchasing of animals or animal food)	58	48.33
3.	Organisational Constraints :		
	Inappropriate Training	18	15.00
	Inadequate transport facilities	32	26.66
	Irregular meetings	12	10.00
	Lack of administrative experience	54	45.00
	Lack of group consensus	34	28.33
	No rotation of leadership	54	45.00
	Lack of team management	42	35.00
4.	Marketing Constraints		
	Inability to catch market for producers	58	48.33
	High cost of raw material	18	15.00
	Difficulty in getting raw material	24	20.00
5.	Economic Constraints		
	High rate of interest	16	13.33
	Loan not received in time	34	28.33
	Lack of timely and adequate credit in group	12	10.00
	Inappropriate distribution of benefits	38	31.66
	Short duration of repayment of loan	42	35.00
6.	Social Constraints		
	Lack of communication	42	35.00
	Conflict among group members	44	36.66
	Unfavourable attitude of the neighbours/society	26	21.66

Responses were multiple

Regarding organizational constraints 45.00 percent farmers reported lack of administrative experience and no rotation of leadership in both categories followed by 35.00 percent farmers who revealed lack of team management.

The data analysis further revealed few marketing constraints as inability to catch market for producers, high cost of raw material and difficulty in getting raw material was revealed by 48.33 percent, 15.00 percent and 20.00 percent farmers respectively.

Regarding economic constraints the major constraint was of short duration of repayment of loan reported by 35.00 percent farmers followed by 31.66 percent farmers who reported appropriate distribution of benefits and 28.33 percent farmers reported loan not received on time. Regarding Social constraints 36.66 percent farmers reported conflict among group members followed by 35.00 percent farmers who revealed about lack of communication and another 21.66 percent farmers who reported unfavourable attitude of the neighbours/society. Pradeep etal (2019) also concluded and confirmed in their study that by being a member of SHG there is possibility for better participation, decision making, planning for future by inculcating management skills in financial matters. Sangvikaretal(2019) also concluded that SHGS members faced many challenges and majorly have problems regarding lack of awareness about government schemes, lack of training and skills, and lack of funds. Singh etal (2017)concluded in their study thatthere is no doubt that microfinance has positive impact on income and employment level of rural poor people especially women in Haryana. Despite all, there is also a need for some innovative policies/strategies and initiatives to be taken in this region regarding microfinance programme so that rural poor can enhance their level and for the betterment of their livelihood.Naiketal (2017) reported that threris lack of Stability and Unity Especially among women SHGs: Enormous workload of women, especially on account of their family obligations, leads to poor productivity of women member of SHGs. In the case of SHGs dominated by women, it is found that there is no permanence of the groups as; many married women are not in a position to associate with the group due to the change of their place of residence. In addition to it, there is no unity among women members owing to personal reasons.

REFERENCES

1. Meenu Maheshwari and Shobhna Goyal (2016) Socio- Economic empowerment of women through self help groups : An Empirical Analysis.Vol 8 Issue 8 pp-87-100.
2. Pal, Anirban; and Singh,Piyush Kumar(2021)Do socially motivated self help groups perform better ? Exploring determinants of micro credit groups performance in Eastern India.Annals of Public and Cooperative Economics.Vol 92 Issue 1:pp 119-146.
3. Varsha ,P.S; Gayathri, Reddy K; Sudheendra Rao, L.N ;Kumar , Amit; (2019) Impact of self help groups , capacity building measures and perceived tension on women empowerment-an empirical study.Asian Journal of Empirical Research Vol 9 Issue 3:pp 65-87.
4. M Srikanth / P Saravanan The Hindu,Bussiness line .How self help groups can sustain during covid .Updated on May 11th 2020.
5. https://www.clearias.com....
6. Carly Nichols (2021)Self groups as platforms for development:The role of social capital . World Development 146 (2021)105575.
7. Pradeep M.D and Rakshitha Rai R.P (2019) Women Empowerment through Self Help Groups-Interventions towards Socio–Economic Welfare. Innovative Practices in IT, Management, Education and Social Sciences ISBN:978-81-929306-8-8.

8. Rana , Kiran ;Ansari ,M.A;(2017) Self Help Group & Woman Empowerment: A Study On Some Selected SHGS In Dehardun District . International Journal of Current Science and Technology .Vol.5, Issue,12.
9. Gugerty, M. K., Biscaye, P., & Leigh Anderson, C. (2019). Delivering development? Evidence on self-help groups as development intermediaries in South Asia and Africa. Development Policy Review, 37(1), 129–151. https://doi.org/10.1111/ dpr.2019.37.issue-110.1111/dpr.12381.
10. Narang Uma (2012) Self Help Group: An Effective Approach To Women Empowerment In India. InternationalJournal of Social Science & Interdisciplinary ResearchVol.1Issue 8 pp 8-16
11. Nayak Madanant and Rodrigues Anthony (2017) Women Empowerment Through Self Help Groups: Realities And Challenges. IOSR Journal Of Humanities And Social Science (IOSR-JHSS) Volume 22, Issue 6, Ver.12 pp 1-9
12. Singh, Tej and Mittal Parul (2017) Self Help Groups in Haryana:An Analysis of Trends and Schemes. Management Insight Vol 13 ,(1) pp54-68.
13. Tyagi,Rashmi and Kathpalia, Jatesh (2021) Role of self-help groups in women empowerment rural communities of Haryana. The Pharma Innovation Journal, Vol. 10, issue 4S, pp. 416-426.

EFFECT OF INNOVATION AND TECHNOLOGY ON PRODUCTIVITY AND PROFITABILITY IN NEPALESE COMMERCIAL BANKS

Sarita Adhikari and Radhe Shyam Pradhan

Abstract

This study examines theeffect of innovation and technology on productivity and profitability of Nepalese commercial banks. Bank productivity and profitabilityare the dependent variables. The independent variables are mobile banking, e-payment, internet banking, ATM banking, and POS banking. The primary source of data is used to assess the opinions of respondents regarding innovation and technology in Nepalese commercial banks. The study is based on 160 respondents from 25 commercial banks of Nepal. To achieve the purpose of the study, structured questionnaire is prepared. The multiple regression models are estimated to test the relationship and importance of innovation and technology on productivity and profitability in Nepalese commercial banks.

The study showed that internet banking has a positive impact on bank productivity and profitability. It indicates that increase in internet banking leads to increase in the bank productivity and profitability. Similarly, ATM service has a positive impact on bank productivity and profitability. It means that better ATM service leads to increase in bank productivity and profitability. The result also shows that mobile banking has a positive impact on bank productivity and profitability. It means that better mobile banking services leads to increase in bank productivity and profitability. Likewise, point of sale has a positive impact on bank productivity and profitability. It indicates that increase in point of sale services in retail stores leads to increase in bank productivity and profitability. Similarly, e-payment technology has a positive impact on bank productivity and profitability. It means that better e-payment technology leads to increase in bank productivity and profitability.

Keywords: *Productivity, Profitability, Mobile banking, e-payment, Internet Banking, ATM Banking and POSBanking*

Introduction

Employee performance is vital to any organization as it is a form of measurement of a company's success. There are various methods or approaches to enhance employee performance and one of them is through innovation. Innovation activities improve administrative process, increase efficiencies and make work management more effective (Benner and Tushman, 2002). Employee performance improves firm performance indirectly through innovation as employee generates ideas for new products or services to improve competitiveness of the firm. The competition is fierce in the economy and particularly in banking sector. Consumer is shifting from tradition channels to digital ones and the multichannel model now is the popular trend in the banking industry. Internet banking is an innovative service in the banking industry. Internet banking is a service with great potential. It would become a decent source of profits for banks; reduce bank's operating expenses so ultimately enhance bank performance. To date, internet banking is not just an element to compete for market share but becomes an essential service to provide, if not banks would face the chance of losing their market share or bad effects to their brand. The banks should focus on improving the productivity through operational efficiency, adopting efficient banking system, and efficient resource generation and allocation to survive in such a competitive market. This could eventually contribute positively to financial performance. Banks that sustain continuous improvements in performance show better ratio of human capital efficacy (Singh and Kamlesh, 2013).

The applications of technology and internet banking have brought great changes in the banking industry. Agboola (2006) emphasized that banks have to invest in technology, modernize their systems to improve quality, efficiency and speed in delivering services; otherwise they may lose their positions in the competitive race with the rivals. Customer expectations are changing and shifting due to advances in technology. To satisfy those subtle needs, multichannel delivery model is applied and proven to be a success. Such a system employs a unified interface across all channels. Customer's preferences and activities are transferred across mediums and thus ensure functionality remains reliable regardless of the customer's preferred device. This forms and enhances customer's trust and loyalty to the banks which is increasingly important to banks in the integration trend. Besides from those indirect impacts, a modern service such as Internet banking can have direct impacts on banks' performance such as bank income, operating costs, and in turn bank profitability. Employees are directly related to banking activities and are crucial in the development, productivity enhancement, and success of banking institutions. Devising technology-driven strategies that facilitate knowledge discovery and enhance the skill sets of employees is vital because the success of banking institutions and the realization of their objectives depend largely on human resources. Improvements in the skills and competence of employees influence employee productivity that manifests in service offering responsiveness and customer satisfaction (Singh and Kaur, 2011).

In the banking industry, providing high-quality innovative outputs improve the satisfaction level of employees that eventually increases the productivity of these employees (Obeng and Mkhize, 2017). Efficient use of information technologies increases labour productivity levels (Sabherwal and Chan, 2001). Complementing information technology and innovation activities could lead to higher improvements in employee productivity than applying them individually since technology can only contribute to increased productivity when used with other resources effectively (Dauda and Akingbade, 2011). Banking institutions must play a significant role to develop technological innovation-driven economy. The financial services institutions among the industries are most affected by the technological revolution. The financial services industry relies on the exchange of information, which itself depends heavily on communications technology and information (ICT) in order to obtain, analyze and provide data for all users concerned. Financial institutions continuously update their marketing strategies and technologies in order to satisfy the desires and demands of their clients in a safe environment (Rust and Kannon, 2003).

Dzombo *et al.* (2017) found that branchless banking such as automated teller machines banking, phone banking, internet banking (IB) and point of sale banking have significant positive effect on financial performance of commercial banks. In addition, the availability of automated teller machines (ATM), cards, telephone banking, personal computer banking and internet banking have positive impact on financial performance of banking system (Narteh, 2014). Mahdi and Mehrdad (2010) determined the impact of e-banking in Iran. The study showed that there is a positive correlation between e-banking and profitability of banks. Similarly, Rafael and Francisco (2007) investigated the impact of various regional banking sector developments and innovations during 1986-2001 in Spain. The study found out that product and service delivery innovations contribute positively to regional gross domestic product, investment and gross savings growth. In addition, Simpson (2002) revealed that electronic banking is motivated largely by the prospects of operating costs minimization and operating revenues maximization. The adoption of internet banking leads to cost reduction and hence likely to increase banks' profitability.

Polatoglu and Ekin (2001) concluded that online banking has a positive impact on the profits of Turkish banks. Online banking has changed the dimensions of competition in the retail banking sector. It has also provided opportunities for emerging a gradual process. DeYoung *et al.* (2007) observed the change in financial performance of internet community banks in U.S. during 1999-2001. The results showed that internet adoption improved community banks' profitability, particularly through increased revenues from deposit service charges. Internet adoption was also associated with movements of deposits from checking accounts to money market deposit accounts, increased use of brokered deposits and higher average wage rates for bank employees. The findings suggested that internet adoption was associated with an economically and statistically significant improvement in bank profitability. Cashless payment is a form of financial exchange that takes place between the buyer and seller facilitated by means of electronic communication.

According to Cobb (2004), electronic payments can lower transaction costs stimulate higher consumption and GDP, increase government efficiency, boost financial intermediation and improve financial transparency. Similarly, electronic payments enable customers to handle their daily financial transactions without having to visit their local bank branch. Electronic payments products could save merchants time and expense in handling cash (Appiah and Agyemang, 2006). Kiplangat and Tibbs (2018) found a significant positive influence of mobile banking on financial performance of commercial banks. According to Koivu (2002), uptake of mobile phone in Kenya influences the performance of organization, behavior and decision making of the entire economy. Similarly, Jayawardhena and Foley (2000) showed that internet and mobile banking results in cost and efficiency gains for banks.

In the context of Nepal, Joshi (2019) analyzed the impact of ATM service quality on the customer satisfaction, productivity, profitability in Nepalese banking sector. The study found that the ATM services have positive impact on the productivity and profitability. Further, Sapkota *et al.* (2018) explored the prevailing status of the use of POS banking in commercial banking services in Nepal. The study found that the bank has been providing different services like debit card, ATM card, mobile banking, mobile cash, utility bill payment and internet banking services in the country. Banstola (2007) found that the ATM is the most popular electronic delivery channel for banking services in Nepal. Only few customers are using internet banking facilities. Nepalese financial institutions till date have not faced any kind of electronic fraud or risk.

The above discussion reveals that there is no consistency in the findings of various studies concerning the effect of innovation and technology on productivity and profitability of banks.

The major objective of this study is to examine the effect of innovation and technology on productivity and profitability of Nepalese commercial banks. More specifically, it examines the relationship of independent variables (i.e., mobile banking, e- payment, internet banking, ATM banking, and POS banking) with productivity and profitability in Nepalese commercial banks.

The remainder of this study is organized as follows: section two describes the sample, data, and methodology. Section three presents the empirical results and final section draws the conclusion and discuss the implication of the study findings.

Methodological Aspects

The study is based on the primary data. The data were gathered from 160 respondents through questionnaire. The respondents' views were collected on mobile banking, e-payment, internet banking, ATM banking and POS banking of Nepalese commercial banks. The study is based on descriptive and causal-comparative research designs. Table 1 shows the list of commercial banks along with the number of the respondents selected for the study.

Table 1: Number of Commercial Banks Selected for the Study Along with Number of Respondents

S.No.	*Name of the Banks*	*No. of Respondents*
1	Bank of Kathmandu Limited	5
2	Century Bank Limited	5
3	Citizens Bank International Limited	7
4	Civil Bank Limited	6
5	Everest Bank Limited	5
6	Global IME Bank Limited	9
7	Himalayan Bank Limited	6
8	Kumari Bank Limited	5
9	Laxmi Bank Limited	6
10	Machhapuchchhre Bank Limited	6
11	Mega Bank Nepal Limited	8
12	Nabil Bank Limited	6
13	Nepal Bangladesh Bank Limited	5
14	Nepal Bank Limited	9
15	Nepal Credit and Commerce Bank Limited	7

S.No.	*Name of the Banks*	*No. of Respondents*
16	Nepal Investment Bank	4
17	NIC Asia Bank Limited	5
18	NMB Bank Limited	8
19	Prabhu Bank Limited	5
20	Rastriya Banijya Bank Limited	12
21	Sanima Bank Limited	6
22	Nepal SBI Bank Limited	5
23	Siddhartha Bank Limited	6
24	Standard Chartered Bank Limited Nepal	7
25	Sunrise Bank Limited	7
Total number of respondents		160

Thus, the study is based on the 160 observations.

Model

The study assumes that the bankproductivity and profitability depend upon different factors. The dependent variables selected for the study areproductivity and profitability. Similarly, the selected independent variables are mobile banking, e-payment, internet banking, ATM banking and POS banking. Therefore, the model takes the following form:

$$PD = \beta_0 + \beta_1 MB + \beta_2 EP + \beta_3 IB + \beta_4 ATM + \beta_5 POS + e$$

$$PF = \beta_0 + \beta_1 MB + \beta_2 EP + \beta_3 IB + \beta_4 ATM + \beta_5 POS + e$$

Where,

PD = Productivity

PF = Profitability

MB = Mobile banking

EP = E-payment

IB = Internet banking

ATM = Automated teller machine

POS = Point of sales

Mobile banking was measured using a 5-point Likert scale where the respondents were asked to indicate the responses using 1 for strongly disagree and 5 for strongly agree. There are 5 items and sample items include "I can carry out my banking operations easily using mobile banking", "I trust the network connectivity while doing a transaction using mobile banking" and so on. The reliability of the items was measured by computing the Cronbach's alpha ($\alpha = 0.737$).

E-paymentwas measured using a 5-point Likert scale where the respondents were asked to indicate the responses using 1 for strongly disagree and 5 for strongly agree. There are 4 items and sample items include "E-payment system is better than cash and saves time", "E-payment offers a greater choice for consumer and merchant in the way they sent and receive payments" and so on. The reliability of the items was measured by computing the Cronbach's alpha ($\alpha =0.714$).

Internet banking was measured using a 5-point Likert scale where the respondents were asked to indicate the responses using 1 for strongly disagree and 5 for strongly agree. There are 5 items and sample items include "Internet banking saves time and money", "Internet banking is more reliable and secured than traditional banking" and so on. The reliability of the items was measured by computing the Cronbach's alpha ($\alpha = 0.760$).

ATMbanking was measured using a 5-point Likert scale where the respondents were asked to indicate the responses using 1 for strongly disagree and 5 for strongly agree. There are 5 items and sample items include "ATM banking provides the customers with facility of withdrawing the money 24 hours a day, 7days a week through their debit cards", "My bank has located ATM machines in such place where customer can have easy access to it" and so on. The reliability of the items was measured by computing the Cronbach's alpha ($\alpha = 0.733$).

Point of sales was measured using a 5-point Likert scale where the respondents were asked to indicate the responses using 1 for strongly disagree and 5 for strongly agree. There are 5 items and sample items include "POS in my bank manages employees, and offer customer rewards programs", "POS system maintains much needed accuracy by generating accurate reports in the banks" and so on. The reliability of the items was measured by computing the Cronbach's alpha ($\alpha = 0.769$).

Productivitywas measured using a 5-point Likert scale where the respondents were asked to indicate the responses using 1 for strongly disagree and 5 for strongly agree. There are 5 items and sample items include "Proper implementation of e-banking facilities will help to increase productivity", "E-payment technology offers cost saving opportunity to banks which helps to increase productivity" and so on. The reliability of the items was measured by computing the Cronbach's alpha ($\alpha = 0.820$).

Profitability was measured using a 5-point Likert scale where the respondents were asked to indicate the responses using 1 for strongly disagree and 5 for strongly agree. There are 5 items and sample items include "Mobile banking provides competitive advantage and increase profitability of bank", "New innovation in the bank helps to retain customers and gain long term profitability" and so on. The reliability of the items was measured by computing the Cronbach's alpha ($\alpha = 0.830$).

The following section describes the variables used in this study.

Mobile Banking

Mobile banking refers to provision of banking and bank related financial services with the help of mobile telecommunication devices. Amin*et al.* (2008) examined the adoption of mobile banking in Malaysia. The study showed that adoption of mobile banking by financial institutions is very important in improvement of financial adequacy of commercial banks as well as improving operations, reducing costs in the long run hence increase in earnings. Similarly, Ijeoma (2018) determined the impact of the mobile banking on the financial performance of commercial banks in Kenya. The study found a positive relationship between mobile banking and bank's profitability and productivity. Moreover, Kiplangat and Tibbs

(2018) found a positive influence of mobile banking on financial performance of commercial banks. Based on it, this study develops following hypothesis:

H_1: There is a positive relationship of mobile banking technology with bank productivity and profitability.

E-payment Technology

Electronic payment is also referred as a financial exchange that takes place online between buyers and sellers. Frank and Binaebi (2019) concluded that the adoption of electronic payment improved the returns on equity of Nigerian banks. Similarly, Mustapha (2018) revealed that introduction of electronic payment systems into the financial sector leads to increase in the profitability and productivity of banks. Likewise, Jayawardhena and Foley (2000) showed that internet and mobile banking and electronic payment results in cost and efficiency gains for banks. Based on it, this study develops following hypothesis:

H_2: There is a positive relationship of electronic payment system with bank productivity and profitability.

Internet Banking

Kim *et al.* (2006) defined internet banking as the process whereby the customer is able to access, control and use his or her account over the internet. Murat and Isaac (2019) found that the effect of internet banking on the bank performance is positive and significant. Likewise, Noah *et al.* (2019) found that internet banking has a significant and positive influence on productivity through efficiency and profitability. The study concluded that internet banking leads to strategic advantage against competitors and increases the likelihood of customer loyalty. Similarly, Mateka *et al.* (2016) found that internet banking has a positive impact on bank's productivity and profitability i.e. incomes, operating costs, and loan book and customer deposits. Based on it, this study develops following hypothesis:

H_3: There is a positive relationship of internet banking with bank productivity and profitability.

ATM Banking

Mwai *et al.* (2018) found that online banking has a significant influence on the financial deepening of commercial banks in Kenya. The study found that ATM banking has positive influence on financial performance of the banks. Likewise, Dhungel *et al.* (2012) found that ATM has a positive influence on productivity, profitability and customer satisfaction. Similarly, Abdullai and Nyaoga (2017) concluded that ATMs usage is highly related to the operational efficiency of commercial banks in Kenya. The study showed that the adoption of automated teller machine has a positive influence on operational performance. Based on it, this study develops following hypothesis:

H_4: There is a positive relationship of ATM banking with bank productivity and profitability.

POS Banking

Saleem *et al.* (2019) revealed that due to cashless banking like POS, the profitability of the banking sector results in better economic activity and growth of Pakistan's banking industry. Likewise, Njoroge and Mugambi (2018) revealed that increase in POS leads to an increase in the bank performance in Kenya. Further, the study showed that increase in debit card usage enhances the profitability of banking industry in form of ROA. Increased usage of debit cards has significantly reduced transaction costs and enhanced convenience among credit and debit card users. Furthermore, Okon and Amaegberi (2018) revealed that there is a positive and statistically significant relationship between point of sale banking service and bank productivity in Nigeria. The study indicated that point of sale is a major factor that contributes to the bank profitability and productivity in Nigeria. Based on it, this study develops following hypothesis:

H_5: There is a positive relationship of POS banking with bank productivity and profitability.

Results and Discussion

Correlation Analysis

On analysis of data, correlation analysis has been undertaken first and for this purpose, Kendall's Tau correlation coefficients along with mean and standard deviation have been computed and the results are presented in Table 2.

Table 2: Kendall's Tau Correlation Coefficients Matrix

This table presents Kendall's Tau correlation coefficients between dependent variable and independent variables. The correlation coefficients are based on 160 observations. The dependent variables are PRD (Productivity) and PF (Profitability). The independent variables are MB (Mobile Banking), EP (E-Payment), IB (Internet Banking), ATM (Automated Teller Machine), and POS (Point of Sales).

Variables	*Mean*	*SD*	*PRD*	*PF*	*MB*	*EP*	*IB*	*ATM*	*POS*
PRD	4.249	0.466	1						
PF	4.258	0.442	0.565**	1					
MB	4.284	0.425	0.438**	0.415**	1				
EP	4.128	0.543	0.372*	0.343**	0.443**	1			
IB	4.288	0.422	0.490**	0.410*	0.415**	0.462**	1		
ATM	4.287	0.428	0.392*	0.387**	0.470**	0.372**	0.425**	1	
POS	4.157	0.522	0.428**	0.377*	0.311**	0.342**	0.435**	0.439**	1

Note: The asterisk signs (**) and (*) indicate that the results are significant at one percent and five percent levels respectively.

The result shows that internet banking is positively related to bank productivity indicating that increase in internet banking leads to increase in the bank productivity. Similarly, ATM services are positively related to bank productivity. It means that better ATM services leads to increase in bank productivity. The result also shows that mobile banking is positively related to bank productivity. It means that better mobile banking services leads to increase in bank productivity. Likewise, point of sale is positively correlated to bank productivity. It indicates that increase in point of sale services in retail stores leads to increase in bank productivity. Similarly, e-payment technology has a positive relationship with bank productivity. It means that better e-payment technology leads to increase in bank productivity.

On the other hand, internet banking is positively related to bank profitability indicating that increase in internet banking leads to increase in the bank profitability. Similarly, ATM services are positively related to bank profitability. It means that better ATM services leads to increase in bank profitability. The result also shows that mobile banking is positively related to bank profitability. It means that better mobile banking services leads to increase in bank profitability. Likewise, point of sale is positively correlated to bank profitability. It indicates that increase in point of sale services in retail stores leads to increase in bank profitability. Similarly, e-payment technology has a positive relationship with bank profitability. It means that better e-payment technology leads to increase in bank profitability.

Regression Analysis

Having indicated the Kendall's Tau correlation coefficients, the regression analysis has been carried out and the results are presented in Table 3. More specifically, it shows the regression results of mobile banking, e-payment banking, internet banking, ATM banking and POS banking on productivity in Nepalese commercial banks.

Table 3 shows that the beta coefficients for mobile banking are positive with productivity. It indicates that mobile banking has a positive impact on bank productivity. This finding is similar to the findings of Ijeoma (2018). Likewise, the beta coefficients for e-payment technology are positive with bank productivity. It indicates that e-payment technology has a positive impact on bank productivity. This finding is consistent with the findings of Mustapha (2018). Similarly, the beta coefficients for internet banking are positive with bank productivity. It indicates that internet banking has a positive impact on bank productivity. This result is consistent with the findings of Murat and Isaac (2019). Further, the beta coefficients for ATM are positive with bank productivity. It indicates that ATM has a positive impact on bank productivity. This finding is consistent with the findings of Mwai *et al.* (2018). In addition, the beta coefficients for point of sales are positive with bank productivity. It indicates that point of sales has positive impact on bank productivity. This finding is similar to the findings of Okon and Amaegberi (2018).

Table 3: Estimated Regressions of Mobile Banking, E-payment Banking, Internet Banking, ATM Banking and POS Banking on Bank Productivity

The results are based on 160 observations using linear regression model. The model is $PD= \beta_0 + \beta_1 MB + \beta_2 EB + \beta_3 IB + \beta_4 ATM + \beta_5 POS + \beta$, *where the dependent variable is PD is productivity. The independent variables are MB (Mobile Banking), EP (E-Payment), IB (Internet Banking), ATM (Automated Teller Machine), and POS (Point of Sales).*

Model	*Intercept*	*Regression Coefficients of*					*Adj. R_bar²*	*SEE*	*F-value*
		MB	*EP*	*IB*	*ATM*	*POS*			
1	1.937	0.540					0.299	0.347	68.663
	(6.190)**	(8.286)**							

Model	*Intercept*	*Regression Coefficients of*					*Adj. R_bar²*	*SEE*	*F-value*
		MB	*EP*	*IB*	*ATM*	*POS*			
2	2.420		0.443				0.209	0.368	42.970
	(8.625)**		(6.555)*						
3	1.647			0.607			0. 349	0.335	86.210
	(5.850)**			(9.285)**					
4	2.221				0.473		0.249	0.348	67.345
	(8.935)**				(8.206)*				
5	1.792					0.592	0.312	0.344	73.175
	(6.209)**					(8.554)**			
6	1.550	0.416	0.222				0.332	0.339	40.557
	(5.127)**	(5.496)**	(2.997)**						
7	0.954	0.308	0.054	0.408			0.426	0.314	40.312
	(3.145)**	(4.211)**	(0.715)	(5.157)**					
8	0.806	0.218	0.027	0.354	0.204		0.457	0.305	34.482
	(2.700)**	(2.842)**	(0.368)	(4.501)**	(3.164) **				
9	0.389	0.255	0.017	0.263	0.116	0.292	0.502	0.293	33.018
	(1.272)	(3.439)**	(0.231)	(3.324)**	(1.758)	(3.853)*			

Notes:

i. Figures in parenthesis are t-values.

ii. The asterisk signs (**) and (*) indicate that the results are significant at one percent and five percent level of significance respectively.

iii. Productivity is dependent variable.

Table 4 shows the regression results of mobile banking, e-payment banking, internet banking, ATM banking and POS banking on profitability in Nepalese commercial banks.

Table 4: Regression Results of Mobile Banking, E-payment Banking, Internet Banking, ATM Banking and POS Banking on Bank Profitability

The results are based on 160 observations using linear regression model. The model is $PR = \beta_0 + \beta_1 MB + \beta_2 EB + \beta_3 IB + \beta_4 ATM + \beta_5 POS + \beta$, where the dependent variable is PR is profitability. The independent variables are MB (Mobile Banking), EP (E-Payment), IB (Internet Banking), ATM (Automated Teller Machine), and POS (Point of Sales).

Model	*Intercept*	*Regression Coefficients of*					*Adj. R_bar²*	*SEE*	*F-value*
		MB	*EP*	*IB*	*ATM*	*POS*			
1	2.142	0.494					0.236	0.372	50.092
	(7.127)**	(7.078)**							
2	2.636		0.393				0.154	0.392	29.999
	(8.846)**		(5.477)**						

Model	Intercept	Regression Coefficients of					Adj. R¯bar^2	SEE	F-value
		MB	EP	IB	ATM	POS			
3	1.994			0.528			0. 249	0.369	53.640
	(6.420)**			(7.324)*					
4	2.510				0.408		0.206	0.379	42.146
	(9.265)**				(6.492)**				
5	2.306					0.470	0.184	0.385	36.928
	(7.145)**					(6.077)*			
6	1.819	0.319	0.185				0.256	0.367	28.400
	(5.548)**	(4.763)**	(2.310)*						
7	1.325	0.302	0.047	0.338			0.315	0.353	25.381
	(3.894)**	(3.673)**	(0.548)	(3.804)**					
8	1.212	0.233	0.026	0.297	0.156		0.330	0.349	20.591
	(3.558)**	(2.657)**	(0.037)	(3.301)**	(2.123) *				
9	0.946	0.256	0.002	0.238	0.100	0.186	0.344	0.345	17.702
	(2.625)**	(2.932)**	(0.024)	(2.555)*	(1.288)	(2.088)*			

Notes:

i. *Figures in parenthesis are t-values*

ii. *The asterisk signs (**) and (*) indicate that the results are significant at one percent and five percent level respectively.*

iii. *Profitability is dependent variable.*

The regression results show that the beta coefficients for mobile banking are positive with profitability. It indicates that mobile banking has a positive impact on profitability. This finding is similar to the findings of Amin et al. (2008). Likewise, the beta coefficients for e-payment technology are positive with profitability. It indicates that e-payment technology has a positive impact on profitability. This finding is consistent with the findings of Frank and Binaebi (2019). Similarly, the beta coefficients for internet banking are positive with profitability. It indicates that internet banking has a positive impact on profitability. This result is consistent with the findings of Mateka *et al.* (2016). Further, the beta coefficients for ATM are positive with profitability. It indicates that ATM has a positive impact on profitability. This finding is consistent with the findings of Abdullai and Nyaoga (2017). In addition, the beta coefficients for point of sales are positive with profitability. It indicates that point of sale has positive impact profitability. This finding is similar to the findings of Njoroge and Mugambi (2018).

Summary and Conclusion

Today's every organizations are in need of good technology and innovations for the achievement of goal. There has been high competition among banking sectors to provide better quality services to customers. Banks discretionary devise technology-driven core strategies to leverage trends in information technology to pursue technological innovation in order to improve the productivity of employees. Employee productivity is a considerable unit of measure of a firm's performance and a source of sustaining competition.

This study attempts to examine the effect of innovation and technology on productivity and profitability in Nepalese commercial banks.The study is based on primary data which were collected from160 respondentsfrom25 Nepalese commercial banks.

The study showed that mobile banking, e- payment, internet banking, ATM banking, and POS banking have positive impact on productivity and profitability in Nepalese commercial banks. The study also concluded that internet banking followed by POS banking is the most influencing factor that explains the bank productivity. Similarly, the study also concluded that internet banking followed by mobile banking is the most influencing factor that explain the changes in profitability of Nepalese commercial banks.

References

1. Abdullai, H. M., and R. B. Nyaoga (2017). Effect of automated teller machines usage on operational performance of commercial banks in Nakuru County, Kenya. *InternationalJournal of Economics, Finance and Management Sciences, 5*(3), 162-167.
2. Appiah, E. E., and C. Agyemang (2006). Customers perception on the benefits of a cashless payment system in Ghana. *Journal of Business Research,* 2(1), 65-74.
3. Cobb, A. (2004). The impact of central bank of nigeria cashless policy in Nigeria economy. *Journal of Business and Management,* 12(1), 84-95.
3. Dhungel, A., B. Acharya, and K. U. Dhunge. (2012). Perception of bank customers about Automated Teller Machine (ATM) service quality. *Journal of Banking,* 2(2), 23-38.
4. Frank, B. P., and B. Binaebi (2019). Electronic payment systems implementation and the performance of commercial banks in Nigeria. *European Journal of Business and Management Research,* 4(5), 1-5.
5. Ijeoma, K. R. (2018). Impact of mobile banking on the bank profitability of Kenyan commercial banks. *School of Finance and Applied Economics,* 14(20), 33-35.
6. Joshi, C. (2019). Impact of automated teller machine (atm) service quality on customer satisfaction in the Nepalese commercial banks. *Journal of Marketing Research,* 3(1), 7-18.
7. Kim, B. M., R. Widdows and T. Yilmazer (2006). The determinants of consumers' adoptionof internet banking: Factors determining consumer adoption of internet banking. *Journal of Management Science,* 57(1), 291-307.
8. Mahdi, S., and A. Mehrdad (2010). E-banking in emerging economy: Empirical evidence of Iran. *International Journal of Economics and Finance,* 2(1), 201-209.
9. Mateka, M., J. Gogo, and J. Omagwa (2016). Effects of internet banking on financial performance of listed commercial banks in Kenya. *American Journal of Finance,* 1(2), 53-70.
10. Murat, A., and M. Isaac (2019). Effect of internet banking on the performance of first bank Nigeria Plc Abuja. *The International Journal of Social Sciences and Humanities Invention,* 6(8), 5559-5564.
12. Mustapha, S. A. (2018). E-Payment technology effect on bank performance in emerging economies–Evidence from Nigeria. *Journal of Open Innovation: Technology, Market, and Complexity — Open Access Journal,* 4(43), 1-14.

13. Mwai, A., F. S. Memba, and A. Njeru (2018). The relationship between ATM banking and financial deepening of commercial banks in Kenya. *International Journal of Economics, Commerce and Management,* 6(12), 496- 514.
14. Njoroge, M. N., and F. Mugambi (2018). Effect of electronic banking on financial performance in Kenyan commercial banks: Case of Equity bank in its Nairobi Central Business District branches, Kenya. *International Academic Journal of Economics and Finance,* 3(2), 197-215
15. Noah, A. M., A. O. Jagongo, and F. W. S. Ndede (2019). Effect of internet banking on financial performance of tier one commercial banks in Kenya. *Journal Entrepreneurship and Organization Management, 8*(1), 2-8.
16. Okon, A. N., and M. A. Amaegberi (2018). Mobile banking transactions and bank profitability in Nigeria. *International Journal of Economics, Commerce, and Management,* 6(6), 692-716.
17. Rafael, P., and R. F. Francisco (2007). Modeling financial innovation and economic growth: Why the financial sector matters to the real economy. *Journal of Regional Studies,* 41(3), 311-26.
18. Rust, R. T., and P. K. Kannan (2003). E-service: A new paradigm for business in the electronic environment. *Communications of the ACM,* 46(6), 37-42.
19. Saleem, Z., U. Akhter, I. Baber, I. Bashir, and S. A. Haider (2019). Impact of cashless banking on profitability in banking industry of Pakistan. *Journal of Global Scientific,* 7(3), 70-79.
20. Sapkota, N., N. Paudel, D. K. Subedi, R. Bhattarai, and R. Shrestha (2018). Role of point of sales in Nepalese banking industry. *American Scientific Research Journal for Engineering, Technology, and Sciences,* 42(1), 75-88.
21. Simpson, J. (2002). The impact of the internet in banking: observations and evidence from developed and emerging markets. *Telematics and Informatics,* 19(1), 315-330.
22. Amin, H., M. R. A. Hamid, S. Lada, and Z. Anis (2008). The adoption of mobile banking in Malaysia: The case of Bank Islam Malaysia Berhad (BIMB). *International Journal of Business and Society*, 9(2), 43-53.
23. Sabherwal, R., and Y. E. Chan (2001). Alignment between business and IS strategies: A study of prospectors, analyzers and defenders. *Information Systems Research*, 12(1), 11-33.
24. Dauda, D. Y., and W. A. Akingbade (2011). Technological change and employee performance in selected manufacturing industry in Lagos state of Nigeria. *Australian Journal of Business and Management Research*, 12(3), 115-127.
25. Obeng, A. Y., and P. L. Mkhize (2017). An exploratory analysis of employees and customers' responses in determining the technological innovativeness of banks. *The Electronic Journal of Information Systems in Developing Countries*, 80(1), 1-23.
26. Singh, H.,and E. Kamlesh (2013). Employee productivity of private sector banks in India. *International Journal of Management and Social Sciences Research*, 2(10), 64-79
27. Singh, J., and G. Kaur (2011). Customer satisfaction and universal banks: An empirical study. *International Journal of Commerce and Management*, 21(4), 327-348.
28. Agboola, A. (2006). Information and communication technology (ICT) in banking operations in Nigeria: An evaluation of recent experiences. *African Journal of Public Administration and Management*, 25(2), 56-76.
29. Benner, M. J., and M. Tushman (2002). Process management and technological innovation: A longitudinal study of the photography and paint industries. *Administrative Science Quarterly*, 47(4), 676-707.
30. Banstola, A. (2007). Prospects and challenges of e-banking in Nepal. *Journal of Nepalese Business Studies*, 4(1), 96-104.

31. DeYoung, R., W. W. Lang, and D. L. Nolle (2007). How the Internet affects output and performance at community banks. *Journal of Banking and Finance, 31*(4), 1033-1060.
32. Polatoglu, V., and S. Ekin (2001). An empirical investigation of the Turkish consumers' acceptance of Internet banking services. *International Journal of Bank Marketing, 19*(4), 156-165.
32. Kiplangat, K., D., and C. Tibbs (2018). Financial innovations and financial performance of commercial banks. *International Journal of Innovative Research and Development,* 7(5), 36-41.
33. Koivu, T. (2002). Do efficient banking sectors accelerate economic growth in transition countries? *International Journal of Bank Marketing,* 2(3), 24-26.
34. Jayawardhena, C., and P. Foley (2000). Changes in the banking sector: The case of internet banking in the UK. *Internet Research, 10*(1), 19-31.
35. Narteh, B. (2014). Internal marketing and employee commitment: Evidence from the Ghanaian banking industry. *Journal of Finance Services Marketing,* 17(4), 284-300.
36. Dzombo, G. K., M. K. James, and M. James (2017). The effect of branchless banking strategy on the financial performance of commercial banks in Kenya. *International Journal of Financial Research, 8*(4), 167-183.

MANAGING MUNICIPAL SOLID WASTE IN INDIA: A CASE STUDY OF ROHTAK MUNICIPAL CORPORATION

Parmod Malik

Abstract

Municipal solid waste generation in Indian cities is estimated to have more than from 55 million tons in 2020. Municipal solid waste generation reflects not only just income levels but also life styles choices. A paradigm shift towards environmental policy and municipal waste disposal has been observed in India, during swatch Bharat Abhiyan. The 74th constitutional amendment of 1992 transferred the responsibility for collection, treatment and disposal of Municipal solid waste from state government to the urban local bodies. Municipal solid waste rules 2000 and 2016 were promulgated in which Municipal solid waste service from generation to disposal was mandated and local government made responsible for compliance. This research explores the potential benefits of municipal waste disposal legislation in for the sustainable development in developing countries. The current research also explored the challenges faced by developing countries regarding municipal waste disposal legislation and suggested relevant policies to address the identified problems for the sustainable development of the municipal waste disposal. Secondary data regarding municipal waste disposal worldwide were utilized to provide empirical evidence of municipal waste disposal legislation's importance for developing countries. This study also underlined key challenges regarding environmental specifically municipal waste disposal legislation in developing countries. Indigenous methods which were based on principle of prevention is better than cure is the need of the hour. The paper also presents a case study of Municipal solid waste of Rohtak Municipal Corporation, highlighting the unique experiences, lessons learnt, success stories and evolution in managing Municipal solid waste and process of collection, transport and disposal of Municipal solid waste where Rohtak Municipal Corporation is spending Rs. 85 Lakhs for handling Municipal solid waste by assigning tender to M/S Parvati Enterprises for complete sanitation programme of Rohtak Municipal Corporation area.

Keywords: *Municipal Solid Waste, Sanitation, Rohtak, Disposal*

Introduction

India, 2nd largest populated country, 2% of the geographic area of world, having more than 4000 cities and 664,369 villages facing one of the major problem now a day is municipal solid waste. As the urbanization, industrialization process is on the peak it increases the production of municipal solid waste too. Government of India started and thought about MSW first time in fourth 5 year plan which was implemented during 1969 to 1974. Government of India has also appointed high level committee to curb the problem of MSW and finding the solution for the same in 1975 which has given its suggestions and recommendation. National Scheme of Solid Waste Disposal was also started to composting the MSW in some major cities. But in spite of all these efforts, the problem of MSW increased with the pace of time as due to process of urbanization, the production of MSW was higher than disposal. In 1990's National Waste Management Council was constituted by Ministry of environment to curb the MSW management. In 1998, Government of India drafted Recycled Plastic Usages Rules which tried to ban the storing and packaging of food items in plastic bags. These efforts were not enough from sigh of relief as insurmountable mountains of MSW were seen in outskirt of major cities in India, so the high powered committee was constituted to find out the solution to manage MSW. This High Powered Committee also known as Bajaj Committee recommended for door to door collection of wastes/garbage, disposing it in appropriate manner. As per Hon'ble Supreme Court, Barman Committee was appointed and it has framed the MSW rules 2000. As per MSW Rules 2000, Local bodies such as Municipal Corporations were held responsible for collection, transportation and composting, treatment, segregation and disposal of MSW. Landfilling was only allowed for non-biodegradable wastes. The Government enforced the Solid Waste Management Rules, 2016 to monitor the proper and adequate disposal of the solid wastes generated. The Parliamentary standing committee on Urban Development submitted its report on Solid Waste Management Including Hazardous Waste, Medical Waste And E-Waste in 2021 and placed action taken report which recommended for extensively using plastic for road construction. Swachh Bharat Mission (Urban) which was launched by government of India in 2014, central assistance is provided to states and there has been significant improvement in the processing of MSW and door-to-door collection. It is correctly said by Talyan (2008) that despite consistent efforts of government of India and various states and regulatory bodies, the implementation of these rules is still a distant dream.

Municipal Corporation Rohtak – A Case Study

Rohtak one of district and major city of Haryana falls under the category of national capital region. It has population of 4,77,999 in 2022 of which more than 80% literacy rate. It has area of 1,745 Sq. Km There are 20 wards in Municipal Corporation Rohtak, in which both residential and commercial areas are included in door to door collection of garbage and garbage is collected from all these areas. Wet and dry garbage are collected from all areas by engaging by 45 tractors trolleys and 40 garbage tickers and one refuse collector and one dumper placer and placed 100% to solid waste plant. Tenders have been allotted to M/S Parvati Enterprises by way of bid for different wards of Rohtak Municipal Corporations. The rate of tender for collection is about 85 lakhs per months for some wards. It is more than 3 crores of rupees for whole Rohtak municipal corporation territory. There are 4 stages for MSW disposal.

(a) Collection
(b) Transportation
(c) Segregation
(d) Disposal either in Landfill or other manner

M/S Parvati Enterprises has made a MSW disposal plant at village Sunaria District Rohtak. Tender has been allotted to this M/S Parvati Enterprises for Rs. 16,40,000 per month for processing of municipal solid wastes. The tender is given to M/S Parvati Enterprises for waste collection also that has install informal waste picker at solid waste plant. Municipal Corporation Rohtak has entered into agreement with M/S Parvati Enterprises for the same.

As per discussion with the employees of /S Parvati Enterprises, it is observed that there is need of more awareness in Rohtak citizens to segregate between wet and dry garbage before pouring into garbage tickers as it will help them to dispose it off properly.

Suggestions

1. **Awareness Programmes:** Although Swacch Bharat Abhiyan is very much successful for spreading awareness in villages and cities, but consistent efforts are needed for these types of projects. We have to take lessons from some foreign countries and adopt their habits to eradicate such types of problems.
2. **Reward Scheme:** Reward scheme should be initiated to encourage the general public to collection and disposition of wastes.
3. **Penalties:** Time has come to impose penalties to those who are negligent in following these rules. We have no option now as water surpass our head.
4. **Frugal Innovation:** is the ability to do more with less. It is to create significantly more business and social value while minimizing the use of diminishing resources such as energy, capital and time.
5. **Create sustainable mode of disposing MSW:** More R and D is needed for inventing the sustainable use of resources and disposing the wastes.
6. Institutional Training Mechanism for all persons concerned with environmental department.
7. **Investment in R and D:** We can see that composting is only method of disposing MSW. We have to devise new technology to cure and dispose off MSW. But based on the principle of 'Prevention is better than cure' will be far effective than finding out solution. We the people of India have to take pledge that we should create minimum to minimum garbage and waste and dispose it as per rules and recommendations of the governments.
8. **Public access to Decision Making:** Environmental issues are best handled with the participation of all concerned citizens at relevant level.
9. **Latest Technology and new innovative methods:** Landfilling is not solution. We have to devise the technologies which help us to convert these non-biodegradable waste to some utilization. As it is stated that India generated more than 65 million tonnes of MSW every year of which only 20% is processed. It is matter of concern for us. So government of India and state government should come together and find out easy and cheap sustainable processing methods of disposal.
10. **Waste Minimization:** Basis on the principle of prevention is better than cure, we have to work on the root cause i.e. creation of garbage. We have to use indigenous mode of living which have no wastage way. Recycle, Reusing and recreate should be future for us otherwise we have no space to live and take breath.

11. **Public-Private Partnership:** There is need of entering public- private partnership between government and private bodies for collection and disposing the MSW. Rohtak and some other cities are example of this. PPP mode is need of the hour. Municipal Corporations are levy tax in bill as per cooperative mode. We cannot blame government always. It is our fundamental duty also to value and preserve the rich heritage of our composite culture and to protect and improve the natural environment including forests, lakes, rivers, wildlife and to have compassion for living creatures;
12. **Corporate Social Responsibility:** It is time for corporation also to come forward and contribute to the society by spending some part of their earning in municipal Solid Wastes. They can also contribute by way of not producing solid waste also in their premises.

The 17 identified sustainable goals adopted by 193 countries of the world on 25 September 2015 also assured about the availability and sustainable management of water and sanitation for all and to ensure sustainable consumption and production pattern. It is correctly said by Ramani that some individual and organization who will experiment to find creative ways of pursuing opportunities. If successful, they will become role models, provoking emulation and imitation, and more than policy they will be the agents of transformative change.

The management of municipal solid waste is one of the main functions of all Urban Local Bodies as directed by Parliament. all Urban Local Bodies are required to meticulously plan, implement and monitor all systems of urban service delivery especially that of municipal solid waste. With limited financial resources, technical capacities and land availability, urban local bodies are constantly striving to meet this challenge. Centre and state government coordination is also required.

References

1. Ramani Shyama V., Innovation in India, Combining Growth with inclusive development, Cambridge University Press, 2014.
2. Radjou Navi and Prabhu Jaideep, Frugal Innovation, How to do better with Less, Hachette India with The Economist, 2015.
3. Malik P., Environment Related Aspects of Intellectual Property Rights, in Intellectual Property Branding in the Developing World, Editors Prof. Vijender Kumar, Satyam Law International, 2021.
4. http://mcrohtak.gov.in/sanitation_wing.htm.
5. https://www.niti.gov.in/sites/default/files/2021-12/Waste-Wise-Cities.pdf.

ROLE OF MICROFINANCE ON WOMEN EMPOWERMENT: A CASE OF KATHMANDU VALLEY

Anita Sapkota and Nar Bahadur Bista

Abstract

This study examines the role of microfinance on women empowerment in Kathmandu Valley. Financial independency, decision making and self-confidence are the dependent variables. The selected independent variables are entrepreneurial skills, access to resources, leadership skills and self-efficacy. The primary sources of data are used to assess the opinions of the respondents regarding the role of microfinance on women empowerment in Kathmandu Valley. The study is based on primary data from 154 respondents. To achieve the purpose of the study, structured questionnaire is prepared. The regression models are estimated to test the significance and importance of microfinance on women empowerment in Kathmandu Valley.

The study showed that entrepreneurial skills have positive impact on financial independency, decision making and self-confidence. It implies that increase in entrepreneurial skills leads to increase in financial independency, decision making and self-confidence of women. Similarly, access to resource has a positive effect on financial independency, decision making and self-confidence. It indicates that increase in access to resources leads to increase in financial independency, decision making and self-confidence of women. The result also showed that leadership skills have positive impact on financial independency, decision making and self-confidence. It indicates that better the leadership skills, higher would be the financial independency, decision making and self-confidence of women. Similarly, self-efficacy has a positive effect on financial independency, decision making and self-confidence. It indicates that increase in self-efficacy leads to increase in financial independency, decision making and self-confidence.

Keywords: *Financial Independency, Decision Making, Self-confidence, Entrepreneurial skills, Access to Resources, Leadership Skills and Self-efficacy*

Introduction

Microfinance is a type of banking service which provides access to financial and non-financial services to low income or unemployed people. Microfinance is a powerful tool to self-empower the poor people especially women especially in developing countries. Women empowerment means to let women survive and let them live a life with dignity, humanity, respect, self-esteem and self-reliance. Kabeer (2001) stated that women empowerment is the process to acquire the ability from which those who have been denied the ability to make the strategic life choices. Women empowerment is a continuous process where the powerless people become conscious of their situation and organize to improve it and access opportunities, gain skills, solve problems and develop self-reliance. Snijder (2009) defined empowerment as giving somebody the power or authority to do something. Women empowerment means increased access of women to financial resources, income generating assets or activities, saving, increased financial decision-making power and more economic independence (Mayoux, 2008). Empowerment can be viewed as means of creating a social environment in which one can make decisions and make choices either individually or collectively for social transformation. Empowerment of women is essentially the process of upliftment of economic, social and political status of women in the society. Women empowerment involves building up of a society where women can breathe without the fear of oppression, exploitation, apprehension, discrimination and the general feeling of persecution which goes with being a woman in a traditionally male dominated structure. Chaudhry and Nosheen (2009) revealed that women empowerment is one of issue of present-day development policies in developing countries.

Microfinance institutions are effective institutions providing basic services like saving, microcredit, and training. Microfinance institutions are an important economic development agent intended to benefit women and lower-income people (Duflo, 2012). Microfinance institution has a great role in alleviating economic problem, creating self-employment opportunities, developing businesses for female entrepreneurs. Sarumathi and Mohan (2011) found that microfinance has built confidence, courage, skill development and empowerment among women who are participating in Self-Help Groups (SHG). The study showed that there is a positive improvement in psychological and social empowerment among rural women due to their participation in microfinance programs. Similarly, Banerjee *et al.* (2010) examined that there is no significant impact of microfinance on measures of women's decision-making over issues of household spending, investment, savings, or education.

Bhardwaj and Gebrehiwot (2012) showed that there is an improvement in socioeconomic condition of women who participated in microfinance programs. It has improved the role of women in family and also their ability to take decisions regarding various matters without depending on others. Das (2012) revealed that microfinance programs have a positive influence on the economic status, knowledge, decision-making power and self-worthiness of women participants, with a significant improvement in income, assets/wealth, and standard of living. The study also found that the SHG's have brought social and psychological empowerment. Arora and Meenu (2011) found that microfinance has been successfully contributing to women empowerment at great extent. It has also benefited their families by giving access to credit for housing repair, education and marriage of their children and it has also improve the saving habits of women. Sarkar and Baishya (2012) found that MFIs have contributed to the economic growth and development of woman of Assam, resulting in increase in resources and also well-being of the entire family. The study found that women's access to credit has a significant role in improving their decision-making capacity, work force participation rate and even political and legal awareness, thereby opening opportunity for greater empowerment of women of Assam. Prabhakara (2012) showed that there is a remarkable improvement in the status and recognition of women in the society after joining Self-Help Groups (SHG). Gowda and Manjula (2012) revealed that women were able to increase their income and provide financial help to their families. The study also found that microfinance has brought a positive impact in their economic and social situation, which helped women to take an important role in the decision-making process in their family and also in society.

According to Nader (2008), microfinance plays an important role in women empowerment, especially their inclination towards family wellbeing and children education. Providing access to microfinance for women is considered to be a precondition of poverty alleviation and women's empowerment (Mayoux, 2006). Rehman *et al.* (2020) examined the role of microfinance institutions in women empowerment in the context of Akhuwat, Pakistan. The study identified that age, education levels of women and levels of income are significant factors that influence women empowerment. This study also confirmed that although MF has impact on women's lives but there are other factors as well that are associated to women that affect their decision making ability. Noreen (2011) assessed the role of microfinance in empowerment of female population of Bahawalpur district. The study showed that women empowerment is considerably influenced by age, education of husband, father inherited assets, marital status, number of sons alive and microfinance.

Aruna and Jyothirmayi (2011) explored the role of microfinance in women empowerment: A study on the SHG bank linkage program in Hyderabad (Andhra Pradesh). The findings of the study showed that microfinance has a profound influence on the economic status, decision making power, knowledge and self-worthiness of women participants of self-help group linkage program in Hyderabad. The microfinance related loan availement and its productive utilization have significant differences in women empowerment levels, measured through women empowerment index (WEI), of the loan availed participants as compared to the non- loan availed. Microfinance is the provision of broad range of financial service such as deposits, loans, payments, money transfers and insurance to the low income households and their micro enterprises to break out of their impoverishment (Lazer, 2008). Empowerment of women is one of very important issue in developing countries. As women are integral part of society, her status and participation in decision making as well as economic activities is very low. Microfinance plays role in improving women decision making by contributing in economic activities (Noreen, 2011). Although women access to financial resources has substantially increased yet loans given to women differ in sizes. In spite of this, just financial help not enough to empower women and improve wellbeing but if they are properly designed then they make important contribution to women empowerment (Herath *et al.*, 2015). Microfinance affect women's ability or decision making and self-confidence which is closely linked with knowledge, women's status and gender relations at home. Microfinance program strengthen women's economic autonomy and gives them means to pursue nontraditional activities. Through these programs women escaped from abusive relationship. By providing them opportunity for self-employment, these programs have significantly improved women security, autonomy, self-confidence and status within the household which in turn improves women empowerment. Hunt and Kasynathan (2002) described that microfinance programs for women have positive impact on economic growth by improving women income generating activities.

In the context of Nepal, Adhikari and Shrestha (2013) noticed that participating in microfinance programs increase women power to purchase necessities independently, resist wife-beating, earned respect and participation in community level decisions. The study showed that microfinance is an effective tool for bringing positive impact on the economic status of the women along with their family members. Guvaju and Sherpa (2020) examined the impact of microfinance on women empowerment in Nepal. The study showed that there is a significant relationship between changing lifestyle of women entrepreneur and socio-economic activities with women empowerment. The results also showed that the socio-economic activities are performed well and there was contribution of women entrepreneurs in change the life style of the women. Sharma (2007) found that women's participation in micro-credit programs helps to increase women's empowerment.

The above discussion shows that empirical evidences vary greatly across the studies on the role of micro finance on the women empowerment. Though there are above mentioned empirical evidences in the context if other countries and in Nepal, no such findings using more recent data exist in the context of Nepal. Therefore, in order to support one view or the other, this study has been conducted.

The main purpose of the study is to examine the role of microfinance on women empowerment in Kathmandu Valley. Specifically, it examines the impact of entrepreneurial skills, access to resources, leadership skill and self-efficacy on financial independency, decision making and self-confidence of women in Kathmandu Valley.

The remainder of this study is organized as follows. Section two described the sample, data and methodology. Section three presents the empirical results and the final sections draw the conclusion.

Methodological Aspects

The study is based on primary data. The data were gathered from 154 respondents through questionnaire. The respondent' views were collected on entrepreneurial skills, access to resources, leadership skills, financial independency, decision making, self-confidence and self-efficacy. This study is based on descriptive as well as causal comparative research designs.

The Model

The model estimated in this study assumes that financial independency, decision making and self-confidence depends on different variables such as entrepreneurial skills, access to resources, leadership skills and self-efficacy. Therefore, the models take the following forms:

$$FI = \beta_0 + \beta_1 ES + \beta_2 AR + \beta_3 LS + \beta_4 SE + \beta_{it}$$

$$DM = \beta_0 + \beta_1 ES + \beta_2 AR + \beta_3 LS + \beta_4 SE + \beta_{it}$$

$$SC = \beta_0 + \beta_1 ES + \beta_2 AR + \beta_3 LS + \beta_4 SE + \beta_{it}$$

Where,

FI = Financial independency

DM = Decision making

SC = Self-confidence

ES = Entrepreneurial skills

AR = Access to resources

LS = Leadership skills
SE = Self-efficacy

Entrepreneurial skill was measured using a 5-point Likert scale where the respondents were asked to indicate the responses using 1 for strongly disagree and 5 for strongly agree. There are 7 items and sample item include "I have keen interest in trying or exploring new things to find what works best", "I have the courage to act on my ideas and plan" and so on. The reliability of the item was measured by computing the Cronbach's alpha ($\alpha = 0.904$).

Access to resources was measured using a 5-point Likert scale where the respondents were asked to indicate the responses using 1 for strongly disagree and 5 for strongly agree. There are 6 items and sample item include "I have ability to obtain credit at reasonable rates from traditional sources (collateral)", I have ability to repay the old debts and meeting domestic obligations like marriage, health and education" and so on. The reliability of the item was measured by computing the Cronbach's alpha ($\alpha = 0.868$).

Leadership skill was measured using a 5-point Likert scale where the respondents were asked to indicate the responses using 1 for strongly disagree and 5 for strongly agree. There are 6 items and sample item include "I have ability to make decisions on my own without consulting others", "I am capable of driving creativity and styles productivity while also improving the bottom line of a business" and so on. The reliability of the item was measured by computing the Cronbach's alpha ($\alpha = 0.874$).

Self-efficacy was measured using a 5-point Likert scale where the respondents were asked to indicate the responses using 1 for strongly disagree and 5 for strongly agree. There are 7 items and sample item include "I have ability to perform a particular activity", "I can support my sisters or friends morally if they decide to face a family legal action" and so on. The reliability of the item was measured by computing the Cronbach's alpha ($\alpha = 0.865$).

Financial independency was measured using a 5-point Likert scale where the respondents were asked to indicate the responses using 1 for strongly disagree and 5 for strongly agree. There are 5 items and sample item include "I am able to earn income for my family", "I am involved to promote economic activities" and so on. The reliability of the item was measured by computing the Cronbach's alpha ($\alpha = 0.827$).

Decision making was measured using a 5-point Likert scale where the respondents were asked to indicate the responses using 1 for strongly disagree and 5 for strongly agree. There are 5 items and sample item include "I can make decision regarding health of family members", "I can make decision regarding education of children" and so on. The reliability of the item was measured by computing the Cronbach's alpha ($\alpha = 0.810$).

Self-confidence was measured using a 5-point Likert scale where the respondents were asked to indicate the responses using 1 for strongly disagree and 5 for strongly agree. There are 5 items and sample item include "I feel that I'm a person of worth, at least on an equal plane with others", "I feel that I have a number of good qualities" and so on. The reliability of the item was measured by computing the Cronbach's alpha ($\alpha = 0.741$).

The following section describes the independent variables used in this study along with the hypothesis formulation.

Entrepreneurial Skill

Entrepreneurship is an individual's ability to turn ideas into action. It includes creativity, innovation and risk-taking, as well as the ability to plan and manage projects in order to achieve objectives. Al-Dajani and Marlow (2013) revealed that marginalized subordinated women were empowered through their home-based enterprises. The result showed that entrepreneurial skills have positive impact on women empowerment. Similarly, Ul-Hameed *et al.* (2018) found that entrepreneurial skills and social capital are key elements to enhance women empowerment. Moreover, Paramanandam and Packirisamy (2015) revealed that entrepreneurial skills play significant role to empower women in marketing and production, which are keys to success and for becoming self-reliant. Based on it, this study develops the following hypothesis:

H_1: There is a positive relationship between entrepreneurial skills and women empowerment.

Access to Resources

Access to resources is the opportunity to make use of resources for a larger gain. Access to resources in this study refers to the ability of women to use resources to a greater extent. According to Ackerly (1995), effect of microfinance services is higher when women actually control the resources acquired in their names. Increased control is likely to contribute to women's empowerment, facilitate women's entrepreneurship, assist women in their reproductive tasks and ease their repayment burden. Kabeer (2005) revealed that access to financial resources make positive contribution to the economic productivity and social well-being of poor women and their households. In addition, Hashemi *et al.* (1996) revealed that women's access to credit has positive effect on empowerment. Moreover, Sinha and Matin (1998) found that access to financial services and the resultant transfer of financial resources to poor women over time have led to women becoming more confident and empowered. Based on it, this study develops the following hypothesis:

H_2: There is a positive relationship between access to resources and women empowerment.

Leadership Skill

Leadership skills are the strengths and abilities individuals demonstrate that help the oversee processes, guide initiatives and steer their employees toward the achievement of goals. Leadership skill affect the quality of work life of women and effective leadership skills helps to increase women empowerment (Nanjundeswaraswamy *et al.*, 2020). Govender and Vyas-Doorgapersad (2013) showed that leadership skills improved women empowerment and enhanced gender equality. Leadership skill and capacity continue to strengthen practice, reflection and relationships that provide authentic and rigorous with feedback and support (Das, 2014). Mehta and Sharma (2014) revealed that good leadership skills have a positive relationship with women empowerment. Based on it, this study develops the following hypothesis:

H_3: There is a positive significant relationship between leadership skill and women empowerment.

Self-efficacy

Self-efficacy is an individual's belief in their innate ability to achieve goals. Self-efficacy points at one's work role efficacy or personal mastery; women must feel that they are competent to engage in the behaviors required by the organization or family. Postmus *et al.* (2013) found positive and significant relationships between financial literacy with economic empowerment, economic self-efficacy and economic self-sufficiency. The results also indicated that financial literacy, race, and economic self-efficacy are significant predictors of economic empowerment. Empowerment is about self-actualization and competence. Forrester (2000) revealed that self-efficacy enables the women empowerment. Bandura (1982) found that self-efficacy helps to increase empowerment that combines intention and belief in one's ability into a women's outcome expectation. Al-Qahtani *et al.* (2021) indicated that high self-efficacy has a significant positive relationship with women empowerment. Moreover, Veisi *et al.* (2014) indicated a significant positive correlation between women empowerment and women self-efficacy. Based on it, this study develops the following hypothesis:

H_4: There is a positive relationship between self-efficacy and women empowerment.

Results and Discussions

Correlation Analysis

On analysis of data, correlation analysis has been undertaken first and for this purpose, Kendall's Tau correlation coefficients along with mean and standard deviation has been computed and the results are presented in Table 1.

Table 1: Kendall's Tau Correlation Coefficients Matrix

This table presents Kendall's Tau correlation coefficients between dependent variable and independent variables. The correlation coefficients are based on 154 observations. The dependent variables are FI (Financial independency), DM (Decision making) and SC (Self-confidence). The independent variables are ES (Entrepreneur skills), AR (Access to resources), LS (Leadership skills) and SE (Self-efficacy).

Variables	*Mean*	*SD*	*FI*	*DM*	*SC*	*ES*	*AR*	*LS*	*SE*
FI	3.840	0.694	1						
DM	3.811	0.658	0.617**	1					
SC	3.779	0.562	0.453**	0.492**	1				
ES	3.786	0.787	0.558**	0.473**	0.427**	1			
AR	3.796	0.758	0.550**	0.471**	0.404**	0.568**	1		
LS	3.806	0.710	0.552**	0.561**	0.441**	0.530**	0.559**	1	
SE	3.810	0.696	0.603**	0.488**	0.404**	0.537**	0.532**	0.564**	1

Notes: The asterisk signs (**) and (*) indicate that the results are significant at one percent and five percent level respectively.

The result shows that entrepreneurial skill has a positive relationship with financial independency. It indicates that increase in entrepreneurial skills leads to increase in financial independency of women. Similarly, access to resources has a positive relationship with financial independency. It indicates that increase in access to resources leads to increase in financial independency. The result also shows that leadership skills have a positive relationship with financial independency. It indicates that better the leadership skills, higher would be the financial independency. Similarly, self-efficacy is positively correlated to financial independency. It indicates that increase in self-efficacy leads to increase in financial independency.

Similarly, the result also shows that entrepreneurial skill has a positive relationship with decision making. It indicates that better entrepreneurial skills leads to better decision making ability of women. Likewise, access to resources has a positive relationship with decision making. It indicates that increase in access to resources leads to better decision making ability of women. The result also shows that leadership skills has a positive relationship with decision making. It indicates that good leadership skills leads to better decision making ability of women. Similarly, self-efficacy is positively correlated to decision making. It indicates that increase in self-efficacy leads to better decision-making ability of women.

In addition, entrepreneurial skill has a positive relationship with self-confidence. It indicates that increase in entrepreneurial skills leads to increase in self-confidence of women. Similarly, access to resources has a positive relationship with self-confidence. It indicates that increase in access to resources leads to increase in self-confidence. The result also shows that leadership skills have a positive relationship with self-confidence. It indicates that better the leadership skills, higher would be the self-confidence. Similarly, self-efficacy is positively correlated to self-confidence. It indicates that increase in self-efficacy leads to increase in self-confidence.

Regression Analysis

Having indicated the Kendall's Tau correlation coefficients, the regression analysis has been carried out and the results are presented in Table 2. More specifically, it shows the regression results of entrepreneurial skill, access to resources, leadership skills and self-efficacy on financial independency.

The regression result shows that the beta coefficients for entrepreneurial skills are positive with financial independency. It indicates that entrepreneurial skills have positive impact on financial independency. This finding is similar to the finding of Ul-Hameed *et al.* (2018). Likewise, the beta coefficients for access to resources are positive with financial independency. It indicates that access to resources has a positive impact on financial independency. This finding is consistent with the findings of Hashemi *et al.* (1996). Similarly, the beta coefficients for leadership skills are positive with financial independency. It indicates that leadership skills have a positive impact on financial independency. This finding is consistent with the findings of Mehta and Sharma (2014). Furthermore, the beta coefficients for self-efficacy are positive with financial independency. It indicates that self-efficacy has a positive impact on financial independency. This finding is similar to the findings of Forrester (2000). The result also shows that the beta coefficients of all the explanatory variables are significant at one percent level.

Table 2: Estimated Regression Results of Entrepreneurial Skills, Access to Resources, Leadership Skills and Self-efficacy on Financial Independency

The results are based on 154 observations using linear regression model. The model is FI= $\beta_0 + ß_1$ ES + $ß_2$ AR + $ß_3$ LS + $ß_4$ SE + e, where the dependent variable is FI (Financial independency). The independent variables are ES (Entrepreneurial skills), AR (Access to resources), LS (Leadership skills) and SE (Self-efficacy).

Models	*Intercept*	*Regression Coefficients of*				*Adj. R_ bar2*	*SEE*	*F-value*
		ES	*AR*	*LS*	*SE*			
1	1.330	0.663				0.562	0.459	197.191
	(7.285)**	(14.042)**						
2	1.185		0.669			0.581	452	212.495
	(6.383)**		(14.577)**					
3	0.961			0.756		0.595	0.442	225.592
	(4.930)**			(15.020)**				
4	0.717				0.820	0.673	0.395	315.541
	(4.013)**				(17.763)**			
5	0.931	0.352	0.415			0.641	0.416	137.769
	(5.215)**	(0.068)**	(5.888)**					
6	0.682	0.241	0.255	0.336		0.677	0.395	107.737
	(3.796)**	(3.460)**	(3.302)**	(4.186)**				
7	0.458	0.144	0.136	0.189	0.426	0.724	0.365	101.34
	(2.672)**	(2.145)*	(1.732)**	(2.383)*	(5.169)**			

Notes:

i. Figures in parenthesis are t-values
ii. The asterisk signs (**) and (*) indicate that the results are significant at one percent and five percent level respectively.
iii. Financial independency is dependent variable.

Table 3 shows the regression results of entrepreneurial skill, access to resources, leadership skills and self-efficacy on decision making.

The regression result shows that the beta coefficients for entrepreneurial skills are positive with decision making. It indicates that entrepreneurial skills have positive impact on decision making. This finding is similar to the finding of Al-Dajani and Marlow (2013). Likewise, the beta coefficient for access to resources are positive with decision making. It indicates that access to resources has a positive impact on decision making. This finding is consistent with the findings of Sinha and Matin (1998). Similarly, the beta coefficients for leadership skills are positive with decision making. It indicates that leadership skills have a positive impact on decision making. This finding is consistent with the findings of Das (2014). Furthermore, the beta coefficients for self-efficacy are positive with decision making. It indicates that self-efficacy has a positive impact on decision making. This finding is similar to the findings of Postmus *et al.* (2013). The result also shows that the beta coefficients of all the explanatory variables are significant at one percent level.

Table 3: Estimated Regression Results of Entrepreneurial Skills, Access to Resources, Leadership Skills and Self-efficacy on Decision Making

The results are based on 154 observations using linear regression model. The model is DM= $\beta_0 + \beta_1$ ES + β_2 AR + β_3 LS + β_4 SE + e, where the dependent variable is DM (Decision making). The independent variables are ES (Entrepreneurial skills), AR (Access to resources), LS (Leadership skills) and SE (Self-efficacy).

Models	*Intercept*	*Regression coefficients*				*Adj. R_bar2*	*SEE*	*F-value*
		ES	*AR*	*LS*	*SE*			
1	1.678	0.564				0.451	0.487	126.599
	(8.662)**	(11.252)**						
2	1.572		0.59			0.459	0.484	130.589
	(7.864)**		(11.428)**					
3	1.117			0.708		0.58	0.426	212.443
	(0.593)**			(14.575)**				
4	1.162				0.695	0.538	0.447	179.107
	(5.774)**				(13.383)**			
5	1.349	0.308	0.342			0.509	0.461	80.398
	(6.819)**	(4.088)**	(4.372)**					
6	0.978	0.143	0.103	0.531		0.599	0.416	77.266
	(5.162)**	(1.939)	(1.263)**	(5.908)**				
7	0.834	0.081	0.023	0.405	0.275	0.619	0.406	63.275
	(4.371)**	(1.071)	(0.269)	(4.591)**	(0.275)			

Notes:

i. Figures in parenthesis are t-values

ii. The asterisk signs (**) and (*) indicate that the results are significant at one percent and five percent level respectively.

iii. Decision making is dependent variable.

Table 4 shows the regression results of entrepreneurial skill, access to resources, leadership skills and self-efficacy on self-confidence.

The regression result shows that the beta coefficients for entrepreneurial skills are positive with self-confidence. It indicates that entrepreneurial skills have positive impact on self-confidence. This finding is similar to the finding of Paramanandam and Packirisamy (2015). Likewise, the beta coefficient for access to resources are positive with self-confidence. It indicates that access to resources has a positive impact on self-confidence. This finding is consistent with the findings of Ackerly (1995). Similarly, the beta coefficients for leadership skills are positive with self-confidence. It indicates that leadership skills have a positive impact on self-confidence. This finding is consistent with the findings of Govender and Vyas-Doorgapersad (2013). Furthermore, the beta coefficients for self-efficacy are positive with self-confidence. It indicates that self-efficacy has a positive impact on self-confidence. This finding is similar to the findings of Veisi *et al.* (2014). The result also shows that the beta coefficients of all the explanatory variables are significant at one percent level.

Table 4: Estimated regression results of entrepreneurial skills, access to resources, leadership skills and self-efficacy on self-confidence

The results are based on 154 observations using linear regression model. The model is SC= $\beta_0 + \beta_1$ ES + β_2 AR + β_3 LS + β_4 SE + e, where the dependent variable is SC (Self-confidence). The independent variables are ES (Entrepreneurial skills), AR (Access to resources), LS (Leadership skills) and SE (Self-efficacy).

Models	*Intercept*	*Regression coefficients*				*Adj. R_ bar2*	*SEE*	*F-value*
		ES	*AR*	*LS*	*SE*			
1	2.095	0.445				0.383	0.442	96.004
	(11.938)**	(9.798)**						
2	1.978		0.475			0.405	0.434	105.134
	(11.040)**		(10.253)**					
3	1.747			0.534		0.450	0.417	126.026
	(9.492)**			(11.226)**				
4	1.713				0.542	0.446	0.418	124.269
	(9.096)**				(11.148)**			
5	1.815	0.226	0.292			0.441	0.420	61.376
	(10.049)**	(3.290)**	(4.096)**					
6	1.592	0.127	0.149	0.300		0.483	0.404	48.696
	(8.652)**	(1.778)	(1.884)**	(3.650)**				
7	1.481	0.078	0.086	0.226	0.214	0.499	0.398	39.068
	(7.901)**	(1.066)	(1.051)	(2.611)**	(2.378)*			

Notes:

i. Figures in parenthesis are t-values
ii. The asterisk signs (**) and (*) indicate that the results are significant at one percent and five percent level respectively.
iii. Self-confidence is dependent variable.

Summary and Conclusion

Women empowerment is a broad concept which can be defined as the multidimensional social process that occurs at different levels and come with the relation to others. This is relative process of enhancing the capabilities of an individual, group and community as a whole that assist people to realize and understand their own inner capabilities and exercise it for the welfare of themselves and others.

This study attempts to examine the role of microfinance on women empowerment in the context of Kathmandu Valley. This study is based on primary data with 154 observations.

The study showed that entrepreneurial skills, access to resources, leadership skills and self-efficacy have significant impact on women empowerment. The study also showed that micro finance helps to empower the women in Kathmandu Valley. The study concluded that self-efficacy is the most influencing factor that explains the changes in financial independency of women. The study also concluded that leadership skills is the most influencing factor that explains the self-confidence and decision-making ability of women.

References

1. Ackerly, B. A. (1995). Testing the tools of development: Credit programs, loan involvement, and women's empowerment. *IDS Bulletin*, 26(3), 56-68.
2. Adhikari, D. B., and J. Shrestha (2013). Economic impact of microfinance in Nepal: A case study of the Manamaiju Village Development Committee, Kathmandu. *Economic Journal of Development Issues*, 16(2), 36-49.
3. Al-Dajani, H., and S. Marlow (2013). Empowerment and entrepreneurship: A theoretical framework. *International Journal of Entrepreneurial Behavior and Research*, 19(5), 503-524.
4. Al-Qahtani, A. M., H. A. Ibrahim, W. T Elgzar, H. A. El Sayed, and R. M. Essa (2021). The role of self-esteem and self-efficacy in women empowerment in the Kingdom of Saudi Arabia: A cross-sectional study. *African Journal of Reproductive Health*, *25*(1), 69-78.
5. Arora, S., and D. Meenu (2011). Women empowerment through microfinance intervention in the commercial banks: An empirical study in the rural India with special reference to the state of Punjab. *International Journal of Economic and Research*, 2(2), 35-45.
6. Aruna, M., and M. R. Jyothirmayi (2011). The role of microfinance in women empowerment: A study on the SHG bank linkage program in Hyderabad (Andhra Pradesh). *Indian Journal of Commerce and Management Studies*, *2(4)*, 77-95.
7. Bandura, A., L. Reese, and N. E. Adams (1982). Micro-analysis of action and fear arousal as a function of differential levels of perceived self-efficacy. *Journal of Personality and Social Psychology*, 43(1), 5-21.
8. Banerjee, A., E. Duflo, R. Glennerster, and C. Kinnan (2010). The Miracle of Microfinance? Evidence from a Randomized Evaluation. *American Economic Journal: Applied Economics*, 13(1), 253-268.
9. Bhardwaj, R. K., and K. Gebrehiwot (2012). Microfinance and women empowerment: An impact study of Self-Help Groups (SHGs) - An empirical study in the rural India with special reference to the state of Uttarakhand. *International Journal on Management*, 4(2), 8-16.
10. Chaudhry, I. S., and F. Nosheen (2009). The determinants of women empowerment in southern Punjab (Pakistan): An empirical analysis. *European Journal of Social Sciences*, 10(2), 216-229.
11. Das, N. (2014). The empowering of destitute women at wish home through leadership programs: A case study. *Indian Journal of Health and Wellbeing*, *5*(6), 760-763.
12. Das, S. K. (2012). Socio-economic empowerment of women through SHG-banking linkage program: A boon for development. *International Journal of Management and Business Studies*, 2(1) 39-46.
13. Duflo, E. (2012). Women empowerment and economic development. *Journal of Economic Literature*, 50(4), 1051-79.
14. Forrester, R. (2000). Empowerment: Rejuvenating a potent idea. *Academy of Management Perspectives*, 14(3), 67-80.
15. Govender, S. D., and S. Vyas-Doorgapersad (2013). The implementation of gender equality policies in achieving millennium development goal three in the Sedibeng District Municipality. *Journal of Public Administration*, *48*(1), 105-117.
16. Guvaju, S., and D. K. Sherpa (2020). A study of impact of microfinance on women empowerment in Nepal. *LBEF Research Journal of Science, Technology and Management,* 2(3), 25-32.
17. Gowda, C., & B. G. Manjula (2012). Impact of microfinance on poor people: A study of

living standards, empowerment and poverty alleviation in the Davangere district of Karnataka state. *International Journal of Research in Commerce, Economics & Management*, *2*(5), 56-59.
18. Hashemi, S. M., S. R. Schuler., and A. P. Riley (1996). Rural credit programs and women's empowerment in Bangladesh. *World Development*, 24(4), 635-653.
19. Herath, H. M. W. A., L. H. P. Guneratne, and N. Sanderatne (2015). Impact of microfinance on women's empowerment: a case study on two microfinance institutions in Sri Lanka. *Sri Lanka Journal of Social Sciences*, *38*(1), 51-61.
20. Hunt, J., and N. Kasynathan (2002). Reflections on microfinance and women's empowerment. *Development Bulletin*, *57*(1), 71-75.
21. Kabeer, N. (2001). Conflicts over credit: Re-evaluating the empowerment potential of loans to women in rural Bangladesh. *World Development*, 29(1), 63-84.
22. Kabeer, N. (2005). Gender equality and women's empowerment: A critical analysis of the third millennium development goal. *Gender and Development*, 13(1), 13–24.
23. Lazer, D. (2008). *Microfinance and Poverty Eradication-Indian and Global Experience*. New Delhi: New Century.
24. Mayoux, L. (2006). Women's empowerment through sustainable microfinance: Rethinking "Best Practice". *Eldis Gender Guide*, 1(1), 47-62.
25. Mayoux, L. (2008). Micro-finance and the empowerment of women: A review of the key issues. *ILO Working Papers 993441343402676*.
26. Mehta, P., and K. Sharma (2014). Leadership: Determinant of women empowerment. *SCMS Journal of Indian Management*, 11(2), 5-10.
27. Nader, Y. F. (2008). Microcredit and the socio-economic wellbeing of women and their families in Cairo. *The Journal of Socio-Economics*, *37*(2), 644-656.
28. Nanjundeswaraswamy, T. S., D. R. Swamy., and P. Nagesh (2020). Leadership styles in mediating the relationship between quality of work life and employee commitment. *International Journal for Quality Research*, 14(2), 387-412.
29. Noreen, S. (2011). Role of microfinance in empowerment of female population of Bahawalpur district. *International Journal of Economics and Finance Research*, 4(20), 65-71.
30. Paramanandam, D. A., and P. Packirisamy (2015). An empirical study on the impact of micro enterprises on women empowerment. *Journal of Enterprising Communities: People and Places in the Global Economy*, 9(4), 298-314.
31. Postmus, J. L., S. B. Plummer, S. McMahon, and K. A. Zurlo (2013). Financial literacy: Building economic empowerment with survivors of violence. *Journal of Family and Economic Issues*, 34(3), 275-284.
32. Prabhakara, K.V. (2012). Micro finance empowers women evidence from India NGO. *Online International Interdisciplinary Research Journal*, 2(2), 157-164.
33. Rehman, H., D. A. Moazzam, and N. Ansari (2020). Role of microfinance institutions in women empowerment: A case study of Akhuwat, Pakistan. *South Asian Studies*, *30*(1), 107-125.
34. Sarkar, S., and S. Baishya (2012). Impact of microfinance in women empowerment of Assam. *Barnolipi – An Interdisciplinary Journal*, *5*(1), 47-68.
35. Sarumathi, S., and K. Mohan (2011). Role of micro finance in women's empowerment: An empirical study in Pondicherry region rural SHG. *Journal of Management and Science*, 1(2), 1-8.
36. Sharma, P. R. (2007). Micro-finance and women empowerment. *Journal of Nepalese Business Studies*, 4(1), 16-27.
37. Sinha, S., and I. Matin (1998). Informal credit transactions of micro-credit borrowers in rural Bangladesh. *IDS Bulletin*, 29(4), 66-81.

38. Snijders, A. L. (2009). Women Empowerment in South India. Measurement. *International Journal of Social Economics,* 6(4), 22-24.
39. Ul-Hameed, W., H. Mohammad, and H. K. Shahar (2018). Microfinance institute's non-financial services and women-empowerment: The role of vulnerability. *Management Science Letters*, 8(1), 1103-1116.
40. Veisi, S., A. Azizifar, H. Gowhary, and A. Jamalinesari (2015). The relationship between Iranian EFL teachers' empowerment and teachers' self-efficacy. *Procedia-Social and Behavioral Sciences*, 185(1), 437-445.

PART III: AGRICULTURE AND SUSTAINABILITY

KNOWLEDGE OF FARMERS RELATED TO PADDY STRAW MANAGEMENT TECHNIQUES IN HARYANA

Preeti Sihan, Ashok Kumar, Neelam Kumari and Shivam

Abstract

Rice (Oryza sativa L.) is a vital cereal food crop for more than half of the world's population. In Indian context, rice occupies a pivotal place and contributes about 13 per cent of annual agriculture GDP and provides 43 % calorie requirement for more than 70 % of Indian population. India is the second largest producer of rice after China.Crop residues are the materials which are left in an agricultural field after the crop harvested. These residues involve stalks, stems, leaves and seed pods. The huge quantity of paddy straw after the combine harvesting of paddy has to be managed in 15-20 days to plant next succeeding wheat crop. Traditionally, straw was seen as a versatile by-product of rice cultivation because it was used in many ways including fodder for livestock and as a building material. However, the increase in productivity and area under cultivation of rice has led to a huge production of rice straw. Moreover, mechanization decreased the animal dependency and hence the feed requirement. The most effective way of disposing of the residue in recent days is seen as burning of biomass in the paddy field. So, it has acquired very serious dimensions during the recent past. The problem is severe in irrigated agriculture, particularly in the mechanized rice-wheat system. Haryana is the leading paddy producing state of India. It is being cultivated in an area of about 1.35 million ha and having a production of 4.14 million tonnes. Ambala, Yamunanagar, Kurukshetra, Karnal, Sonipat, Kaithal, Panipat, Jind and Bhiwani are the major paddy-growing districts of the state. However, the cultivation of high yielding varieties of paddy has helped in ensuring food security in the state but at the same time has resulted in production of huge quantities of crop residues. It is also generating around 20 million tonnes of paddy straw in the state. There are diverse set of productive techniques for paddy straw management that can be utilised such as composting, straw as a ruminant fodder, incorporated in the soil, gasification, bailing, mushroom farming, production of bio-fuel, recycling in soil, packing material and bio-char production. Apart from this, paddy straw also used for various purposes i.e., in boilers for parboiling rice in West Bengal, thatching for rural houses, power generation, paper mills and stable bedding or as a raw material in industrial processes, etc. Conservation agriculture also provides a good promise in utilising this abundant paddy straw through the use of different implements e.g.,rotavators, happy seeders, paddy straw chopper, zero–till-drills, etc. for better soil health, increasing productivity, reducing pollution and enhancing sustainability and resilience on agriculture. Moreover, India's first plant to convert paddy straw into biogas that can be utilised as CNG in automobiles will come up at Karnal in Haryana as agencies double effort to stop burning of crop stubble. Several initiatives are also started by the Central and State Government for paddy straw management. Keeping in view the above facts, a study on 'To assess the knowledge of farmers related to paddy straw management techniques in Haryana' was conducted. The present research was conducted in Sonipat and Karnal districts of

Haryana state. These districts were selected purposively. Both the districts were having large area under rice cultivation and are near to National Capital Region (NCR). Two blocks were selected randomly from each selected district i.e., Sonipat, Rai, Karnal and Nilokheri. Two villages were selected randomly from each selected block. Thus, four villages, namely, Chhatera, Bindhroli and Uldepur, Zahiriwere selected from Rai and Sonipat blocks. Whereas Sultanpur, Naraina and Kunjpura, Mohidinpur villages were selected from Nilokheri and Karnal blocks, respectively. From each selected village, 15 farmers were selected through simple random sampling technique. Thus, a total number of 120 farmers were interviewed for the present study. The specific objective of the present research was to assess the knowledge of farmers related to paddy straw management techniques. The data were collected through well-structured interview schedule. Eleven important independent variables, namely, age, education, socio-economic status, land holding, farm Implements, mass media exposure, extension contact, irrigation facilities, risk orientation, cropping system, soil health card and dependent variables, namely, knowledge, adoption and constraints perceived by the farmers in in adoption of paddy straw management techniques were selected for the research. The research revealed that majority of the farmers were associated to middle age category and having general caste, majority of the farmers were educated up to matriculation. Majority were engaged in farming used both submersible pump and canal as source of irrigation. Most of the farmers had medium socio-economic status, farm implements, mass media exposure, extension contact. Mostly farmers were belonged to low category of risk orientation The knowledge level of respondents regarding PSMT associated too high to medium level. Among the techniques of paddy straw domestic purpose, animal fodder, Rotavator, Happy Seeder was well known and most of them adopted were domestic purpose, animal fodder, spreader/ shrub master, super SMS (attached with Combine Harvester). The results of the correlation showed that out of 11 independent variables, education, socio- economic status, mass media exposure and extension contact showed positive and highly significant correlation with the knowledge level of the respondents about PSMT at 0.01 level of probability. While age, risk orientation, cropping system and soil health card showed positive and significant correlation with the knowledge level about PSMT at 0.05 level of probability. However, land holding, farm implements and irrigation facilities showed positive and non-significant correlation with the knowledge level of the respondents about PSMT. All the 11 independent variables jointly contributed to 67.33 per cent (R^2 = 0.6333) of variation in the knowledge level. This means that only 67.33 per cent of the variation in the dependent variable was due to these independent variables and the remaining 32.67 per cent was due to unexplained variables. Further, it was found that one unit change in education, socio- economic status, mass media exposure, risk orientation, extension contact and cropping system experience would result in a corresponding change of 2.022, 0.781, 0.682, 0.575, 2.681 and 0.989 unit change in the knowledge level of paddy straw management techniques, respectively.

Keywords: *Knowledge, Paddy Straw, Farm Implements, Socio-Economic Status*

Introduction

Rice (*Oryzasativa* L.) is a vital cereal food crop for more than half of the world's population. It belongs to the family Graminae/ Poaceae and prefers wet tropical climate for its growth and development. In case of nutritional benefits, rice contains 7% of protein, 36–58% of crude fat, 16–25%of crude ash, 21% of calcium, 47–52% of thiamine, 35-43% of riboflavin, and 45–55% of niacin.More than 90 per cent of the world's rice is produced and consumed in Asia, where it is an integral part of culture and tradition.

In Indian context, rice occupies a pivotal place and contributes about 13 per cent of annual agriculture GDP and provides 43 per cent calorie requirement for more than 70 per cent of Indian population. India is the second largest producer of rice after China and has an area of over about 88.07 million hand production of 117.47 million tonnes with productivity of 2424 kg/ha and approximately 500 million tonnes of paddy straw is generated annually. Among different states, West Bengal, Uttar Pradesh, Punjab, Odisha, Bihar, Chhattisgarh, Andhra Pradesh, Telangana, Haryana, Tamil Nadu are the 10 top leading states in rice production. Whereas in case of crop residue production, Uttar Pradesh (60 Mt) is ranked as highest producer of crop residue followed by Punjab (51 Mt) and Maharashtra (46 Mt) (Anonymous, 2019).

Generally, crop residues are the materials which are left in an agricultural field after the crop harvested. These residues involve stalks, stems, leaves and seed pods. The huge quantity of paddy straw after the combine harvesting of paddy has to be managed in 15-20 days to plant next succeeding wheat crop. Straw is the only organic material available in abundance after the harvest of the rice crop. The total biomass of this straw depends on various factors such as varieties, soils and nutrient management and weather. At harvest, rice straw is piled or spread in the field depending on the harvesting methods, using stationary threshers or self-propelled combine harvesters, respectively. The amount of rice straw taken off the field depends mainly on the cutting height (i.e., height of the stubble left in the field). About 40% of the nitrogen (N), 30-35% of the phosphorus (P), 80-85% of the potassium (K) and 40-50% of the sulphur (S) taken up by rice straw in vegetative plant parts at crop maturity. Although, straw is a significant source of micronutrients such as zinc (Zn) and the most important influence on the cumulative silicon (Si) balance in rice.There is loss of plant nutrients such as Nitrogen (N), Phosphorous (P), Potassium (K), Sulphur (S) and carbon, which are crucial for soil health (Erenstein et al., 2002).More than half of the respondents (51.67%) had medium knowledge level, while 33.33 per cent of them had high knowledge level and 15.00 per cent had low knowledge level regarding rice production (Kirar and Mehta, 2009). Kumar (2010) revealed that majority of the respondents (73.33%) had medium knowledge level, whereas 14.17 per cent of them had high knowledge level and 12.50 per cent of the farmers had low knowledge level about recommended wheat production technology.

Haryana is the leading paddy producing state of India. It is being cultivated in an area of about 1.35 million ha and having a production of 4.14 million tonnes (Anonymous, 2019). Ambala, Yamunanagar, Kurukshetra, Karnal, Sonipat, Kaithal,Panipat,Jind and Bhiwani are the major paddy-growing districts of the state. However, the cultivation of high yielding varieties of paddy has helped in ensuring food security in the state but at the same time has resulted in production of huge quantities of crop residues. It is also generating around 20 million tonnes of paddy straw in the state.

Taking farmers view into account, burning is not only a cost-effective method but it acts as an effective pest control procedure and it also helps to reduce diseases that may occur due to reinjection from inoculums in the straw biomass. But, the burning of rice crop residue causes atmospheric pollution by emitting trace gases which forms 'Black Cloud' adversely affects human health as well as environment (Haysa*et al.*, 2005).Fairhurst (2002) in their research studied that the major effect of straw removal was on the soil K balance.

Keeping in view the above facts, a study on 'Knowledge and Adoption of Paddy Straw Management Techniques in Haryana' was proposed with following specific objectives:

- To assess the knowledge of farmers related to paddy straw management techniques.

Methodology

The present study was conducted in Haryana state. Two districts viz. Sonipat and Karnal were selected purposively because both the districts were having large rice cultivated area and near to National Capital Region (NCR). Two blocks were selected randomly from these districts, namely, Sonipat and Rai blocks were selected from Sonipat district and Karnal and Nilokheri blocks were selected from Karnal district. Two villages were selected randomly from each selected block. Thus, four villages namely - Chhatera, Bindhroli, Uldepur and Zahiri were selected from Rai and Sonipat blocks. Whereas Sultanpur, Naraina, Kunjpura and Mohidinpur villages were selected from Nilokheri and Karnal blocks respectively. From each selected village, 15 farmers were selected through simple random sampling technique. Thus, a total number of 120 farmers were interviewed for the present study (Fig 1).

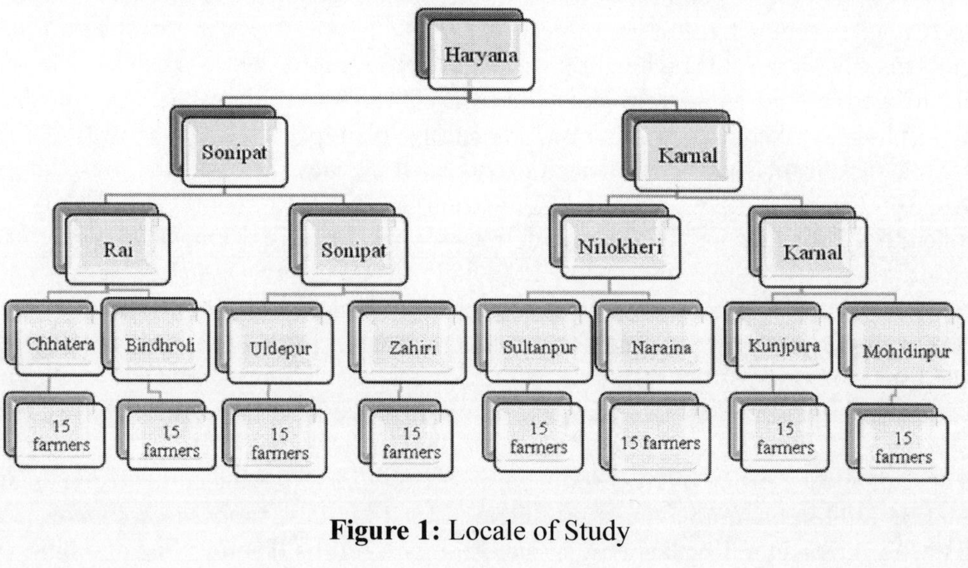

Figure 1: Locale of Study

Analysis of Data

The information collected through the responses of the respondents with the help of schedule was suitably coded and analyzed to draw meaningful inferences by using statistical tools such as frequency, percentage, mean and standard deviation along with correlation and regression.

Statistical Tools used in the Study

Frequency

The number of times an individual item is repeated in a series is called its frequency. The way in which the observations are classified and distributed in the proper class intervals is known as frequency distribution.

Percentage

Percentage is a number or ratio expressed as a fraction of 100. It is often denoted by using the per cent sign, "%", or the abbreviation "pct."; sometimes the abbreviation "pc" is used in the case of quantities in economics. A percentage is a dimension less number (pure number).

Coefficient of Correlation (r)

The Karl Pearsons' coefficient of correlation was applied to test the linear x and y relationship between variables. The formula used is as under:

$$r = \frac{N\,(XY - ((X)((Y)}{(N\,(X^2 - ((X)^2\,(N\,(Y^2 - ((Y)^2}$$

Where,

N = Number of observations

ΣXY = Sum of product of x and y

ΣX = Summation of entries of I[st] variable

ΣY = Summation of entries of IInd variable

ΣX^2 = Sum of square value of each entry of I[st] variable

ΣY^2 = Sum of square value of each entry of IInd variable

Significance of observed correlation coefficient was tested by using:

$$t_{cal.} = \frac{r}{\sqrt{1 - r^2}}\sqrt{n - 2} \sim t_{N-2}$$

if $|t_{cal}|^3$ to t_{tab} then observed coefficient of correlation was significant at 1% or 5% value of t for N-2 or n d.f.

Multiple Regressions

It is used to measure the variables on the dependent variables by the independent variables by fitting the multiple regression equation given by Snedecor and Cochran (1968).

$$Y = a + b_i X_1 + b_2 X_2 \ldots\ldots\ldots\ldots\ldots\ldots\ldots\ldots\; bnXn$$

Where,

Y = Dependent variable

a = Constant

b_i = Partial regression coefficient which represents the amount of change in y

n = Total number of independent variables

Partial regression (b) was tested by using t test as:

$$t_{cal} = \frac{b_i}{SE\ (bi)}$$

if $|t_{cal}|^3$ to t_{tab} then observed regression coefficient was significant at 1% or 5% value of t for N-2 or n d.f.

Where,

N = No. of independent variables

b_i = partial regression coefficient

SE (b) = Standard error of partial regression coefficient

Rank Order

Rank order means that the observation having highest score among all other observations was assigned as rank I.

Results and Discussions

With a view to study the profile of the respondents some of the antecedent factors that were considered to be related with the paddy straw management techniques were included in this study. It includes age, education, caste, family type, family size, socio-economic status, land holding, farm implements, mass-media exposure, extension contact, irrigation facilities, social participation, soil health card, risk orientation and cropping system. The factor wise profile is given below:-

Table 1: Respondents' Personal Profile (n =120)

S No.	*Variables*	*Categories*	*Frequency (percentage)*
1.	Age	Young (up to 35) years	13 (10.83)
		Middle (36-50) years	81 (67.50)
		Old (more than50) years	26 (21.67)
2.	Education	Illiterate	08 (06.66)
		Primary	12 (10.00)
		Middle	20 (16.67)
		Matriculation	52 (43.33)
		Higher secondary	21 (17.50)
		Graduate	06(05.00)
		Post Graduate	01(00.84)
3.	Socio-economic status	Low (<18) score	13 (10.83)
		Medium (18-26) score	79 (65.84)
		High (>26) score	28 (23.33)
4.	Land holdings	Landless (Up to 2.5 acres)	00 (00.00)
		Less than 1 acre	09 (07.50)
		Above 1 and up to 5 acres	62 (51.67)
		Above 5 and up to 10 acres	34 (28.33)
		Above 10 to 15 acres	13 (10.84)
		Above 15 acres	02(01.66)

S No.	*Variables*	*Categories*	*Frequency (percentage)*
5.	Irrigation facilities	Submersible pump Canal Both	24 (20.00) 08 (06.00) 89 (74.00)
6.	Farm implements	Low (<3) score Medium (3 - 6)score High (>6) score	12 (10.00) 75 (62.50) 33 (27.50)
7.	Mass media exposure	Low (<8) score Medium (8-11)score High(>11) score	20(16.67) 66 (55.00) 34 (28.33)
8.	Extension contact	Low (<6)score Medium (6 – 9)score High (>9)score	40(33.33) 62 (51.67) 18 (15.00)
9.	Risk Orientation	Low (< 9) score Medium (9-18)score High (>18) score	57 (47.50) 56 (46.67) 07 (05.83)
10.	Cropping pattern	Mono cropping Inter-cropping Double cropping Multiple cropping	59 (49.16) 08 (06.67) 48(40.01) 05(04.16)
11.	Soil Health Card	Do you have Soil Health Card SHC helps to indicate the soil health SHC encourage judicious application of fertilizers Are you aware about the SHC tenure	72 (60.00) 72 (60.00) 72 (60.00) 41 (34.16)

Age

It is referred to the chronological age of the respondent at the time of investigation. The age of the respondents was recorded as mentioned by them in completed years. The data

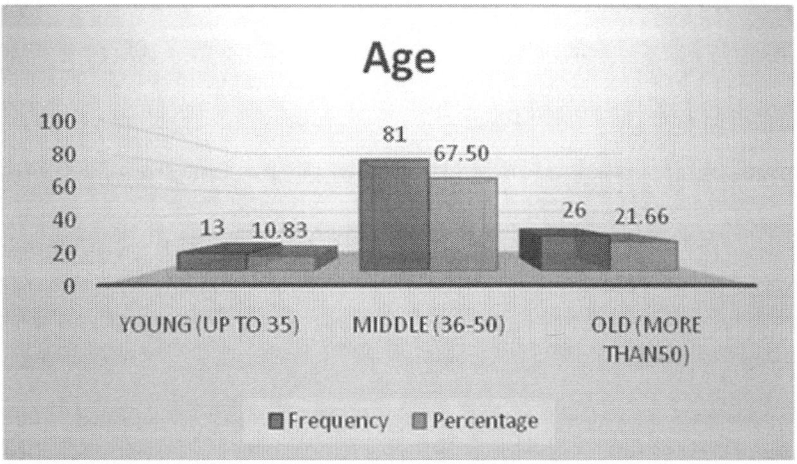

Figure 2: Distribution of Respondents According to their Age

suggested in table 1 revealed that most of the percentage of the farmers were associated to middle age groups (67.50%) followed by old age group (21.67%) and rest (10.83%) of farmers come under young age group. Moreover, age plays an essential role in adoption or rejection of an innovation.

Education

It was a significant element which effect the adoption of respondents. The result obtained has been presented in table and it reveals that (43.33 %) respondents were qualified to matriculation followed by (17.50%) completed their higher secondary schooling, (16.67%) came under middle category while (10.00%) were educated up to primary, (06.66%) of them were illiterate and graduate (5.00 %) followed by (00.84%) of the respondents were educated up to post graduation level. It could be collected that most of the respondents were qualified up to matriculation respectively in the study area.

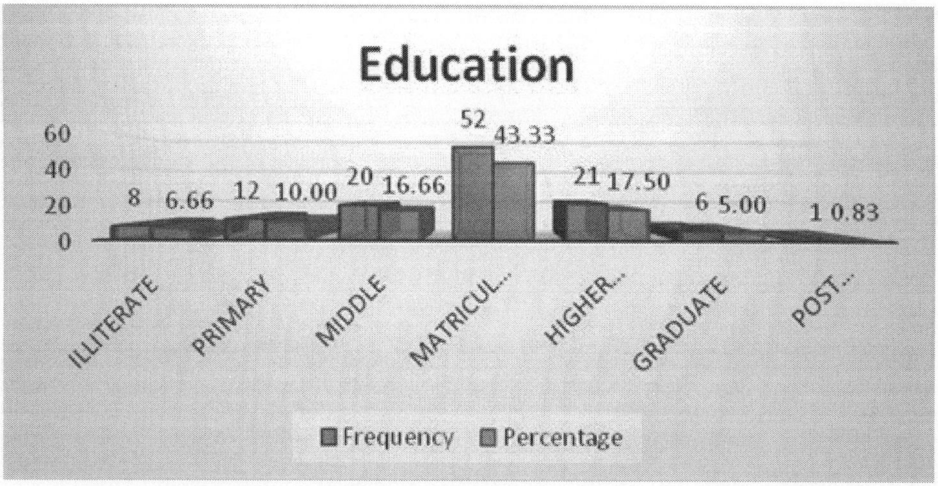

Figure 3: Distribution of Respondents According to Their Education

Socio-Economic Status

Socio-Economic status is an economic and sociological combined total measure of a person's work experience and of an individual's or family's economic and social position in relation to others. When analysing a family's SES annual income, social participation, caste, family type, family size and risk orientation are examined, whereas for an individual's SES only their own attributes are assessed. Majority of the farmers (65.84%) had medium category as socio-economic status followed by high category (23.33%) and low category (10.83%) (Figure 4).

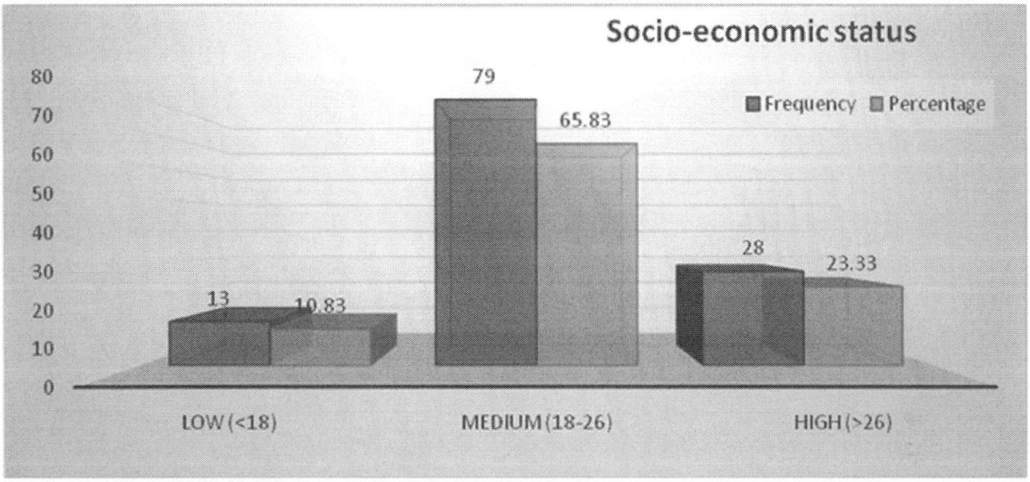

Figure 4: Distribution of Respondents According to Their Socio-Economic Status

Land Holdings

It is a piece of land owned or rented. A perusal of data shown in table 4.1 reported that about half of the farmers (51.67 %) were having above 1 and up to 5 acres of land followed by (28.33%) had above 5 and up to 10 acres.While (10.84%) farmerswere found in above 10 to 15 acresfollowed by (07.50%) with having less than 1 acre.Above 15 acres were to the tune of (01.66%) pursued by (00.00%) come under landless (Fig. 5).

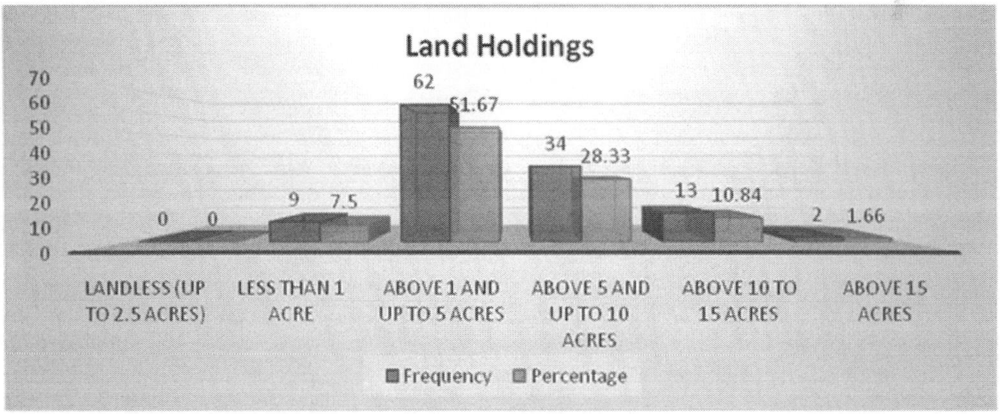

Figure 5: Distribution of Respondents According to Their Land Holdings

Irrigation Facilities

The data shown in the Table 1 Demonstrates that majority of the respondents (74.00%) used both submersible pump and canals irrigation followed by (20.00%) used submersible pump for irrigation and (06.00%) farmers used canals on their farmland for irrigation (Fig. 6).

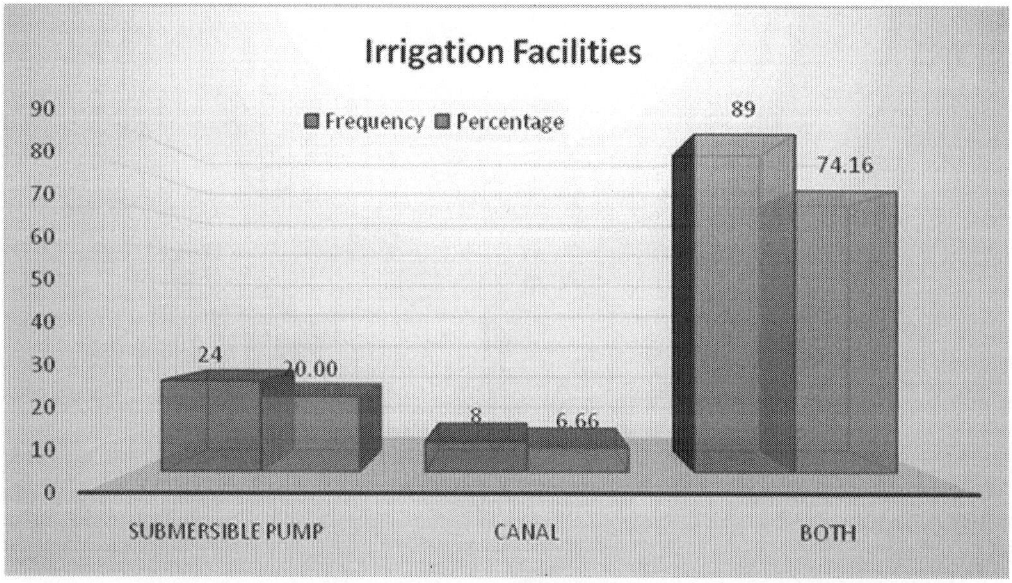

Figure 6: Distribution of Respondents According to Their Irrigation Facilities

Farm Implements

It is evident from the data included there in table 1 that most of the farmers (62.50%) were reported under medium category followed by (27.50%) high category, (10.00%) was found under low category of having farm implements (Fig. 7).

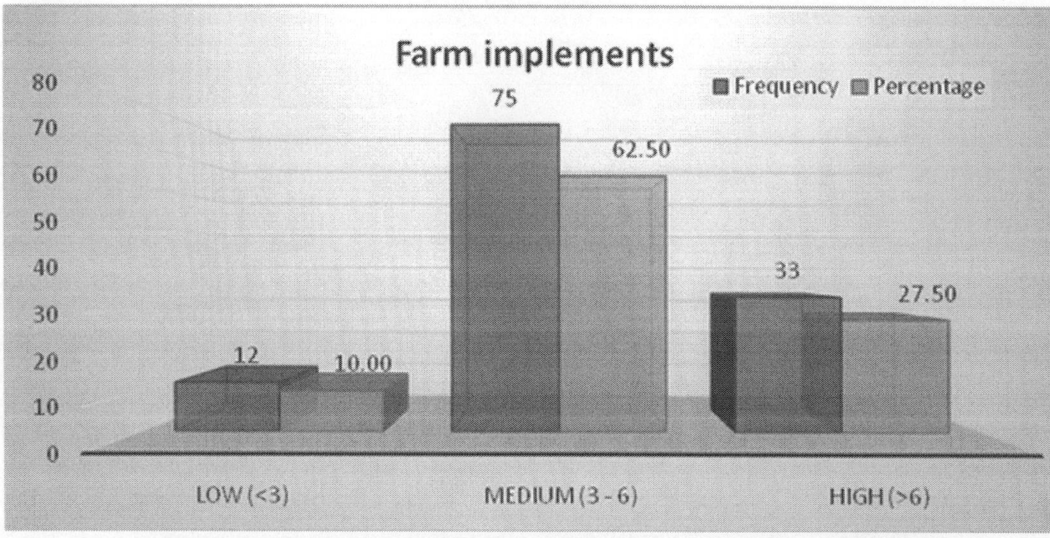

Figure 7: Distribution of Respondents According to Their Farm Implements

Mass Media Exposure

It is a medium of communication that is designed to reach the mass of the people.Mass media is the written, spoken and visual technology which carry information from its source to receivers, readers, listeners and viewers. The data in Table 1 show about the information pursuing behaviour of the farmers, it was observed that medium category was found with (55.00 %) followed by high with (28.33 %), (16.67 %) with low category (Fig. 8).

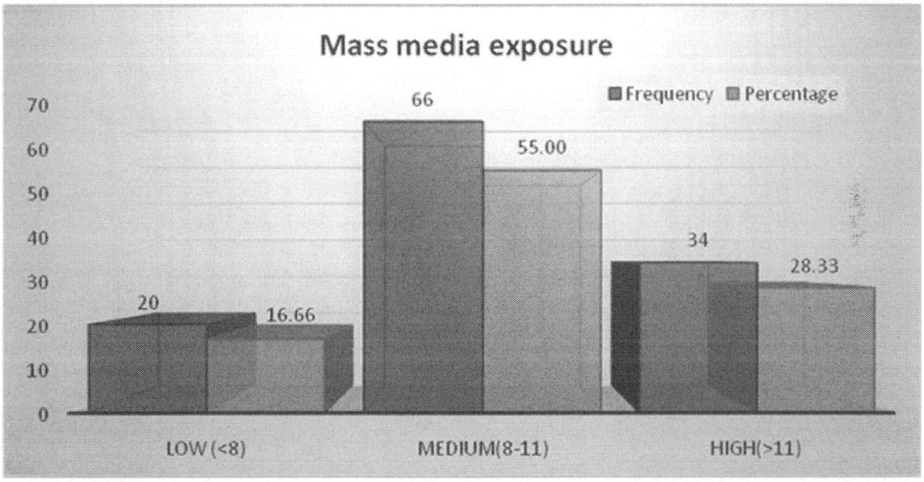

Figure 8: Distribution of Respondents According to Their Mass Media Exposure

Extension Contact

The data represented in table 1 showed that majority of the respondents was found in medium with (51.67%), low with (33.33%) and high category with (15.00%) (Fig. 9).

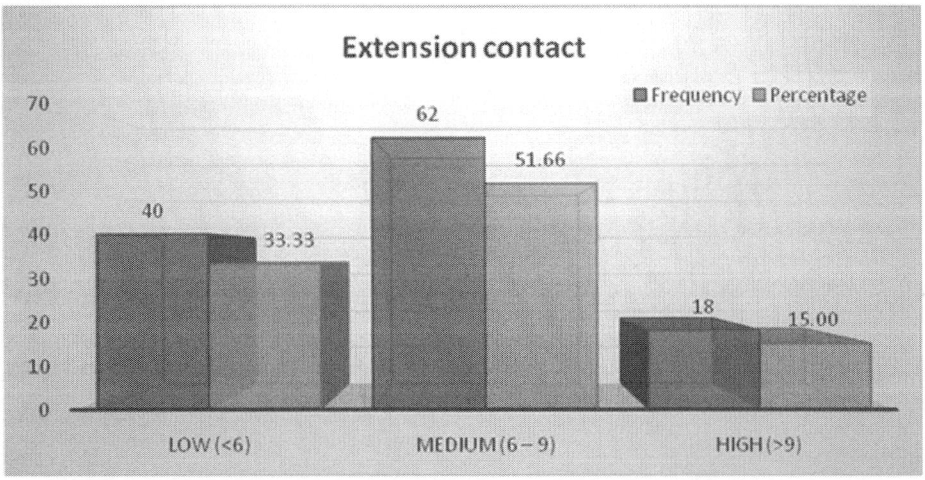

Figure 9: Distribution of Respondents According to Their Extension Contact

Risk Orientation

The data regarding risk orientation behaviour of farmers presented in Table 1 show that majority of the respondents (47.50%) belong to low category followed by medium category (46.66%) and high category with (05.83%) (Fig. 10).

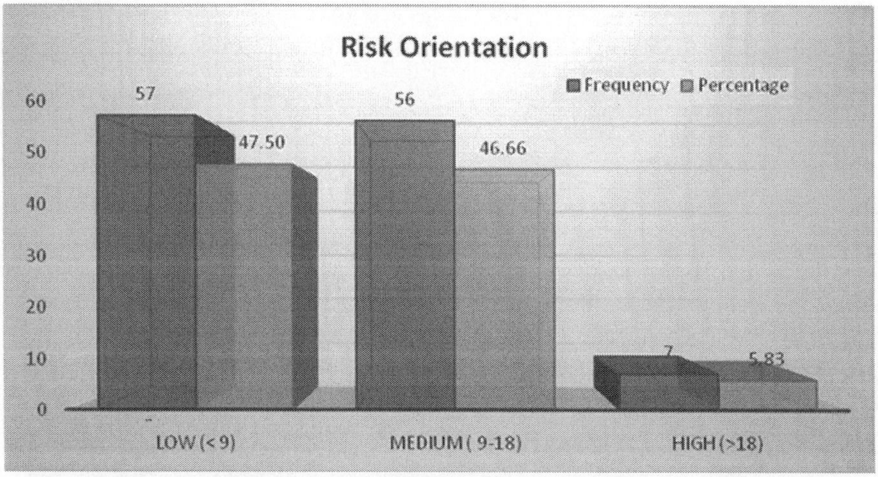

Figure 10: Distribution of Respondents According to Their Risk Orientation

Cropping System

Cropping system refers to the **crops, crop sequences and management techniques used on a particular agricultural field over a period of years.** The data shown in Table 1 states that majority of respondents had monocropping with (49.16%) followed by double cropping (40.01%). Intercropping system was used by 6.67% farmers followed by multiple cropping systems (4.16%) (Fig. 11).

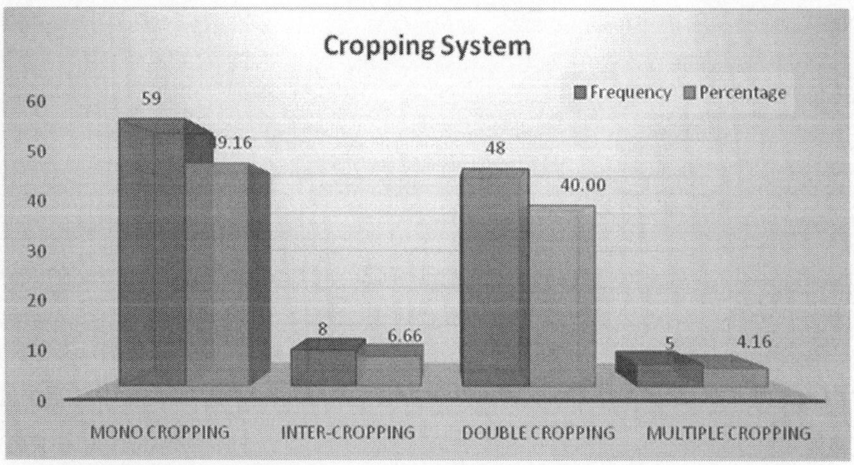

Figure 11: Distribution of Respondents According to Cropping System

Soil Health Card

Awareness is essential idea which entails the awareness of a person to a specific event. Awareness of the respondents regarding soil health card was estimated by a questionnaire. The data mentioned in table 1 indicated that majority of the respondents (60.00%) were having Soil Health Card, helps to indicate soil health (60.00%), encourage judicious application of fertilizers (60.00%) followed by (34.16%) which were aware about SHC tenure (Fig. 12).

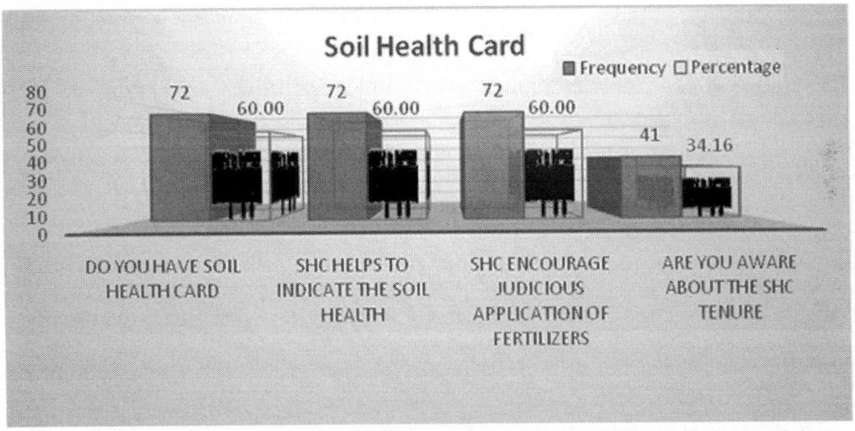

Figure 12: Distribution of Respondents According to Their Soil Health Card

Knowledge Level of Farmers Related to Paddy Straw Management Techniques

Overall Knowledge of Farmers' Regarding PSMT

It is revealed from the table 2 that 65.84 % of the farmers had high level of knowledge followed by 28.33 % with medium level and 5.83% respondents had low level of knowledge regarding PSMT (Fig.13).

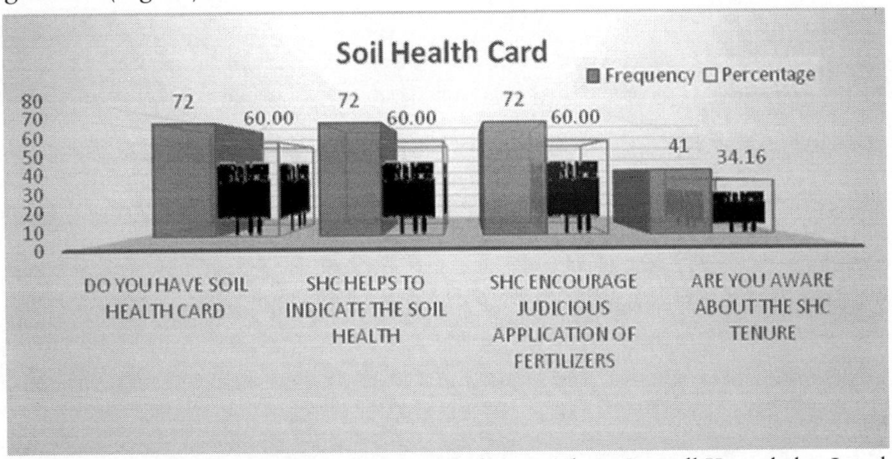

Fig. 13: Distribution of Respondents According to Their Overall Knowledge Level

Table 2: Distribution of Respondents According to Their Overall Knowledge Level About PSMT in Haryana (n = 120)

S. No.	*Category*	*Frequency*	*Percentage*
1.	Low (< 12 score)	7	5.83
2.	Medium (12 -24 score)	34	28.33
3.	High (> 24score)	79	65.84

Knowledge of Farmers Regarding PSMT

The data from the Table 3 revealed that all of the respondents had full knowledge about domestic purpose which got Ist rank with weight mean score of 2.00 followed by animal fodder (1.96), packing material (1.73), soil incorporation (1.38), composting (1.33), mulching (1.14), mushroom farming (0.95), bailing (0.65), biomass plant (0.45) and biofuel (0.03) with ranks II, III, IV, V,VI,VII,VIII, IX and X, respectively. Whereas none of the respondent found to have knowledge regarding biochar (0.00) and got last rank i.e., XI.

Table 3: Knowledge of Farmers Regarding PSMT (n = 120)

Particular	*Full Knowledge*	*Partial Knowledge*	*No Knowledge*	*Total Score*	*Weighted Mean Score*	*Rank Order*
Mulching	62(51.6)	13(10.8)	45(37.6)	137	1.14	VI
Soil incorporation	71(59.16)	24(20.00)	25(20.84)	166	1.38	IV
Animal fodder	116(96.7)	4(3.33)	00(0.00)	236	1.96	II
Bailing	33(27.5)	12(10.00)	75(62.5)	78.00	0.65	VIII
Composting	61(50.83)	38(31.67)	21(17.5)	160	1.33	V
Biochar	0(0.00)	0(0.00)	120(100.00)	0.00	0.00	XI
MushroomFarming	18(15.00)	78(65.00)	24(20.00)	114	0.95	VII
Domestic purpose	120(100.00)	0(0.00)	0(0.00)	240	2.00	I
Packing material	94(78.4)	20(16.67)	6(5.00)	208	1.73	III
Biomass plant	21(17.5)	12(10.00)	87(72.5)	54.00	0.45	IX
Biofuel	0(0.00)	4(3.33)	116(96.7)	4.00	0.03	X

Knowledge About Implements Use in PSMT

When asked about the knowledge about implements in PSMT, the data shows that all of the respondents were found to have knowledge of rotavator with weighted mean score of 2.00 got rank 1st followed by happy seeder with weighted mean score of 1.75 got rank 2nd. Whereas baler (1.53), mulcher (1.50), ZT seed drill (1.37), super SMS (attached with combine harvester) (1.33), spreader/shrub master (1.29), super seeder (1.18), paddy straw chopper (1.11), raker (0.90), reversible MB plough (0.71) with ranks III, IV, V, VI, VII, VIII, IX, X and XI, respectively in table 4.

Table 4: Knowledge about implements use in PSMT (n = 120)

Sr. No.	*Implements*	*Fully Knowledge*	*Partial Knowledge*	*No Knowledge*	*Total Score*	*Weighted Mean Score*	*Rank Order*
1.	Spreader/Shrub Master	62(51.66)	31(25.84)	27(22.5)	155	1.29	VII
2.	Super SMS (attached with Combine Harvester)	60(50.00)	40(33.33)	20(16.67)	160	1.33	VI
3.	Paddy straw Chopper	53(44.2)	28(23.33)	39(32.5)	134	1.11	IX
4.	Mulcher	69(57.6)	43(35.83)	8(6.66)	181	1.50	IV
5.	Happy Seeder	98(81.7)	15(12.5)	7(5.83)	211	1.75	II
6.	Rotavator	120(100.00)	0(0.00)	0(0.00)	240	2.00	I
7.	Reversible MB plough	39(32.5)	8(6.7)	73(60.83)	86	0.71	XI
8.	ZT seed drill	77(64.16)	11(9.16)	32(26.7)	165	1.37	V
9.	Raker	48(40.00)	13(10.83)	59(49.2)	109	0.90	X
10.	Baler	72(60.00)	40(33.33)	8(6.7)	184	1.53	III
11.	Super seeder	67(55.83)	8(6.66)	45(38)	142	1.18	VIII

References

1. Anonymous. (2019). State wise area, production and yield of rice (2018-19).Directorate of Economics and Statistics, Ministry of Agriculture, Govt. of India. 2019, pp. 151-152.
2. Anonymous. (2019). Crop residue. Available at*en.wikipedia.org/wiki/Crop residue*. Last accessed *January 2019).*
3. Dobermann, A., & Fairhurst, T. H. (2002). Rice straw management. *Better Crops International*, **16**(1), 7-11c. economictimes.indiatimes.com.
4. Erenstein, O. (2002). Crop residue mulching in tropical and semi-tropical countries: An evaluationof residue availability and other technological implications, Soil and Tillage Research. 67: 115-133.
5. Haysa M D, Finebm P M, Eronam G C D, Kleemanc M J, Brian K and Gulletta B K. (2005). Open burning of agricultural biomass: Physical and chemical properties of particle – phase emissions. *Atmos. Environ*. **39**(36):6747-6764.
6. Kirar and Mehta (2009) observed that more than half of the respondents (51.67%) had medium knowledge level, while 33.33 per cent of them had high knowledge level and 15.00 per cent had low knowledge level regarding rice production technology.
7. Kumar, D. (2010). A study on adoption of recommended wheat production technology among the farmers of Bilaspur district of Chhattisgarh state. Doctoral dissertation, Indira Gandhi Krishi Vishwavidyalaya, Raipur).

LASER LEVELLING TECHNOLOGY FOR SUSTAINABLE IRRIGATION IN PUNJAB: AN ECONOMIC ANALYSIS

Priya and Jaswinder Singh Brar

Abstract

Sustainable agriculture essentially provides profitability at the same time as the balance requirements of the present and future generations. This study analyses the economic impact of Laser Levelling Technology (LLT) upon water productivity, associated cost, and crop yield in the case of the wheat crop from the Jalandhar district. It also attempts to understand the social-economic determinants of the adoption of farm households. The analysis is based on secondary and primary data and also a comparative study. In primary data, there were a limited number of 56 farm households as a sample size with 36 which adopted this technology and 20 non-adopters as the control group. The analysis of data establishes that the farmers who had adopted this technique realized better water productivity, saved on the front of cost, and realized better returns. Moreover, highly educated and large farm households have adopted more of the latest irrigation technique. The study, overall, argued for the adoption of this technology with apparent benefits. Therefore, the government needs to adopt policies and incentives aimed at water use to ensure sustainable development of the agricultural sector.

Keywords: *Sustainable Agriculture, Irrigation Water, Economic Analysis, Punjab, India*

Introduction

Sustainable agriculture essentially encompasses balancing the needs of current and future generations while simultaneously ensuring profitability; environmental, social, and economic justice. That is why sustainability practically works through netting and nesting the economic, social, and environmental dimensions by suitable technological interventions. Agricultural production structures and associated food systems have been facing growing competition with alternative use of limited natural resources. The availability of the resources has been laid low with the prolonged grip of ongoing unsustainable practices. Water continues to be the main natural resource for agriculture production systems all over. Many communities around the world face water scarcity because water is not sufficient both in terms of desired quantity and quality; which necessitates its rationale use and conservation.

India is an agricultural economy, and the country's overall economic performance is highly dependent on the performance of the agricultural sector. India's economic growth rate is influenced by everything that happens to its agriculture. Given the great need for food security in India and its rapidly growing population, this is also a national priority. India's food security is threatened by several issues, including water shortages that require urgent attention. Solutions aimed at addressing food security issues, such as improved varieties and improved management practices, cannot be fruitful without water.

Water development and conservation have become a major concern of India, as some parts of India are suffering from severe water shortages. Water problems are worsened by increased consumption in the summer. With increasing demographic pressure, the development of appropriate institutional arrangements surrounding water is crucial to the conservation and sustainability of the country's water resources. India has taken several steps to save water in agriculture by producing alternative crop mixtures to ensure optimal water use. The Union Minister Jal Shakti recently said, the total groundwater available, 6 per cent is used for household use and an additional 5 per cent is used for industrial use. The remaining 89 per cent is used for agriculture. "He said, out of 178.7 million rural households, only 32.7 million (18 per cent) received tap water. And by 2050, India will become a global hotspot for "water insecurity." It is further held that the focus should shift from land productivity to irrigation water productivity so that farmers can work on saving water (Bakshi, 2019). Keeping water management in view, the study is divided into five sections. The next section second describes the water issues in Punjab agriculture. Section 3, provides in detail the data and methodology. The results are presented in Section 4 with detailed focus on cost, productivity and returns. The final section concludes and provides some policy recommendations.

Water Issues in Punjab Agriculture

Water is what humans need. People working in different fields need water for different purposes, such as agriculture, industry, and home. Due to the inadequate availability of water of the required quantity and quality, water shortages are faced in many parts of the world, requiring careful use and conservation of water needs. Water conservation refers to the proper use of water with caution, strategies, and policies to prevent waste, as water is in great need for the current population and future generations.

Irrigation development plays an important role in improving farmers' incomes through improving agricultural productivity, cultivation intensity, employment opportunities, and wage rates. The supply of irrigation water can be improved by adding new reservoirs and by adjusting for irrigation water loss. One of the options available to regulate field loss and increase farm water productivity is to replace traditional irrigation systems with modern irrigation systems.

Punjab's agricultural system, based on the mono-cropping pattern of rotation of paddy and wheat, requires intensive use of water for irrigation throughout the year. The Punjab state contributes 36.8 per cent of wheat and 27.3 per cent of rice to the country's central pool of food grains (GOP, 2016). The future of food production in the state will be seriously threatened by unsustainable groundwater use, which at present is open flooding of fields, and thereby in itself is a case of poor water use and hence saving when viewed in the context of emergent irrigation technologies in many parts of the world. The demand for water in the state has been growing and it remains a major issue as the state is a predominantly agricultural-driven economy. During 2017, it was reported that total water (ground and surface) availability in Punjab was 35,109.97 Million Cubic Meter (MCM); of which groundwater constituted 20,698.94 MCM and surface water 14,411.03 MCM. It was further estimated that by 2020, the water demand will rise to 44,227.87 MCM with a water deficit in the state equivalent to 14,715.11 MCM (GOP, 2017). Noticeably, it is reported that groundwater level has dropped in about 85 per cent of the areas where groundwater is fresh and suitable for irrigation. The groundwater table rose in about 15 per cent of brackish and salt-containing areas. In the Central Plain Zone of Punjab, the water table is declining at a rate of 54 cm (0.54 m) per year in some patches during 2004 (Aulakh, 2004). The decrease in 2019 was 37 cm (0.37 m) per year (Bharti, 2019). The excessive decline in groundwater levels has affected the economic viability of small and marginal landowners.

The fast depletion of the groundwater table has been emerging as a big social and political issue also as it involves the economic future of the state. Therefore, the emergent water distress has prompted the state the adoption of irrigation water-saving technologies for the last decade or so. Many attempts are underway with the combined efforts of state, market, and civil society for encouraging water-efficient irrigation practices. Many ways have been suggested and practiced to save irrigation water during agricultural operations, such as using central or side-moving sprinklers, minimizing evaporation, use of overhead irrigation methods to avoid a surface runoff, deep seepage, along underground drainage, and also other micro-irrigation techniques mainly drip systems also.

Materials and Methods

Keeping in view the precarious subsoil water position of the state the present study focuses upon the water-saving practices adopted with a specific focus upon irrigation by scientifically leveling the field. The study analyses the economic impact of the adoption of the Laser Levelling Technology (LLT) upon water productivity, associated cost, and crop yield in the case of the wheat crop. It also attempts to understand the social and economic characteristics of its adoption by farm households. The foremost purpose of this study is to explore the irrigating behavior of farmers by inspecting elements that affect their irrigation choices. It needs to be understood here is that sustainable irrigation water means improving water use efficiency or water productivity by maintaining production level also. The efficient use of irrigation water, alongside its saving, is extraordinarily essential for the sustainability of food security under heavy demographic pressure. The use of irrigation water for agricultural production calls for modern and sustainable research and the correct switch over to water-saving technologies. The study draws its added importance also from the fact that the Government of India has adopted 17 Sustainable Development Goals (SDGs) in 2015, of which managing water resources occupy a central position (GOI, 2015). The study is limited to the Central Plain Zone of the Punjab state where a significant decline in groundwater levels has been observed. With a total area of 34, 42,000 hectares, this zone occupies 43.42 per cent of the state's total area (GOP, 2011). This zone consists of eight districts (ENVIS Environment Information System, PSCST, 2020)with the annual average drop in groundwater level (meter per year) from June 1984 to 2017 was as follows: Amritsar (0.30), Tarn Taran (0.39), Kapurthala (0.32), Jalandhar (0.51), Ludhiana (0.33), Fatehgarh Sahib (0.46), Sangrur (0.81) and Patiala (0.73) (Ground Water Resources of Punjab, 2020). Importantly, the water table in this zone has dropped by more than 15 meters between June 1984 and June 2016 (Water

Resources Department, 2018). In addition, depending on groundwater conditions as of March 31, 2017, all 65 blocks in this zone were classified in the 'over exploited' category (out of 109 over-exploited blocks in the state) and the rest in the 'safe' category (Water Resources Department, 2018).

The study has been focused on both the secondary as well as primary data. The secondary data related to groundwater are provided by two government agencies: Central Ground Water Board, North Western Region, Chandigarh, and Water Resources and Environment Directorate, Water Resources Department Punjab, Mohali with state-specific publication namely Ground Water Resources of Punjab State.

Farmers using modern irrigation systems are much scattered overall with no definite pattern in the selected zone. The techno-economic nature of the study requires repeated visits and follows up to generate adequate data set. The data with suitable questionnaire has been collected by incorporating both open-ended and close-ended questions by method of personal interviews for one crop season. The data on output has been obtained directly from farmers for the selected crop wheat from Jalandhar district which has been selected purposely as in this district the LLT has been adopted extensively. The analysis is based on the comparative study of a limited number of 56 farm households as a sample size with 36 which adopted this technology and 20 non-adopters as the control group.

The economic analysis has been based on Benefit-Cost Ratio (BCR). The BCR is estimated by dividing the present value of the estimated benefits by the estimated costs. Similarly, the Water productivity is estimated by using the ratio of yield (kg/acre) to consumed irrigation water (cubic meters/acre). Water usage is estimated by taking into account many factors such as irrigation frequency, well motor output, drilling depth, and flow tube diameter. The information gathered from the primary data is further processed and analyzed to identify the determinants of the adoption of the latest irrigation practices.

The water use impact of new technique has been examined by using the concept of Water Productivity (WP). It is a term commonly used "to describe the relationship between water (input) and agricultural product (output)". It is often used to express the effectiveness of irrigation water use and delivery. The water productivity is estimated as the ratio of output (kg/acre) and irrigation water used (cubic meter/acre):

$$WP\ (kg/m^3) = [Output\ (kg/acre)]\ /\ [Irrigation\ water\ used\ (m^3/acre)]$$

Therefore, to measure groundwater usage by farmers we used an approximate estimation model following Eyhorn et al. (2005), Srivastava et al. (2009), and Watto et al. (2015), Razzaq et al. (2018). The information on the number of irrigations, duration of each irrigation, tube well engine horsepower, the diameter of the suction pipe, and boring depth was collected from farmers to incorporate in the following model to measure the volume of water in liters which was then converted to cubic meters.

$$Q = \frac{t \times 129574.1 \times BHP}{[d + (255.5998 \times BHP^2)/d^2 \times D^4)]}$$

Where; Q is the volume of water in liters, t is the total duration of irrigations, d denoted the boring depth, D is the diameter of the suction pipe, and BHP is the engine power of the tube well. This formula gave the extraction of water in liters which we converted to m^3.

Results and Discussion

This section provide the results of the study such as the socio-economic profile of respondents, installation and working costs, estimated values of BCR, and water productivity under LLT and non LLT users. The analysis of data establishes that the farmers who had adopted this technique realized better water productivity, saved on the front of cost, and realized better returns. Moreover, highly educated and large farm households have adopted more of the latest irrigation technique.

Production Costs of LLT versus Non-LLT Users

Table 1 shows the average cost per hectare of wheat production for farmers irrigating wheat crops using LLT and Non-LLT methods of irrigation. The results show that there was a difference in the cost of various activities between the two types of agricultural systems. Irrigation costs for LLTs are lower than for irrigated farms under the Non-LLTs. Labour costs for LLTs irrigated farms were lower than for Non-LLTs farmers who had used more labour to harvest their crops. Machines accounted for the highest cost of all of the above, but there were also differences in other costs of both LLTs and Non-LLT users, and LLT users cost less than those of Non-LLT users. The LLT user has incurred comparatively lower costs than that of non-LLT users in case of each and every cost. The maximum difference was noted in case of Agro-Chemicals (77.82 per cent) followed by irrigation (78.03 per cent). The use of LLT results in the saving of all types of costs for the farm households. It proved to be cost efficient method of growing wheat with numerous economic benefits.

Similarly, as per Table 2, there was a significant difference between yields and revenues for LLT and Non-LLT users. The yield and revenue for LLT users were higher than those of Non-LLT users, which indicates that LLTs balanced supply of water to crops than Non-LLTs, ultimately resulting in higher wheat yields and therefore revenue also. This makes a strong case for the wider benefits of adoption of laser levelling technique as it not only saves water but also gives better yield and reduces cost and makes it better economic choice for the producers. This also indicates about the better balance between private profits and social interest in form of the long-term sustainability of water.

Table 1: Average Cost of Production in Wheat Crop under LLT and Non-LLT Users, Rupee per Acre

Costs	*LLT Users* 1	*Per Cent* 2	*Non-LLT Users* 3	*Per Cent* 4	*Cost Gap (Per cent)* 5=1 to 3
Land Preparation	1784	7.94	2045	8.28	87.24
Seeds	2330	10.37	2580	10.45	90.31
Fertilizers	5810	25.85	6014	24.36	96.61
Agro-Chemicals	1200	5.34	1542	6.25	77.82
Irrigation*	2056	9.15	2635	10.67	78.03

Costs	*LLT Users 1*	*Per Cent 2*	*Non-LLT Users 3*	*Per Cent 4*	*Cost Gap (Per cent) 5=1 to 3*
Machinery (Manual Cutting+ Harvester+ Thresher+ Tractor +Other)	7716	34.34	8146	33.00	94.72
Hired Labour	1576	7.01	1783	7.22	88.39
Total Costs (TC)	22,472	100.00	24,687	100.00	91.03

Note: *Includes repair, maintenance, and depreciation of owned irrigation machinery excluding diesel charges, if any. It also includes charges of hired irrigation.
Source: Primary Survey.

Table 2: Crop Yield and Revenue of LLT and Non-LLT Users

Category	*Yield (qt/ acre) (1)*	*Price (Rs/ qt) (2)*	*By product/ acre (Turi Straw) (qt/acre) (3)*	*Price (By- product) (Rs/qt) (4)*	*Total Revenue (TR) (Rs/ acre) 5= (1)(2) +(3)(4)*
LLT Users	23	1975	15	1200	63,425
Non-LLT Users	21	1975	12	1200	55,875

Source: Primary Survey.

Table 3 shows the Benefit-Cost Ratio (BCR) results for LLTs and Non-LLTs farms. It emerged that the gross return of the LLTs users was higher than the gross return of the Non-LLTs users. The BCR values for LLTs and Non-LLTs on wheat crop were greater than 1. The values were 1.82 and 1.26, respectively. These results showed that LLTs and non-LLTs both were economically viable options for wheat harvesting but the LLTs was comparatively more beneficial. The BCR results proved that a high-efficiency irrigation system (LLT) is an economically more viable and sustainable option particularly related to the scare resource that is water.

The water productivity on LLTs wheat farms was 0.51 kg/m^3 which was much higher than those of Non-LLTs farmers who had water productivity of 0.42 kg/m^3 only. Our results show that LLT has significant potential to increase water productivity in the Punjab province of India. The higher water productivity basically seems to result from balanced spread of water on a highly levelled field which lead to equal supply of water to all plants with no over or under watering across the patches as is the case with uneven fields.

Table 3: Gross Return, BCR Values and Productivity Values of LLT and Non-LLT Users.

Category	*Gross Return (GR) (TR-TC)*	*BCR Values*	*Water Productivity Kg/m^3*
LLT Users	40,953	1.82	0.51
Non-LLT Users	31,188	1.26	0.42

Source: Primary Survey.

Social and Economic Characteristics

Tables 4, 5 and 6 show the socio-economic characteristics of current adopters of LLTs users to design practical policies to encourage the use of such systems. The age of farmers did not show any significant variation among farmers under both the LLTs and Non-LLTs users. This finding indicated that the age of a farmer did not affect the choice of irrigation system. But, within the LLT users, it is important to note that about 22 per cent were in the age group of less than thirty years. It means it could also be interpreted that the younger lot of farmers have started realizing the benefits of better techniques and this trend will all likely to go up as the demonstration impacts are increasing with the better spread of social media etc. The household size of respondents ranged from 7-8 persons for all types of farmers, so the family size was also found to be neutral in determining farmers' attitudes toward the choice of irrigation technology. The education of farmers revealed that farmers using LLTs were relatively more educated than those who used Non-LLTs to irrigate their crops. Therefore, education might be a factor affecting the farmers' choice of LLTs. This factor is quite noticeable and would exert more pressure in coming years as they would be better understanding the potential of new technology by more interacting with peer groups.

Table 4: Social and Economic Characteristics of Respondents using LLT and Non-LLT Users

Particulars	*LLT users*		*Non-LLT users*	
	Number	*Per Cent*	*Number*	*Per cent*
Religion				
Hindu	0	0	0	0
Sikh	36	100	20	100
Other	0	0	0	0
Social Category				
General	21	58.33	10	50
SC	6	16.66	4	20
OBC	4	11.11	3	15
EWS	5	13.88	3	15
Other	0	0	0	0
Gender				
Male	36	100	20	100
Female	0	0	0	0
Age (Years)				
Less than 30	8	22.22	10	50
30-50	10	27.77	2	10
50-70	4	11.11	2	10
More than 70	14	38.88	6	30

Source: Primary Survey.

Table 5: Family Profile of the Respondents using LLT and Non-LLT Users

Particulars	*LLT users*		*Non-LLT users*	
	Number	*Per Cent*	*Number*	*Per cent*
Family Type				
Nuclear	32	88.88	17	75
Joint	4	11.11	3	15
Family Size				
4 or less	32	88.88	18	90
5-8	2	5.55	1	5
More than 8	2	5.55	1	5
Marital Status				
Married	35	97.22	18	90
Unmarried	0	0	0	0
Other	1	2.77	2	10

Source: Primary Survey.

Table 6: Education and Occupation Profile of the Respondents using LLT and Non-LLT Users

Particulars	*LLT users*		*Non-LLT users*	
	Number	*Per Cent*	*Number*	*Per cent*
Education level				
Illiterate	6	16.66	2	10
Up to primary	2	5.55	2	10
Up to matric	8	22.22	10	50
Up to secondary	9	25	2	10
Up to graduate	7	19.44	2	10
Up to postgraduate	4	11.11	2	10
Other	0	0	0	0
Occupation				
Farming	33	91.66	17	85
Business	1	2.77	1	5
Government job	1	2.77	1	5
Private job	1	2.77	1	5
Other	0	0	0	0

Source: Primary Survey.

Conclusions and Policy Recommendations

Punjab is a water-scarce state, and its agriculture sector needs irrigation water to feed the rapidly growing population. Also, the water demand for non-agricultural uses is expected to grow more than its agricultural uses. Therefore, a shift to water-saving technologies is needed to maintain the balance in the use of this precious resource in its competitive uses. Modern irrigation systems, e.g. LLT, provide numerous other benefits along with the huge water-saving potential. The low adoption of these technologies in Punjab might be due to several limiting factors. Farmers in Punjab are reluctant to adopt the technology because they might perceive it as an expensive technology that offers water savings only. However, the inefficient water pricing system fails to induce the farmers to adopt modern water-saving technologies for the sole purpose of water-saving. The farmers could be incentivized through the economic benefits for the adoption of the LLT.

Based on the findings of this study, it is concluded that modern irrigation systems provide substantial increases in yield and water productivity of wheat farms. The results of our study further showed that most of the farmers using LLT were large farmers. The present subsidies and other incentives offered by the government for the adoption of LLT may not be enough to encourage the small farmers to adopt LLT partly due to a lack of awareness about the economic benefits of LLT. In addition, the low education status of conventional growers found in this study could also be a limiting factor in the adoption of LLT. The economic analysis of LLT using Benefit-Cost Ratio confirmed the economic feasibility of modern irrigation technologies in the study area. The use of lase levelling has proven benefits in all respects from saving of water, to reduction in cost, improving of yield and ultimately generation of better returns. Importantly, the largescale use of laser levelling in the end will result in huge saving of irrigation water at the macro level for the state and the country. The largescale adoption, apart from monetary incentives, much depends upon the strength of extension services in the state, which as of now are not up to mark because of decline of the public extension services amidst on going resource crunch and change of priorities of the state in favour of the private services which are supposed to fill the vacuum. The extension system makes better impact in situation of demonstration of new technologies by adoption of better platforms. The better return dimension of new technology need to be more highlighted for the producers so that in situation of stagnating farm incomes they may feel more attracted towards it. The policymakers could use the findings of this study to educate the farmers about the economic benefits of adopting LLT. The study, overall, argued for the adoption of this technology with apparent benefits. Therefore, the government needs to adopt policies and incentives aimed at water use to ensure sustainable development of the agricultural sector.

Note: *The paper is based on the ongoing doctoral research work of the first author. These are preliminary results based on limited sample and as such not to be quoted. The authors benefitted a lot from technical discussion held with experts in the area of water resources and hence all those deserve special thanks.*

References

1. Agro-Climatic Zones of Punjab (2020). *ENVIS Environment Information System, PSCST*. June 4, URL: http://punenvis.nic.in/index1.aspx?lid=5617&mid=1&langid=1&linkid=1257
2. Aulakh, K.S. (2004). "Resource Conservation and Sustainability under Punjab Conditions", *The National Symposium on Resource Conservation and Agricultural Productivity,* 46(4), pp. 22-25.

3. Bakshi, Gorky (2019). "Water Conservation in India: How to Manage Water and What to Learn from Israel"? The Union Minister of Jal Shakti, September 9, *Jagran Josh*, URL: jagranjosh.com/current-affairs/water-conservation-in-India-water-management-and-what-India-can-learn-from-Israel-1567845801-1
4. Bharti, Vishav (2019). "Water Table Declining Alarming, Government Steps go Down the Drain", September 7, *The Tribune*, Chandigarh; URL: https://www.tribuneindia.com/news/archive/punjab/water-table-decline-alarming-govt-steps-go-down-the-drain-725015
5. District-wise Yearly Rate of Fall/ Rate of Rise of Water Level - June 1984 to June 2017. *Ground Water Resources of Punjab*, June 23, 2020, URL: http://punenvis.nic.in/index2.aspx?slid=5815&mid=1&langid=1&sublinkid=996
6. Eyhorn, Frank., Mäder, Paul., Ramakrishnan, Mahesh (2005). "The Impact of Organic Cotton Farming on the Livelihoods of Smallholders, Evidence from the Maikaal BioRe Project in Central India", Organic cotton research report, pp. 1-75.
7. GOP (2011): Environment Statistics of Punjab, ESO, Government of Punjab, Chandigarh. November 4, Official Website, URL: https://irrigation.punjab.gov.in/Water-Resources.aspx
8. GOI (2015): Sustainable Development Goals, Government of India, New Delhi
9. GOP (2016): Statistical Abstract of Punjab, Economic and Statistical Abstract of Punjab, ESO, Government of Punjab, Chandigarh.
10. GOP (2017). "State Irrigation Plan Punjab". Punjab Agriculture University, Ludhiana.
11. Razzaq, A., Rehman, A., Qureshi, A.H., Javed, I., Saqib, R. and Iqbal, M.N. (2018). "An Economic Analysis of High Efficiency Irrigation Systems in Punjab, Pakistan", *Sarhad Journal of Agriculture*, 34(4), pp. 818-826.
12. Srivastava, S.K., Kumar, Ranjit., and Singh, R.P. (2009). "Extent of Groundwater Extraction and Irrigation Efficiency on Farms under Different Water-Market Regimes in Central Uttar Pradesh", *Agricultural Economics Research Review,* 22(1), pp. 87-97.
13. Watto, M.A. and Mugera, A.W. (2015). "Econometric Estimation of Groundwater Irrigation Efficiency of Cotton Cultivation Farms in Pakistan", *Journal of Hydrology: Regional Studies,* 4(1), pp. 193-211.
14. Water Resources Department (2018). *Ground Water Resources of Punjab State (As On 31st March, 2017)*, Water Resources & Environment Directorate, Water Resources Department, Punjab, Mohali, and Central Ground Water Board, North Western Region, Chandigarh.

DRIP IRRIGATION TECHNOLOGY IN CITRUS CULTIVATION FOR SUSTAINABLE CROP PRODUCTION

Vinod Kumari and Subhash Chander

Introduction

Agriculture is the backbone of Indian rural society. Water scarcity is becoming more prevalent, limiting agricultural development in India and throughout the world. Water use efficiency is critical for the survival of a growing population as well as the nation's vertical development. For increasing agricultural production, the importance of irrigation is fully realized, but the proper use of water is seldom practised in our country. World Bank predicted that by the year 2035, three million people will live in tough conditions because of water shortage (World Bank, 2009). With this population increase, the major concern would be the demand management mechanism in water-scarce as well as water-stressed areas (Kumar, 2008). Narayanamoorthy (1994) mentioned water efficiency in agriculture can be done after adopting micro-irrigation technologies like Drip Irrigation and Sprinkler Irrigation. In these methods, water losses occurring through evaporation is completely absent. Firstly, the solution to the water problem is through management practices like watershed development, water resources development through major, medium and minor irrigation projects, etc. The second is through efficient use of the available water both in the short-run and long-run perspectives. This includes drip irrigation and other improved water management practices. Recognising the importance of sustainable water-use efficiency in agriculture, several demand management strategies (like water pricing, water users association, turnover system, etc.) have been introduced since the late-1970s to increase the water-use efficiency, especially in the use of surface irrigation water. India is the largest user of groundwater in the world using 260 cubic km per year, i.e. 25% of all groundwater extracted globally, ahead of China and the USA. Out of the total net annual groundwater availability, 90% is used in irrigation while the rest 10% is used for domestic and industrial purposes (Government of India, 2019).

One of the demand management mechanisms is the adoption of micro-irrigation such as drip and sprinkler methods of irrigation. Shreds of evidence show that the water-use efficiency increases to a great extent in a properly designed and managed drip irrigation system. The drip method helps in achieving saving in irrigation water, increased water-use efficiency, decreased tillage requirement, higher quality products, increased crop yields and higher fertilizer-use efficiency (Qureshi et al., 2001; Sivanappan, 2002; Namara et al., 2005, Panigrahi and Srivastava, 2017, Hendre et al., 2020 and Raja et al., 2020)). In India, the major crops under drip irrigation are cotton, sugarcane, banana, grapes, pomegranate, coconut and vegetables like cabbage, cauliflower, chilli, ladies finger and brinjal (Kumar, 2016). Sprinkler method of irrigation is used for field crops like sorghum, pearl millet, groundnut and mustard (Kumar, 2016). MIS is viable for horticultural crops and orchards as even a marginal increase in yield results in a significant rise in crop value for high valued crops (Dhawan, 2000). About 50 per cent saving in water and 20 to 30 per cent yield increase in coconut was seen in Coimbatore district of Tamil Nadu after using drip (Palanichamy et al., 2002).

The objective of the present study is to know the adoption and impact of an efficient water use technology for sustainable crop production known as Drip irrigation. Drip irrigation effectively delivers water directly to the root zone and reduces water wastage and is considered a feasible alternative for crops requiring a lot of water.

Methodology

Citrus is a highly irrigated crop and requires water as well as nutrients all the year for greater yield and productivity. Water shortage is one of the significant worries in the citrus developing areas of the world. Among different irrigation methods, micro-irrigation system (MIS) in general and drip irrigation system (DIS), in particular, has received considerable attention from researchers, policymakers, sociologists and economists. Drip Irrigation is also called trickle irrigation and involves dripping water on the soil at a very low rate from a system of small diameter plastic pipes fitted with outlets called drippers. Drip Irrigation system delivers water to the crop using a network of mainliner, sub-mains and lateral lines with emission points spaced along their lengths. Drip irrigation technology is technically feasible, particularly when the farmers depend on groundwater sources. The study was conducted in Haryana state's two districts, namely Sirsa and Fatehabad, the major citrus growing districts. For assessing the adoption and impact of drip irrigation in citrus crops, data were collected by personal interviews with the respondents at their homes/farms. The interview of every individual was taken separately so that the others did not influence the answer and analysed. In this paper, intensive research works by different researchers as well as by the authors regarding drip irrigation technology in citrus crops have been reviewed and discussed so that a definite perception may be generated for the farmers as well as future researchers.

Knowledge Levels and Adoption of Drip Irrigation

The knowledge level of farmers was analysed at the micro-level and the overall drip irrigation system's knowledge was also assessed (Kumari et al, 2022). The majority of sampled farmers had a high (61.67%) and moderate (31.67%) levels of knowledge of drip irrigation (Table 1). Only 6.6% of farmers had a low knowledge base regarding drip irrigation. Swetha et al. (2019) in their work found medium to low levels of knowledge which led to a medium extent of use and maintenance of drip irrigation systems. The work of Prajapati et al. (2016) pointed out that the knowledge about the Drip Irrigation System was found to be moderate to high and the majority of respondents were having moderate to high levels of adoption of management practices of Drip Irrigation System. The study was undertaken by Swadia (2017) among Chilli growers of Ahmedabad and Gupta & Rao (2019) also points to the fact that the majority of respondents had medium or high adoption levels of drip irrigation systems.

The findings of the work done by the authors and results from other studies indicated that the knowledge level of the majority of farmers about the drip irrigation system was high followed by a moderate level of knowledge while about two-fifths of farmers were having a high level of adoption of drip irrigation followed by a low and moderate level of adoption. On the account of the association of socio-economic factors with the knowledge level, it was found that the knowledge levels were associated with age, education, landholding, income, mass media exposure, type and size of family and Socio-Economic status of farmers (Kumari et al., 2022). Swetha et al. (2019) in their work also looked at the education levels, age, innovations, aspirations, social participation and extension contracts that have a bearing on the knowledge level of farmers. Misra and Kaur (2019) also reported the role of age, education and overall owned area were associated with the awareness parameters.

As far as the size of the family is concerned, the large family sizes were having a high level of adoption. This can be accorded to a variety of reasons, of which economic status and exposure to mass media are few. It was seen in the study undertaken by Mohan, et al. (2012) that farmers' income, size of landholding, education and Kisan Credit Card were having a statistically significant and positive impact on Drip Irrigation. This can be seen as the cornerstone towards improving their overall socio-economic conditions. Verma and Sharma (2017) also highlighted that the variables like knowledge, education, social participation, annual income, economic motivation and mass media exposure were found positively and significantly associated with the adoption of Drip Irrigation by the farmers. While other indicators such as experience in farming and irrigation potentiality were found non-significantly associated with the adoption of Drip Irrigation by the farmers.

An overall outlook regarding the price expenditure levels of adoption of Drip Irrigation has been analysed by Shaik and Mistry (2018). They found out that before the adoption of the drip irrigation system, the majority of drip owners spent more than Rs. 10001 on the purchase of fertilizers. The paradigm shift was seen once the Drip Irrigation system fully came under use. The amount farmers spent on fertilizers reduced significantly after Drip Irrigation. A host of academic research work is done on analysing the correlation between various socio-economic indicators and the knowledge and adoption of Drip Irrigation. It was seen that the size of landholdings had a positive relationship with the adoption of Drip Irrigation. Two-Fifths of the large farmers had a high level of adoption of Drip Irrigation. It was observed that as the size of landholding increased, the level of adoption of drip irrigation also increased simultaneously (Kumari et al., 2022).

The findings of the work done by the authors and results from other studies indicated that the knowledge level of majority of farmers about the drip irrigation system was high followed by moderate level of knowledge while about two fifth farmers were having high level of adoption of drip irrigation followed by low and moderate level of adoption. Efficient utilization of water and nutrients need an integrated approach to promote the technique of drip irrigation system among farmers to achieve quality and quantity production. Various socio- economic factors like income, landholding, mass media exposure, education and socio-economic status were found significantly associated with the level of knowledge and adoption of drip irrigation. Drip irrigation technology not only saved water and electricity but it also increased productivity of crop, increased the total cropped area, extended area under irrigation and increased cropping and irrigation intensity. Investment on DIS was found financially feasible by farmers.

Table 1: Knowledge Level of Respondents About Drip Irrigation

Level of Knowledge	
Low (30-38)	04 (06.67)
Moderate (39-47)	19 (31.67)
High (48-57)	37 (61.67)

Impact of Drip Irrigation

Drip Irrigation, if preferred by farmers not only delivers a greater return on investment as compared to other irrigation methods, it also gives farmers an efficient and simple way to operate their farms. Other benefits of drip irrigation are higher consistent quality yields, huge water savings: no evaporation, no runoff, no waste, proper land utilization, irrigates uniformly in any topography and soil type. Drip saves energy as drip irrigation works on low pressure, efficient use of fertilizer and crop protection with no leaching and less dependency on weather, greater stability and lower risks. A host of other positives associated with Drip Irrigation can be gauged by the dwindling groundwater levels and how Drip Irrigation has tackled that particular problem. A study by Kumar et al., (2004) conducted a benefit-cost analysis of using drip irrigation which resulted that the incremental net returns were higher for cash crops like cotton, groundnut and banana than food crops like bajra and wheat. About 50 per cent saving in water and 20 to 30 per cent yield increase in coconut was seen in Coimbatore district of Tamil Nadu after using drip (Palanichamy et al., 2002). Discounted flow techniques were used to study the economic viability of growing capsicum in West Bengal, and the net present worth was found to be Rs. 3,09,734.90 (Singh, 2008). In Karnataka, net return per acre for crops under drip irrigation was found to be higher than conventional irrigation where it was Rs.26,208 for tomato, Rs.7,621 for mulberry and Rs.52,084 for grapes (Chandrakanth et al., 2013). Using drip irrigation system in capsicum resulted in increased yield by 57% and net income by 54% and benefit-cost ratio was found to be 2.44 in drip irrigation system against 2.01 for conventional irrigation (Paul et al., 2013).

Narayanamoorthy et al. (2016) found in their study that the productivity of green chillies increased by 52.45% with drip irrigation, where the cost of cultivation was reduced by 29.14% and net profit increased by 142.15%. Vaibhav and Makwana (2017), conducted impact analysis in terms of water saving, fertilizer and pesticide usage and yield increase in Kodinar region of Gujarat. Maximum water saving was found to be in sugarcane (6195 m3 /ha). Shaik and Mistry (2018) observed that majority of farmers had medium level of socio economic impact followed by nhigh and low. The impact of the adoption of Drip Irrigation can be gauzed by the works of Kaarthikeyan and Suresh (2019) that analysed and reported that almost all the farmers who adopted DIS were very much aware of the benefits that drip irrigation entails. The other benefits of using MIS were increased water use efficiency (50% to 90%) due to reduction in conveyance losses, reduced energy utilization (30.50%)

and saving fertilizer consumption by 28.50%, increased productivity of crops and fruits by 42.40% and 52.70% respectively. Kishore et al. (2019) found that the Sprinkler method of irrigation significantly improved crop yield (21%), water productivity (34%), increased technical efficiency (20%) and saved water use (15%) and energy utilization (8%) in the Bundelkhand region of Uttar Pradesh. Kiruthika and Kumar (2020) found that it increased total crop area(6.54%) and increased cropping intensity(69.19%) and irrigatioin intensity (70.95%).

The overall environmental costs associated with traditional irrigation systems had rendered Indian Agriculture backwards with pressure on the productive land increasing. Micro Irrigation Systems such as Drip Irrigation has taken off major water scarcity challenge. Now, the focus is on precision agriculture with additional impetus on zero water wastage policy. Other than the environmental impact and the increased earning for the farmers, a lot of other things have also popped up which has uplifted the overall status of the farmers. With the increase in the overall income level of the households due to the implementation of Drip Irrigation, the fruits are spilt over to other areas as well. The Purchasing Power of the farmer increased, he can raise the living standards, better education etc for the children. An integrated Drip Irrigation system, therefore, is a boon for the farmers and their communities.

Social and economic changes observed by farmers after adopting drip irrigation was assessed by knowing their improvement in SES, social recognition, health services availed, quality education for children, increase in house hold assets and land, increase in urban and extension contacts, change in dress pattern, mass media exposure, etc. Scores were assigned and categorised as low, moderate and high level of cumulative socio-economic impact. Results revealed that about fifty per cent farmers had high while one third had medium level of cumulative socio-economic impact of drip irrigation. The socio- economic factors like age, income, landholding, mass media exposure, education and socio-economic status were found significantly associated with the commutative impact of drip irrigation. Low price in crop season, non-existence of cooperative society, frequent clogging of dripper, marketing, requirement of time to time attention and fruit dropping are the problems faced by farmers for adoption of DIS in citrus crops. Low level of adoption was mainly due to low level of education, small size of landholdings, low mass-media exposure, low socio-economic status and lack of knowledge and technical support. However, cost of subsidy by the government and forced investment on wells are two major factors of social cost in adoption of drip irrigation technology.

Constraints in Adoption of Drip Irrigation

With the advancement of agricultural techniques, the farmers can realise the overall increase in their standard of living due to better agricultural practices. There are, although certain constraints as was even seen during the Green Revolution. The revolution in irrigation techniques has heralded a new dawn in Indian Agriculture but closer scrutiny made us realise the hidden costs/ hidden externalities/constraints associated with it. A few of the constraints are discussed below-

1. **Economic Constraints:** The initial expenses associated with the Drip Irrigation System installation was felt to be the major roadblock. The farmers were put off by the heavy capital that is required to set up the Drip Irrigation System. Parmar and Thorat (2016) also, have looked at the heavy initial expenses and equipment of Drip Irrigation as a major deterrent. Balasubramaniam et al.(2009) in their study in Tamil Nadu reported that damage done to the pipes by rats/rodents, high cost of spare parts and inadequate technical inputs are major constraints.
2. **Technical Constraints:** Drip Irrigation System is altogether different from the conventional irrigation practices. The technical nature of DIS, therefore, acts as a deterrent. Verma and Sharma (2017) talked about the technical constraints like "clogging of drippers by suspended materials", Low information of Fertigation Schedule, Lack of awareness about crop water requirement, lack of technical know-how, blockage of water pipelines, frequent maintenance etc. as the main technical constraints. Our focus should also be on the complicated technology, difficulty in inter culturing etc. as well.
3. **Administrative Constraints:** Chaudhari (1995) reported that the inadequate and uncertainty in power supply, lack of proper training, non-availability of spare parts, lack of after sell services as major administrative (extension) challenges. Similarly, Parmar and Thorat (2016) have also pointed out non-availability of technical guidance in time, clumsy procedural work, low subsidy rates, delay in loan sanctioning etc. as the major hurdles towards the applicability of Drip Irrigation Systems. To overcome these constraints, it was observed to provide a regular supply of electricity, increase in subsidy by Govt, and training should be imparted to farmers regarding operations, maintenance repair and application of water-soluble fertilizers (Barse et al., 2010).
4. **Climatic and Geographical Constraints:** Jitarwal (2007) in his findings noted that areas which are highly saline was major constraint. Further constraints included inability to minimize temperature of atmosphere while using DIS. Also, the Drip Irrigation System might not be highly useful while dealing with the clayey soil. The small particles of clay can reach the drippers through irrigation water due to which the drippers get clogged and water supply to the root zone is disturbed as well.
5. **Socio-Psychological Deterrents:** Other than the Economic, Technical and Administrative constraints, our focus shall also be on the minor deterrents because an overall change in attitude is required to motivate more and more farmers to take up Drip Irrigation System. Lack of spirit among the farmers regarding DIS, Lack of Motivation, Resistance from family members, frustration due to failure of DIS in work etc are a few of the personal constraints which ultimately makes farmers stick to their traditional/conventional methods.

Conclusion and Implications

There is a need to improve the socio-economic indicators in rural areas to improve the adoption level of drip irrigation among farmers. On the whole, it was found that factors like age, general caste status, level of education, size of landholdings, mass-media exposure and socio-economic status played an important role in the adoption of drip irrigation in citrus crops. Therefore, there is a need to improve, mass-media exposure, extension contacts and training and education, etc. in rural areas to improve the adoption level of drip irrigation among farmers. There is a need to address the constraints faced by farmers to improve the adoption and impact of drip irrigation among farmers. A regular supply of electricity, increase in subsidy and training to farmers regarding operations, maintenance, repair and water-soluble fertilizers are necessary for the successful adoption of the Drip Irrigation System. This water-saving technology must be expended to all regions to elucidate the benefit of drip irrigation through proper extension services so that farmers can get higher crop productivity using limited resources of water and also benefit economically.

References

1. Balasubramaniam, P., Vijayaraghavan, P., & Ravichandran, V. (2009). Merits and Limitations of Water Management Practices in Sugarcane. Kanpur: IIT Kanpur.
2. Barse, K. N., Gohad, V. U., & Lunge, M. R. (2010). Adoption of Drip Irrigation System by Orange Growers in Amravati Taluka. *Agriculture Update* 5(3&4), 346-348.
3. Chaudhari, V. M. (1995). Knowledge and Adoption of Drip Irrigation System by the farmers of North Gujarat. GAU.
4. Gupta, S. K., & Rao, G. M. (2019). The Extent of Adoption of Selected Contemporary Water Management Innovations by Farmers in the Dryland Ecosystem. *Indian Journal of Extension Education*, 139-143.
5. Jitarwal, R. (2007). Impact of Drip Irrigation Technology among farmers in Jaipur Region of Rajasthan. Ph.D. Thesis.
6. Kaarthikeyan, G. M., & Suresh, A. (2019). A Study on understanding the Adoption of Water Saving Technology: A Case Study of Drip Irrigation. *International Journal of Recent Technology and Engineering*, 1123-1130.
7. Kishore, P., Jain, R., & Singh, D. K. (2019). Irrigation in India: Status, Challenges and Options. *Journal of Soil and Water Conservation.*
8. Kumar, M. (2008). Managing Water in the face of Growing Scarcity, Inequity and Declining Returns: Exploring Fresh Approaches. 7th Annual Partners Meet. ICRISAT. Hyderabad: IWMI.
9. Kumari, Vinod, Chander, S. and Sharma, S. (2022). Knowledge and adoption of drip irrigation in citrus crops among farmers of western Haryana. *Indian journal of Extension Education.* 58(1): 151-156.
10. Misra, A., & Kaur, M. (2019). Adoption of Drip Irrigation Technique by Sugarcane Growers of Rajasthan. *Indian Journal of Extension Education* 55(2), 74-79.
11. Mohan, G., Misra, R., Fukushi, K., Besse, R. A., Perarpu, L. N., Chapagain, S. K., & Sudarma, I. N. (2012). Factors Affecting Farmers Perception of Adoption of Water Saving Irrigation Technologies in Semi-Arid States of India. Madras: IIT Madras.
12. Narayanamoorthy, A. (1994). Evaluation of Drip Irrigation System in Maharashtra. *Mimeograph Series No. 42.*
13. Narayanamoorthy, A., Devika, N., & Bhattarai, M. (2016). More Crop and Profit per Drop of Water: Drip Irrigation for Empowering Distressed Small Farmers. *IIM Kozhikode Society and Management Review.*
14. Parmar, S. D., & Thorat, G. N. (2016). Constraints Faced by Farmers in Drip Irrigation System. *Agriculture Update*, 229-233.

15. Prajapati, V. V., Kaid, S. V., Prajapati, R. C., & Thakkar, K. A. (2016). Adoption Behaviour of Drip Irrigation Technology among the Pomegranate Growers of North Gujarat. *International Journal of Agriculture Sciences*, 1443-1447.
16. Shaik, M. S., & Mistry, J. J. (2018). Socio-Economic Impact of the Adoption of Drip Irrigation System on Drip Owners of Aravalli District. *International Journal of Current Microbiology and Applied Sciences* (6), 2174-2180.
17. Swadia, B. U. (2017). Study of Adoption Behaviour of Drip Irrigation System on Chilli Crop in Ahmedabad District of Gujarat. *Recent Trends*, 15-20.
18. Swetha, M., Sudha Rani, V., & Rao, I. S. (2019). Influence of Profile Characteristics on Knowledge level about Drip Irrigation System. *Indian Journal of Extension Education*, 51-54.
19. Verma, H. L., & Sharma, S. K. (2017). Constraints faced by farmers in adoption of DIS in Bikaner District of Rajasthan. *Agriculture Update*, 643-648.
20. Verma, H., & Sharma, S. (2017). Factors Associated with the Adoption of a Drip Irrigation System by the Farmers in the Bikaner District of Rajasthan. *Asian Journal of Agricultural Extension*, 142-144.
21. Yadav, K., Yadav, J. P., & Bijarniya, S. (2019). Adoption of a Drip Irrigation System by the Farmers in Jijhotwara Panchayat Samiti of District Jaipur, Rajasthan. *Indian Journal of Extension Education 55(3)*, 5-8.

ADOPTION OF HAPPY SEEDER FARM TECHNOLOGY AND ECONOMIC BENEFITS FOR SUSTANABLE AGRICULTURE DEVELOPMENT – A SOCIOLOGICAL STUDY

Jatesh Kathpalia, Rashmi Tyagi, Vinod Kumari and Anil Kumar Saroha

Introduction

India has a total geographical area of 329 million hectares (m ha), with gross cultivated and net sown areas of 195 and 140 m ha, respectively. However, the net irrigated area is only 83 m ha, with the remainder being rainfed. Rice–wheat is the most important crop in the Indo-Gangetic Plains (IGP) of south Asia, where it is farmed on 14 million hectares. Haryana being a small state in India has played a vital role in highest food grain production. The farmers of Haryana state have adopted the rice-wheat crop rotation. Paddy- wheat crop rotation is dominant in the state covering about 28.40 lakh hectares of cultivable land. (Singh et al., 2009). Farmers gain more profit from this system but they degraded the most of natural resources like under-ground water, soil fertility, soil fauna and flora etc. The Happy Seeder is a tractor-mounted machine that cuts and lifts rice straw, sows wheat into the bare soil, and deposits the straw over the sown area as mulch. It therefore allows farmers to sow wheat immediately after their rice harvest without the need to burn any rice residue for land preparation. The wheat crop with happy seeder can be sown in standing stubbles of rice which avoids the preparatory tillage of the field and the crop can be sown 7-10 days earlier as compared to traditional method of sowing. Heat generated by burning paddy straw kills useful microbes in the soil leading to poor soil health and loss of soil fertility. They also disturbed the agro ecosystem by incomplete bio chemical cycles, resistance development in insect pests and diseases, reduction in soil organic matter etc. This crop rotation is supposed to produce about 40 million tone of crop waste every year. Out of this wheat straw is mostly used as dry fodder for cattle, a small part of paddy straw is utilized in generating power at biomass thermal plants while rest about 20 million tonne of the paddy straw is set on fire in the fields. Owing to high silica content, paddy straw cannot be directly fed to animals. Crop residues, or plant pieces left over after crop harvesting, are a good source of soil nutrients. It is not a waste product, but rather a valuable natural resource that accounts for the majority of agricultural harvests and contains significant amounts of carbon as well as other nutrients such as nitrogen (N), phosphorous (P), potassium (K), sulphur (S), and others. Rice–wheat system output expanded quickly between 1960 and 1990, owing to increased yield and area as a result of the introduction of highly fertiliser-responsive rice and wheat cultivars, irrigation expansion, improved management, and government support for rice and wheat prices. As a result, massive amounts of rice and wheat wastes are produced. (Sidhu et al 2007) Wheat and rice straw were traditionally collected from the fields to be used as cow fodder, livestock bedding, thatch, and fire. However, in the north-west, rice–wheat farming is now completely mechanised, removing the requirement for draught animals, and straw thatching has been substantially replaced by alternatives. The Punjab and Haryana state governments introduced the Preservation of Subsoil Water Act, 2009 in 2009 with the goal of controlling groundwater levels and reducing water loss to the atmosphere through transpiration. Farmers were prohibited from sowing rice seeds before 10 May and transplanting rice seedlings before 10 June under this act due to high ambient temperatures. The state governments also established provision for deciding the rice crop transplantation date any time after June 10th, based on advice from the concerned department (s). Datta et al. (2020) This shortened the time between rice harvest and wheat seeding in the region by around 5 to 10 days, giving 15 to 25 days for the activity. Delaying the sowing of wheat beyond the optimum date results in significant yield loss .Residue burning is a part of the rice-wheat cropping system' (RWCS) that is the dominant cropping system in Haryana. This system involves growing rice and wheat in rotation throughout the year. Keeping in view the advantages and utility of Happy seeder the study was carried out with following objectives:

1. To assess the adoption level of Happy seeder farm technology among farmers along with factors affecting adoption level.
2. To know the comparative economic benefits of Happy seeder with conventional practices.
3. To find out the reasons for adoption and non-adoption of Happy seeder.
4. To assess the socio-economic impact of Happy seeder along with constraints in adoption of Happy seeder

Concept/Methodology

Wheat cropping system is one of the major cropping system of Haryana. To tackle the issue of stubble burning a technology was required for in-situ residue management and timely sowing of the next wheat crop. as conducted in western climatic zone of Haryana i.e Fatehabad. From this district, three blocks namely Bhuna, Ratia and Fatehabad were selected where maximum no. of farmers had adopted Happy Seeder. On the whole, a total of 80 Happy Seeder adopters and 80 non-adopters farmers were selected for the study. Interview schedule was prepared to collect the desired information as per objectives of the study. Finally selected farmers were surveyed with the help of interview schedule. Statistical techniques like frequency, chi square, and weighted mean scores were used as per the nature of data.

Results

Contextual Matrix of the Respondents

Data in Table 1 shows that 40% of the conventional farmers were above 50 years of age while 22.50% Happy seeder adopters were in this age category, On the other hand 32.50% adopter farmers were from the young age group and only 22.50% young farmers were doing conventional farming. Caste distribution shows that 3/4th of the farmers were from the general caste and more than fifty percent of the conventional farmers were from general caste, only 10% of the respondents were from scheduled caste. It was found that maximum number of the adopter farmers were educated upto secondary and senior secondary level (33.75%) and graduation level (32.50%). More than one fourth of the adopter farmers were having land between 4-10 ha while only 2.5% had this category of land while 60% of the farmers were marginal farmers who were doing farming with conventional methods. It was found that in rural areas number of nuclear families are also increasing .Regarding size of family maximum number of adopter farmers were having upto 4 members in their families and equal number of the farmers (23.75%) were having large size of families. Regarding income, 33.75% of the adopter farmers were having income more than 3 lakh while 45% of the conventional farmers had income between Rs. 75,000–1,50,000/per annum, 62.50% of the conventional farmers and 40%0f the adopter farmers were not member of any social organization. Near about fifty percent of the adopter and conventional farmers had medium level of mass media exposure and socio economic status.

Table 1: Contextual Matrix of the Respondents (n = 160)

Sr. No.	*Variables*	*Adopters (n=80)*		*Conventional (n=80)*		*Total*
		Frequency	*Percentage*	*Frequency*	*Percentage*	
1.	Age					
	Up to 35 years	26	32.50	18	22.50	44(27.50)
	36-50 years	36	45.00	30	37.50	66(41.25)
	Above 50 years	18	22.50	32	40.00	50(31.25)
	Total	80	100	80	100	160(100.0)
2.	Caste					
	General Caste	60	75.00	42	52.50	102(63.75)
	Backward Class	12	15.00	20	25.00	32(20.00)
	Schedule Caste	8	10.00	18	22.50	26(16.25)
3.	Level of Education					
	Illiterate	12	15.00	19	23.75	31(19.37)
	Up to middle school level	15	18.75	29	36.25	44(27.50)
	Secondary and Senior secondary level	27	33.75	20	25.00	47(29.38)
	Graduation and above	26	32.50	12	15.00	38(23.75)
4.	Subsidiary occupation of the Family					
	Nil	34	42.50	26	32.50	60(37.50)
	Business and service	22	27.50	26	32.50	48(30.00)
	small scale enterprise	24	30.00	28	35.00	52(32.50)
5.	Size of land holding					
	Marginal (up to 1 ha)	18	22.50	48	60.00	66(41.25)
	Small (1-2 ha)	21	26.25	22	27.50	43(26.88)
	Semi-medium (2-4 ha)	19	23.75	08	10.00	27(16.87)
	Medium (4-10 ha)	22	27.50	02	2.5	24(15.00)
6.	Type of Family					
	Nuclear	47	58.75	45	56.25	92(57.50)
	Joint	33	41.25	35	43.75	68(42.50)

Sr. No.	*Variables*	*Adopters (n=80)*		*Conventional (n=80)*		*Total*
		Frequency	*Percentage*	*Frequency*	*Percentage*	
7.	Size of Family					
	Up to 4 members	31	38.75	25	31.25	56(35.00)
	5-8 members	30	37.50	36	45.00	66(41.25)
	Above 8 members	19	23.75	19	23.75	38(23.75)
8.	Annual Income					
	Between Rs.75,000-1,50,000/-	16	20.00	36	45.00	52(32.50)
	Rs.1,50,001-3,00,000/-	37	46.25	28	35.00	65(40.63)
	Above Rs. 3,00,000/-	27	33.75	16	20.00	43(26.87)
9.	Social organization Participation					
	No membership	32	40.0	50	62.50	82(51.25)
	Membership of one organization	29	36.25	27	33.75	56(35.00)
	More than one organization	19	23.75	03	03.75	22(13.75)
10.	Mass media exposure					
	Low (up to 9)	16	20.00	26	32.50	42(26.25)
	Medium (10-17)	41	51.25	37	46.25	78(48.75)
	High (above 17)	23	28.75	17	21.25	40(25.00)
11.	Socio-economic Status					
	Low (12-18)	20	25.00	22	27.50	42(26.25)
	Medium (19-24)	41	51.25	41	51.25	82(51.25)
	High (25-31)	19	23.75	17	21.25	36(22.50)

Adoption Level of Happy Seeder Adopters

Adoption level of the respondents has been shown in Fig. 1 About half of the respondents (48.75%) had high level of adoption while 32.50% had medium and rest (18.75%) of the respondents had low level of the adoption.

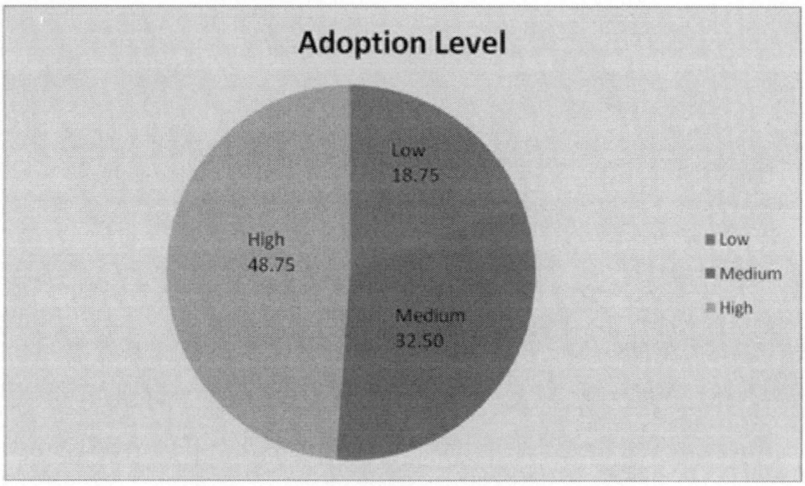

Figure 1. Adoption Level of the Respondents

Table 2: Adoption Level of Respondents Regarding Happy Seeder (n = 80)

S. No.	*Adoption level*	*Frequency*	*Percentage*
1.	Low	15	18.75
2.	Medium	26	32.50
3.	High	39	48.75

Association Between Socio-economic Variables and Adoption Level of Happy Seeder Adopters

Factors affecting adoption level with socio economic status of the farmers have been shown in Table 3. Age was found significantly associated with adoption level. In young age group very high level of adoption (80.77%) while in old age low (55.56%) and medium level (33.33%) of adoption was found among respondents. Education association showed that two-third illiterate respondents had low level (75.00%) of knowledge while senior secondary educated and graduates & above had medium (51.85%) and high (69.40%) level of adoption respectively significant association was found between education and adoption level of the respondents. Size of land holding was found significantly associated with adoption level. Small and semi- medium land holders had low level of adoption while medium level i.e., 4-10 ha land holders had high level of adoption (54.50%). Annual family income, mass media exposure and were found significantly associated while caste and social participation were non-significantly associated with adoption level of Happy Seeder. On the other hand, socio-economic status was found highly significantly associated with level of adoption regarding Happy Seeder.

Table 3: Socio Economic Factors Affecting Adoption Level of the Respondents (n = 80)

Socio-economic Variables	*Adoption Level*			
Age	*Low*	*Medium*	*High*	*Total*
up to 35 yrs.	1(3.85)	4(15.38)	21(80.77)	26(32.50)
36-50 yrs.	4(11.12)	16(44.44)	16(44.44)	36(45.00)
above 50 yrs.	10(55.56)	6(33.33)	2(11.11)	18(22.50)
Total	15(18.75)	26(32.50)	39(48.75)	80(100.0)
χ^2 Cal= 31.46*				
Caste				
General Castes	10(16.67)	23(38.33)	27(45.00)	60 (75.00)
Backward Class	2(16.67)	2(16.67)	8(66.66)	12 (15.00)
Scheduled Castes	3(37.50)	1(12.50)	4(50.0)	8 (10.00)
χ^2 Cal= 4.23				
Level of Education				
Illiterate	9(75.00)	1(8.30)	2(16.70)	12(15.00)
Up to Middle	4(26.67)	4(26.67)	7(46.66)	15(18.75)
Secondary and Senior Secondary	1(3.71)	14(51.85)	12(44.44)	27(33.75)

Socio-economic Variables	*Adoption Level*			
Age	*Low*	*Medium*	*High*	*Total*
Graduation and above	1(3.70)	7(26.90)	18(69.40)	26(32.50)
χ^2 Cal= 37.65*				
Size of land holdings				
Marginal (up to 1 ha)	7(38.89)	6(33.33)	5(27.78)	18(22.50)
Small (1-2 ha)	6(28.57)	5(23.80)	10(47.63)	21(26.25)
Semi-medium (2-4 ha)	2(10.53)	7(36.84)	10(52.63)	19(23.75)
Medium (4-10 ha)	--	8(36.37)	14(63.63)	22(27.50)
χ^2 Cal= 7.81*				
Annual Income				
Between Rs.75,000 - 1,50,000/-	8(50.00)	5(31.25)	3(18.75)	16(20.00)
Between Rs.1,50,000 - 3,00,000/-	5(13.52)	11(29.72)	21(56.76)	37(46.25)
Above Rs. 3,00,000/-	2(7.40)	10(37.05)	15(55.55)	27(33.75)
χ^2 Cal= 15.51*				
Mass media exposure				
Low (up to 9)	6(37.50)	5(31.25)	5(31.25)	16(20.00)
Medium (10-17)	5(12.19)	12(29.27)	24(58.54)	41(51.25)
High (above 17)	4(17.40)	9(39.10)	10(43.50)	23(28.75)
χ^2 Cal= 5.98*				
Social Participation				
No membership	10(31.26)	11(34.37)	11(34.37)	32(40.00)
Member of one organization	4(13.79)	9(31.04)	16(55.17)	29(36.25)
More than one organization	1(5.26)	6(31.58)	12(63.16)	19(23.75)
χ^2 Cal= 7.42				
Socio-economic Status				
Low (12-18)	10 (50.0)	6 (30.0)	4 (20.0)	20(25.00)
Medium (19-24)	3 (7.3)	15 (36.6)	23 (56.1)	41(51.25)
High (25-31)	2 (10.5)	5 (26.3)	12 (63.2)	19(23.75)
χ^2 Cal= 19.087**				

*Significant at 5% level of significance
*Figures in parentheses indicate percentage

Reasons for Adoption of Happy Seeder

Table 4 depicts the reasons for adoption of Happy Seeder as reported by more than 3/4th of the respondents that adoption of Happy Seeder (77.50 %) Saves time and money as there is possibility of sowing wheat crop just after harvesting of rice followed by increased yield than conventional method (72.50%) and it is environment friendly technology (70%) as with the burning of rice residues produced gases create very harmful situations for our environment and it can reduce air pollution followed by increased in yield as compared to conventional methods.

Regarding other reasons higher net return, reduce fuel and labour cost and helps to recycle the plant nutrients present in paddy residues leading to improved soil health (60%, 55% and 53.75% respectively). So overall it was observed a beneficial technology in the favour of the farmers. Gathala et al. (2009) concluded that Happy Seeder technology provides an alternative to burning for managing rice residues and allows direct drilling of wheat in standing as well as loose residues. Both on-farm and on-station trials were conducted to evaluate the feasibility of direct-drilling of wheat in the presence of heavy loads of rice residue using the Happy Seeder and the effects of tillage and residue management methods on crop productivity and soil physical properties.

Table 4: Reasons for Adoption of Happy Seeder (n = 80)

Sr. No.	*Aspects*	*Reasons for Adoption*		
		Agree	*Neutral*	*Disagree*
1.	It is environment friendly technology as with the burning of rice residues produced gases create a very harmful situations for our environment but it can reduce air pollution	56(70.00)	15(18.75)	9(11.25)
2	Higher net return by adoption of Happy Seeder	48 (60.00)	20(25.00)	12(15.00)
3.	Reduce fuel and labour cost	44(55.00)	22(27.50)	14(17.50)
4.	Saves time and money as there is possibility of sowing wheat crop just after harvesting of rice	62(77.50)	12(15.00)	6(7.50)
5.	Increased yield than conventional method	58(72.50)	10(12.50)	12(15.00)
6.	Helps to recycle the plant nutrients present in paddy residues leading to improved soil health.	43(53.75)	32(40.00)	5(6.25)

Figures in Parentheses indicate percentage.
Responses were multiple.

Comparative Benefits between Happy Seeder Adoption and Conventional Practices

A comparative analysis regarding benefits of Happy Seeder and conventional practices has been shown in (Table 5) which indicates that adoption of Happy Seeder is 80% time saving, fuel saving(69%),labour requirement (79%), and 65% of saving in cost of sowing. Yield by Happy Seeder was reported 58q/ha and by conventional practices it was 55q/ha means 5.45% of yield difference was observed. Saving in gross return from grain and straw was reported 5.45% and 6.06% respectively.

The cost of operation with Happy Seeder was Rs 80600/ha while in conventional practices Rs 84500/ha. A saving of 23.77% in net return with total Benefit over conventional Practice 11225 Rs/ha) was observed. In a study conducted in Punjab, the total comparison of Happy seeder with traditional farming revealed that the normal sown wheat fields cost Rs. 924.50 per acre more than the happy seeder sown wheat fields. Apart from avoiding the burning of paddy straw, the happy seeder technology was able to save Rs. 2311.25 per hectare during the field preparation, sowing, and management activities of the crop when compared to conventionally seeded wheat. Kathpalia *et al.* (2020) conducted a study in Kaithal, Haryana and concluded that Happy Seeder is a profitable technology for the farmers which saves on an average 80% time than conventional practices .Other savings were ; Labor saving (79%), saving in the cost of sowing (71%), extra yield (7%), net return (20%), water savings (20%) as reported by the adopters. Regarding knowledge and adoption level 50% and 55% of adopters had medium level respectively. It was found that marginal farmers spend the profit amount of Happy Seeder on social ceremonies (66%) and others on quality education of children, on social ceremonies and on household assets etc. Half of the respondents were agreed that sowing of wheat crop is difficult with high moisture in straw and soil condition.

Table 5: Comparative Benefits between Happy Seeder Adoption and Conventional Practice (n = 160)

	Happy Seeder	*Conventional Practices*	*Saving (%)*
Time(h/ha)	2.8	14.0	80%
Fuel (l/ha)	15.0	48.3	69%
Labour requirement (man-h/ha)	5.8	28.2	79%
Cost of Sowing (Rs /ha)	2100	6000	65%
Benefit in cost of saving (Rs)	3900	-	-
Yield (q/ha)	58	55	5.45
Increase in yield (q)	3	-	
Gross return from grain(Rs/ha)	114550	108625	5.45
Gross return from straw(Rs/ha)	24500	23100	6.06%
Total gross return (Rs/ha)	139050	131725	5.5
Cost of operation (Rs/ha)	80600	84500	4.62
Net return(Rs/ha)	58450	47225	23.77
Total Benefit over conventional Practice (Rs/ha)	11225		

All the agronomic practices remain same in both the practices

Reasons for Non-Adoption of Happy Seeder

Results (Table 6) regarding reasons for non- adoption of Happy Seeder as revealed by more than 3/4th of the respondents (77.50%) that Happy Seeder is unaffordable for a single farmer because of high cost and rent of Happy Seeder. Other reasons for non-adoption are like single Happy Seeder can't till land beyond 8 acres per day which makes it time consuming process, seed wastage and inability of farmers to manage the straw in a short duration between rice harvest and wheat sowing to catch up the right sowing time (48.75%, 56.25% and 35.00).

Also, 27.50% farmers also mentioned the reason of the old age perception that it is a good practice to burn the field which will keep the insects, diseases, weed seeds getting killed in the process.

Table 6: Reasons for Non-adoption of Happy Seeder (n = 80)

Sr. No.	*Aspects*	*Reasons for Non-adoption*		
		Agree	*Neutral*	*Disagree*
1.	High cost and rent of Happy Seeder	62(77.50)	10(12.50)	08(10.00)
2	The old age perception that it is a good practice to burn the field which will keep the insects, diseases, weed seeds getting killed in the process.	22(27.50)	13(16.25)	45(56.25)
3.	Inability of farmers to manage the straw in a short duration between rice harvest and wheat sowing to catch up the right sowing time.	28(35.00)	18(22.50)	34(42.50)
4.	Single Happy Seeder can't till land beyond 8 acres per day	39(48.75)	15(18.75)	26(32.50)
5.	The machine is unaffordable for a single farmer.	52(65.00)	22(27.50)	06(7.50)
6.	Seed Wastage	45(56.25)	18(22.50)	17(21.25)

Cumulative Socio-economic Impact of Happy Seeder

The multiple cumulative socio economic impact of using Happy Seeder as perceived by .Marginal farmers are like (Table 7) performed social ceremonies by the benefit amount of Happy Seeder (22.22%), investment on quality education of their children, Increase in agricultural land on lease (16.67% each) and 11.11% of the medium farmers observed increase in household assets. Small farmers also invested on education of children (23.85%) on social ceremonies (14.28%). 9.10% medium farmers also improved the quality of medical

Table 7: Cumulative Socio-economic Impact of Happy Seeder Adoption on Farming Families (n = 80)

Sr. No.	*Socio-economic Impact*	*Marginal Farmers (18)22.50%*	*Small Farmers (21)26.25%*	*Semi-medium Farmers (19)23.75%*	*Medium Farmers (22)27.50%*
1.	Investment on quality education of their children	3(16.67)	5(23.85)	3(15.78)	8(36.36)
2.	Expenditure on Performance of social ceremonies like marriage, death etc. Increased	4 (22.22)	3(14.28)	3(15.78)	6 (27.27)
3.	Increase in household assets	2(11.11)	5(23.85)	4 (21.05)	2 (9.10)
4.	Increase in quality of medical treatment	2(11.11)	1 (4.76)	2(10.54)	2 (9.10)
5	Increase in agricultural land on lease	3(16.67)	2 (9.50)	4(21.05)	-
6.	Increase in mass media exposure	2(11.11)	1 (4.76)	-	-
7.	Increase in urban and extension contacts	-	2(9.50)	2 (10.54)	4 (18.17)
8.	Any others	2 (11.11)	2 (9.50)	1 (5.26)	-

Figures in Parentheses indicate percentage.

treatment. Semi-medium (15.78%) and medium farmers (36.36%) also reported investment on quality education of their children. Analysis of study depicted the multiple cumulative socio economic impact of using Happy Seeder as perceived by farmers. 18.17% of medium farmers also reported increase in urban and extension contacts and semi- medium farmers (21.05%) observed an increase in agriculture land on lease and increase in household assets each.

Constraints about Happy Seeder Technology

Regarding agro technical problems constraints in adoption of Happy Seeder (Table 8) respondents (51.25%) were agreed that sowing of wheat crop is difficult with high moisture in straw and soil condition which got rank I, other constraints reported by respondents were choking of machinery while working and Sowing of wheat in the starting shows not good results which leads to stress (II) and non-availability of Happy Seeder when required got rank III.

Some of the educational problems reported by the respondents were inadequate extension contacts with ADOs and SDOs (rank I) followed by lack of adequate training programmes II rank and shortage of information on Happy Seeder III rank respectively.

In the same way in financial problems 46.25% and 40.00% respondents were agreed and somewhat agreed that higher cost of Happy Seeder or more custom charges they have to pay for Happy Seeder with mean score 2.32%.

Table 8: Constraints in Adoption of Happy Seeder Technology (n = 80)

Sr. No.	*Constraints*	*Agree (3)*	*Somewhat Agree (2)*	*Don't Agree (1)*	*WMC*	*Mean score*	*Rank*
1.	Agro – technical problems						
a.	Sowing of wheat crop is difficult in high moisture straw and soil condition.	41(51.25)	24(30.00)	15(18.75)	186	2.32	I
b.	Sowing of wheat in the starting does not show good results which leads to stress	31(38.75)	24(30.00)	25(31.25)	166	2.07	II
c.	Non availability of Happy Seeder when required	28(35.00)	28(35.00)	24(30.00)	164	2.05	III
d.	Choking of machinery while working	31(38.75)	24(30.00)	25(31.25)	166	2.07	II
2.	Educational problems						
a.	Inadequate extension contacts with ADOs and SDOs	29(36.25)	27(33.75)	24(30.00)	165	2.06	I
b.	Shortage of information on Happy Seeder	11(13.75)	13(16.25)	56 (70.00)	115	1.43	III
c.	Lack of adequate training program	18(22.50)	25(31.25)	37(46.25)	141	1.76	II
3.	Financial problem						
a.	Higher cost of Happy Seeder/ More custom charges	37(46.25)	32(40.00)	11(13.75)	186	2.32	I

Figures in Parentheses indicate percentage.(Responses were multiple.)

Conclusion

It is concluded that 48.75% of the respondents had high level of adoption while 32.50% had medium and rest (18.75%) of the respondents had low level of the adoption of Happy seeder farm technology.Factors affecting adoption level with socio economic status of the farmers revealed that age,education, annual family income, land holding and mass media exposure were found significantly associated with adoption level Yield by Happy Seeder was reported 58q/ha and by conventional practices it was 55q/ha means 5.45% of yield difference was observed. Saving in gross return from grain and straw was reported 5.45% and 6.06% respectively. Reasons for adoption of Happy Seeder in Fatehabad district reported by 77.50 % of farmers were like it saves time and money as there is possibility of sowing wheat crop just after harvesting of rice, followed by increased yield than conventional method (72.50%) and it is environment friendly technology (70%).

Regarding agro technical problems constraints in adoption of Happy Seeder respondents (51.25%) were agreed that sowing of wheat crop is difficult with high moisture in straw and soil condition which got rank I, other constraints reported by respondents were choking of machinery while working. Overall Happy Seeder is a feasible technology in regard to its eco friendly environment.

References

1. Bimbraw,A.S (2019) Generation and Impact of Crop Residue and it Management. *Current Agriculture Research Journal*, 7(3):304-309.
2. Brar, N.K., Jason C., Jeffrey, E. and Singh, Y. (2010) Nitrogen management in wheat sown in rice straw as mulch in North-West India. In Proc: *19th World Con-gress of Soil Science, Soil Solutions for a Changing world Brisbane, Australia.* August 1-6, 2010, Published on DVD.
3. Datta, A, M A Emmanuel, N K Ram and S Dhingra. 2020. Crop Residue Management: Solution To Achieve Better. Air Quality. TERI publication, New Delhi.
5. Dhillon, G.S (2016) Comparative evaluation of happy seeder technology versus normal sowing in wheat (Triticum aestivum) in adopted village Killi Nihal Singh of Bathinda district of Punjab. *Journal of Applied and Natural Science*, 8 (4): 2278-2282 .
6. Gathala, M. K., Pathak, H., Ladha, J. K., Kumar, V., Mishra, D., Blackwell, J., Roth, C., Kumar, V., Kumar, V. and Sharma, S. (2009). Happy Seeder technology provides an alternate to burning for managing rice loose straw after combine harvest. *Indian Council of Agricultural Research and National Academy of Agricultural Sciences.* https://researchoutput.csu.edu.au/en/publications/happy-seeder-technology-provides-an-alternate-to-burning-for-mana.
7. Kathpalia, J. & Tyagi, R. (2020). Crop residue management with reference to Happy Seeder in Kaithal district – A Sociological study, *Technical Programme of work 2020-2021, Department of Sociology*, CCSHAU Hisar-125004.
8. Sidhu, H.S., Singh, M., Humphreys, E., Singh, Y., Singh, B., Dhillon, S.S., Blackwell J., Bector, V., Singh, M. and Singh, S. (2007). The happy seeder enables direct drill-ing of wheat in to rice stubble. *Australian Journal of Experimentals Agriculture,* 47: 844-854
9. Singh, N. and Chahal, S.S. (2009). A study on the extent of adoption of various recommended technologies in wheat cultivation in Punjab. *Agric Econ. Res rev,* **22**: 218-30.